P9-AOW-088

INSIDE AN AMERICAN CONCENTRATION CAMP

INSIDE AN

AMERICAN CONCENTRATION CAMP

Japanese American Resistance at Poston, Arizona

Richard S. Nishimoto

SELECTED AND EDITED, WITH AN INTRODUCTION AND AFTERWORD BY

Lane Ryo Hirabayashi

The University of Arizona Press Tucson

The University of Arizona Press

⊗This book is printed on acid-free, archival-quality paper.
Manufactured in the United States of America
99 98 97 96 95 5 4 3 2 1

Library of Congress Cataloging-in-Publication Data

Nishimoto, Richard S. (Richard Shigeaki), 1904–1956.
Inside an American concentration camp : Japanese American resistance at Poston, Arizona / Richard S. Nishimoto ; selected and with an introduction and afterword by Lane Ryo Hirabayashi.
p. cm.
Includes bibliographical references and index.
Partial Contents: Autobiography : Nishimoto's letter to Dr. Alexander M. Leighton, Nov. 1, 1942—Labor : Nishimoto's report on the Firebreak Gang—Leisure : Nishimoto's report on gambling at Poston—Demands: Nishimoto's study of the All Center Conference.
ISBN 0-8165-1420-8 (cloth).—ISBN 0-8165-1563-8 (paper)
1. Japanese Americans—Evacuation and relocation, 1942–1945. 2. World War, 1939–1945—Concentration camps—Arizona—Poston. 3. World War, 1939–1945—Personal narratives, American. 4. Passive resistance—Arizona—Poston. 5. Poston Relocation Center (Poston, Ariz.) 6. Poston (Ariz.)—History. I. Hirabayashi, Lane Ryo. II. Title.
D769.8.A6N57 1995
940.53'1503956073—dc20 95-21635
CIP

British Cataloguing-in-Publication Data

A catalogue record for this book is available from the British Library.

To Yuji Ichioka

and Jim Hirabayashi,

who helped me start this book;

and to Evelyn Hu-DeHart

and Marilyn Alquizola,

who helped me finish it.

CONTENTS

FIGURES

PREFACE

The heart of this book consists of an autobiographical statement and three reports, all written by Richard Shigeaki Nishimoto while he was incarcerated during World War II in the Colorado River Relocation Center, located near Parker, Arizona. Nishimoto's autobiographical statement (as of 1942) allows readers to meet and evaluate him on his own terms and to better appreciate the reasons for the power of his writing. The three reports—on work (1942), gambling (1943), and the All Center Conference (1945)—present a fascinating portrait of the daily life of ordinary Japanese Americans in Poston and document their efforts to retain a sense of meaning and dignity under conditions of mass incarceration. The introduction that follows indicates what makes the studies offered here a unique and valuable contribution to the literature on the camps even though Nishimoto did not hold advanced degrees in history or social science.

Beyond this, my interest in Nishimoto has continued to grow over the years I have studied his life and writings. They make it possible for me to obtain a wider perspective on the man and his work than is presently the case for any of the other fieldworkers—Euro-American and Japanese American—who were on the scene.

One of the things that initially attracted me to Nishimoto's writing was his reflexive bent. His field diary and notes, letters, reports, and autobiography made it clear that he took the time to reflect on his own psychological and intellectual makeup. Because he did so, and because he left various written accounts along these lines, we can appreciate more fully the fact that his research entails a fascinating and unusual combination of autobiography, auto-ethnography, and ethnography.

Nishimoto's research on daily life at Poston was guided by the conventions and techniques of the social sciences of his day. Although he was not formally trained in a graduate program in anthropology or sociology, the evidence strongly indicates that Nishimoto's participation in two different professionally run research projects in Poston gave him more than adequate training in this regard, training comparable to what was being provided to graduate students in the social sciences at the best universities in the United States. His writings make it clear that Nishimoto systematically carried out fieldwork in Poston in which he engaged in observation, interviewing, participant observation, archival and secondary research, and the compilation of censuses and other quantitative databases over a sustained period of time. The use of each of these techniques is documented in Nishimoto's extensive field diary and notes. That he employed all of these methods in his research, as well as sometimes recording his own thoughts and actions, is the basis for my contention that Nishimoto was in fact producing a type of auto-ethnography—an empirically based description and interpretation of a people or a group to which one belongs and in which one may be playing an active role, which is also put on the record. Finally, Nishimoto's lengthy field reports on specific topics indicate that he was much more than a mere data collector for the University of California's Japanese American Evacuation and Resettlement Study (JERS) project.

At another level, however, it is difficult to determine whether most academic anthropologists would agree that Nishimoto's work is ethnography, that is, a holistic description of a people's culture and lifeways, guided and informed by the discipline of anthropology. Unlike most anthropologically trained ethnographers, Nishimoto studied only one sociocultural group (Japanese Americans) in depth, and thus his reports contain no cross-cultural or even comparative generalizations. Another reason that Nishimoto's work (at least as it appears in the archives) might not be considered ethnography is that the three reports that I have selected for publication here are not systematically related to one another, especially in terms of an overarching concept or theme, and maintaining such a relationship is a key step in the ethnographic enterprise, at least from a mainstream academic viewpoint. Perhaps Nishimoto's research reports are best considered field reports that were each written to address a specific topical focus. Moreover, Nishimoto's research on the firebreak gang, gambling, and the All Center Conference are clearly not in the final form that he would have achieved had he been given the chance to publish his work, so some of the above criticisms may not be entirely fair.

The process of selecting, juxtaposing, and commenting on Nishimoto's texts, however, brings with it the opportunity to examine possible underlying relationships among the documents and thus to identify and heighten their thematic coherence. In this sense, the thesis that the Poston residents' experience can be seen in terms of Japanese Americans' resistance to the injustices of mass removal and mass incarceration reflects a conceptual synthesis that Nishimoto himself did not fully develop. Further, it is fitting to acknowledge that my selections and interpretations are highly motivated by my conclusion that popular resistance by Japanese Americans in WRA camps during World War II has been underreported and often misinterpreted. In short, this project provided me with a perfect vehicle to place the nature and extent of popular resistance back on the record, an admission that is fully consistent with Nishimoto's own penchant for self-examination.

The need for this admission occurred to me as I worked with Nishimoto's own comments about his life and personality, especially as I drew from them in writing the brief account of his life in the introduction to this book. Reflecting on the process of writing Nishimoto's biography, as well as on the strengths and limitations of his data, has made me deeply aware of the fundamentally constructed nature of the four forms of writing about people discussed here and below: biography, autobiography (which I comment on more fully in my introduction to Nishimoto's 1942 letter to Alexander Leighton), auto-ethnography, and ethnography.

This is not to argue that each form is not constructed in relation to (if not on the basis of) facts or that the assessment and evaluation of each cannot be based on comparing assertions to a body of independently verifiable data. Rather, my point here is that any writing that purports to describe oneself, another person, a people or group that one belongs to, or another people or group is inherently and necessarily selective and provisional. By adapting such a perspective, I have gained a much deeper understanding of the fact that my interventions in writing this book—my biographical account on Nishimoto and my selection and interpretation of his research reports—are constructs too and should be openly acknowledged as such.

This leads to a final point, which is of paramount importance for the historiography of the Japanese American experience during World War II: given the pressures, conflicts, and damage that mass removal and mass incarceration generated among Japanese Americans, it can be very difficult to resolve diametrically opposed descriptions and interpretations of individuals, groups, and events. A classic example concerns the question of whether the behavior of the Japanese American Citizens League during the 1940s was heroic (according to the autobiography of Mike Masaoka) or villainous (according to various essays by Frank Chin and his colleagues). Among all the self-serving hyperbole that has been issued by both camps, how is one to discern where the truth of the matter lies?

At one level, Nishimoto's or anyone else's data and interpretations can and should be compared with the record. Because Nishimoto wrote on-site and in such detail about the people of Poston during the war, and because his data stand up well when compared with a range of other sources, his research can be considered valuable at this level alone. On another, more important level (following the ideas Gunnar Myrdal set forth in *Objectivity in Social Research*), it must be emphasized that premises and values undergird all interpretations in history and the social sciences. In this light, what makes Nishimoto's work even more valuable than its factual content is the fact that, since one can examine his corpus in terms of historical, biographical, autobiographical, auto-ethnographic, and ethnographic dimensions, one is in a much better position to determine what values and premises influenced the constructions that give Nishimoto's varied writings their form, content, and emphases. As Myrdal indicates, there is no greater means of securing objectivity in the social sciences than to make the values and premises behind data collection and interpretation explicit, and this is precisely why Nishimoto is a more valuable source of information about what went on in the camps than other researchers of his day or many who have followed. We can determine what his basic orientations and biases were and can thus take these into account consciously and systematically when we study, evaluate, interpret, and use his research.

Much of this argument is, of course, also drawn from critical commentary about the ethnographic enterprise that is now common to interpretive anthropology and sociology, women's studies, and scholarship attentive to postmodernist perspectives. My claim to originality is that this book illustrates how and why biography, autobiography, and in Nishimoto's case auto-ethnography fully complement the ethnographic enterprise. Each can be used—singly or more powerfully in tandem—by authors or readers to heighten their recognition of the inherent selectivity that is entailed in writing about people. Because it helps to make the principles of selection explicit, reflexivity offers a measure of control over both conscious and unconscious biases that can distort the production of social research. Such an effort here makes Nishimoto's contributions an even more useful and powerful source of information concerning the nature and implications of the period of crisis represented by World War II. Ultimately, then, this rationale has informed the construction of this book by its reflexive dimensions.

In any case, readers are sure to find Nishimoto's Poston writings fascinating in their own right. They should be read critically, but there is no doubt that Nishimoto's contributions offer a rich and valuable resource for scholars, students, and members of the general public who want to explore different perspectives on American history, the West, and Arizona, especially the significance of a federal policy that allowed the mass incarceration of over 110,000 persons, more than half of whom were U.S. citizens.

ACKNOWLEDGMENTS

Over the course of this project, many people have been generous with their time, information, and ideas. I would especially like to thank Professor Yuji Ichioka of the University of California, Los Angeles, who in late 1985 first suggested that I prepare a paper on Richard S. Nishimoto for a conference on the Japanese American Evacuation and Resettlement Study he was planning. I also thank, with much appreciation, my father, James A. Hirabayashi. An anthropologist and chief curator of the Japanese American National Museum, he was a co-author of an earlier essay on which the present introduction and afterword draw. I have relied on his scholarly training in Japanese studies, his personal insights as a Nisei (he and his family were prewar residents in the Kent-Auburn area in the state of Washington and were incarcerated at the northern California camp at Tule Lake), and his own research in the fields of anthropology and ethnic studies in conducting much of my own research on the Japanese American experience.

Others, too, have contributed to my research. Early on, Noriko Sawada Bridges provided fascinating insights about the Poston camp and its inhabitants that have proved invaluable to this study. Roberta Shiroma, Richard Nishimoto's eldest daughter, has been very generous with her time and advice, and with personal documents and photographs in her possession. Under her sponsorship, the Nishimoto family kindly agreed to cooperate with this project and also to allow me to publish the manuscripts that appear herein.

Many others have helped me over the years. First and foremost have been the dedicated librarians and staff at the Bancroft Library of the University of California, Berkeley, where the bulk of Richard Nishimoto's letters, notes, journals, and research reports are held. I would also like to thank Dr. Bonnie Hardwick, head of the Manuscripts Division at the Bancroft Library, who also granted me permission to publish the documents that make up chapters 1 through 4 of the present volume.

I could not have finished this manuscript without the support and encouragement of Professor Evelyn Hu-DeHart, Director of the Center for Studies of Ethnicity and Race in America at the University of Colorado in Boulder. At her behest I obtained assistance from the CSERA staff during the summer of 1993, especially Karen Moreira and Tina Le, who transcribed Nishimoto's reports and essays for me. Marilyn C. Alquizola helped by providing cogent comments on a working draft. Two reviewers, whose names I do not know, worked through the manuscript and offered many good suggestions for revision. I would also like to thank my mother, Joanne V. Hirabayashi, for proofreading the manuscript in its entirety. Sally Bennett carried out the arduous task of compiling an index. I am very grateful to Alan M. Schroder of the University of Arizona Press for his tireless work on this project. His many queries and suggestions helped me enormously as I finalized the manuscript.

Finally, I would like to acknowledge the financial support of the Committee on Research and Creative Work of the Graduate School of the University of Colorado at Boulder, which enabled me to visit key archives as I was completing this book; and the Implementation of Multicultural Perspectives and Approaches to Research and Teaching (IMPART) program, and its director, Professor Albert Ramirez, for their help in underwriting other expenses that this project entailed.

A NOTE ON TRANSCRIPTION AND TERMINOLOGY

The four texts by Nishimoto that appear below are presented in essentially their original form as they were found in the Japanese American Evacuation and Resettlement Study (JERS) archives in the Bancroft Library at the University of California, Berkeley.[1] Although this approach entails the retention of grammatical mistakes, the preservation of Nishimoto's original language provides a constant reminder of exactly who this man was and of the cultures, indeed the worlds, that his experience encompassed.

The faithful reproduction of these four texts, however, is complicated by the fact that, although the Bancroft Library is the primary depository for JERS materials, the manuscripts are apparently only copies of the originals, which may not be extant. The only indication that I have been able to find regarding why this might be so is found in personal correspondence between Nishimoto's colleague and JERS fieldworker Tamie Tsuchiyama and the JERS director, Dorothy Thomas.[2]

On February 1, 1943, Tsuchiyama mailed a letter and various reports to Thomas, one of which was Nishimoto's "Firebreak Gang" report. According to Tsuchiyama, Nishimoto said it was the first report that he had written in English since leaving Stanford University some thirteen years before, and he was apologetic about his writing skills. Tsuchiyama indicated that if Thomas was sufficiently interested, she could have a copy made for herself and then return the original. Subsequently, along with a handwritten letter dated May 26, 1943, Tsuchiyama sent Nishimoto's paper on gambling in Poston to Thomas, indicating that it was a rough draft but suggesting that Thomas might like to see it before it was rewritten. In addition, Tsuchiyama noted that "Since this is the only copy we have will you please write comments along the margins wherever you encounter ambiguous statements and mail it back to us? If you feel that a revision is unnecessary please send us a carbon copy for our files."[3]

The fact that essentially the same procedure was followed with all four of Nishimoto's texts reproduced here can be partially verified by examining the documents themselves. Nishimoto's letter to Alexander Leighton of November 1, 1942, closes with "Very truly yours" and is not signed. The letter is full of very obvious typing errors.[4]

Although Nishimoto himself may have reviewed the copy of the "Firebreak Gang" manuscript (since Japanese characters appear alongside the romanized Japanese versions of Japanese phrases in note 1 there), documents (such as the map described in the original note 8) are missing from its appendix. Note numbers were also written on the text by hand, although I cannot determine by whom.

The extant manuscript of "Gambling at Poston" also appears to be a copy of an original. The cover of the report lists the author only as "R.S.N." An illustration of "eighty Chinese ideographs" described in the text is missing from the version in the archives.

The "All Center Conference" report also appears to be a copy. No author is listed on the front of the archival copy. The text is full of cross-references like "*infra*, p. xxx," with the page number left unspecified. These references are probably to two other lengthy reports Nishimoto wrote as background to his All Center Conference study reproduced below. Finally, in contrast to the other documents discussed here, the "All Center Conference" report has the most extensively corrected text, with most of the notations and typing corrections handwritten on the copy. Nishimoto's distinctive printing of the letter *e* indicates that he personally made the handwritten corrections in this case, although by no means did he do a thorough job of catching errors.

In all probability then, all four of the texts were copied by a stenographer (or possibly various stenographers) from the study's secretarial pool. In the course of reproducing these texts, however, many mistakes crept into the documents, including a great many minor typing errors as well as sections where words, phrases, and even sentences appear to have been dropped when the copy was generated.

In sum, the autobiographical letter and the three research reports are best seen as works in progress that Nishimoto would most certainly have corrected if he had had an opportunity to publish them. For this reason, while Nishimoto's manuscripts are reproduced here in essentially their original form in order to capture the spirit of the man and his work, minor typing errors have been corrected silently.[5]

Nishimoto's terminology in regard to mass removal and mass incarceration has not been made consistent or amended in any way. In the introductory sections, I have avoided the euphemistic terms *evacuation* (which, according to Okamura, implies a temporary removal in order to protect the population in question), *relocation* (which implies a long-term removal along the same lines), and such associated terms as *evacuee, assembly center,* and *relocation center.*[6]

It is also relevant here that the term *internment camp* (along with its derivations such as *internee*) is technically inappropriate for the WRA camps because the United States Department of Justice set up and ran special maximum-security camps to imprison Japanese, Italian, and German nationals who had been swept up in the weeks following the attack on Pearl Harbor and whose loyalties were deemed suspect. These special camps were called internment camps by the Justice Department, and this convention has generally been followed in the scholarly literature to differentiate them from the camps run by the WRA.

As described in the research and publications of a number of scholars, the process that more than 110,000 Japanese Americans were subjected to was mass incarceration, and the facilities that they were placed in were American-style concentration camps.[7] The term *concentration camp* certainly describes conditions in a camp like Poston from the point of view of many of the Japanese Americans, none of whom, even if they were U.S. citizens, were given a fair trial before they were forced to leave their businesses, homes, and communities. Protests against unjust conditions at Poston could be investigated at any time by FBI agents, who were not under the direct control of the WRA and who had the authority to identify "troublemakers," subject them to interrogation, and remove them from Poston for incarceration at another institution. We now know that the FBI placed Japanese American agents inside Poston in order to report on anyone considered a troublemaker, so the Japanese Americans' concern over and anger at *inu,* or spies, was not just paranoia.

Use of the term *concentration camp* is in no way intended to denigrate or minimize the experience of Jews and other minorities in Europe during World War II, millions of whom perished in German death camps. In his historically based explanation justifying the application of the term to the WRA camps, historian Richard Drinnon notes that no less an authority than Hannah Arendt once developed a tripartite typology of concentration camps, dividing them into, first, "milder types"; second, slave labor camps; and, third, camps where torture and execution were routine. On the basis of Arendt's typology, Drinnon proposes that the prisons and reservations developed for North American Indians—as well as camps developed by the Spanish in Cuba, the British in South Africa, the Americans in the Philippines, and the WRA for Japanese Americans during World War II—all fall squarely into the first of Arendt's types, although he notes that "[l]ike Eisenhower and Myer at the time and since, Americans have commonly rejected parallels between their camps and those elsewhere."[8]

In sum, I agree with Drinnon and many other scholars that the OIA/WRA camp at Poston was indeed a concentration camp—that is, according to *Webster's Third New International Dictionary*, "a camp where persons (as prisoners of war, political prisoners, refugees, or foreign nationals) are detained or confined and sometimes subjected to mental and physical abuse and indignity." Further, although he only occasionally used the term himself, Nishimoto's writings on conditions at Poston thoroughly document the psychological dimensions of abuse and indignity Japanese Americans faced at Poston. Finally, the secondary literature cited throughout the introductions to the documents provides ample evidence that physical abuse was always a tangible threat facing anyone at the camps who actively resisted injustice.

Notes

1. For the importance of preserving the original text in documentary editing, see Mary-Jo Kline, *A Guide to Documentary Editing* (Baltimore: Johns Hopkins University Press, 1987).

2. Correspondence between JERS staff members (including Richard Nishimoto, Tamie Tsuchiyama, James Sakoda, and S. Frank Miyamoto) and the JERS director, Dorothy Thomas, is held as part of the JERS collection, though some restrictions apply to its use. They may have been included in the collection because the letters are a rich source of information about the day-to-day work of the members of the study. At the same time, and perhaps not surprisingly, some letters contain information and comments that might be considered personal and private, which leads one to suspect that the Japanese American staff may not have been fully aware that their correspondence would be preserved and eventually made available to researchers. Some of the correspondence in the files is original, but some letters were copied, as indicated by a type-

written closing along the lines of "Tamie Tsuchiyama (signed)." Even more interesting is the fact that correspondence in some of the files appears to have been intentionally or unintentionally edited. Some letters are mentioned in exchanges between Tsuchiyama and Thomas but are missing from the collection, for example.

3. By this time Nishimoto may have been receiving feedback on his writing from Tsuchiyama, although I have been unable to find any reference to this in the documents or their correspondence.

4. As explained below, Nishimoto wrote this letter to Leighton while Nishimoto was an employee of the Bureau of Sociological Research (BSR) and before he began to work for JERS. Like the "Firebreak Gang" report, which was also written while he was a BSR employee, Nishimoto's earlier research found its way into the JERS files and subsequently the JERS archival collection.

5. The only exception to the rule of leaving the Nishimoto text essentially unchanged is the use of pseudonyms at certain points in the text to protect the identity of people whose reputations might otherwise be tarnished. Should researchers wish to check the archival documents, they can be found in the JERS collection under the following call numbers: the autobiographical letter, J 6.25; the "Firebreak Gang" report, J 6.07; the "Gambling at Poston" report, J 6.09; and the "All Center Conference" report, J 6.05. As of 1994 the Bancroft Library was engaged in a two-year project to microfilm the entire JERS collection, which should make access to its materials easier than has previously been the case.

A useful guide to the JERS materials is Edward N. Barnhart's *Japanese American Evacuation and Resettlement: A Catalog of Materials in the General Library* (Berkeley: University of California, Berkeley, Library, 1958). Although most JERS materials have since been transferred to the Bancroft Library and although some of the items listed in the catalog (such as photographic slides of the WRA camp called Granada, or Amache) have apparently disappeared, the call numbers listed in the Barnhart catalog remain the same.

6. Raymond Y. Okamura has written a thoughtful critique of the government euphemisms, including the key terms *evacuation* and *relocation* (which, interestingly enough, the Nazis also used to describe their activities); see "The American Concentration Camps: A Cover-Up through Euphemistic Terminology," *Journal of Ethnic Studies* 10 (1982): 95–108.

7. Edison Uno was one of the first researchers to document the number and range of federal and local officials who called the institutions in which Japanese Americans were incarcerated concentration camps; see his article "Concentration Camps American-Style," *Pacific Citizen*, Special Holiday Edition, December 1974. Others have added names, such as that of Franklin D. Roosevelt, to this list.

8. Richard Drinnon, *Keeper of Concentration Camps: Dillon S. Myer and American Racism* (Berkeley: University of California Press, 1987), 6, 273. Also see the work of historian Roger Daniels: *Concentration Camps, U.S.A.* (New York: Holt, Rinehart and

Winston, 1971); *Concentration Camps: North America; Japanese in the United States and Canada during World War II* (Malabar, Fla.: Krieger, 1989). In his most recent book on the subject, *Prisoners without Trial: Japanese Americans in World War II* (New York: Hill and Wang, 1993), 46–47, Daniels continues to defend his choice and use of the term *concentration camps* to describe the WRA camps.

INTRODUCTION

Why Read Nishimoto?

Some fifty years after the fact, the reader might well inquire: Why bother to read Richard Nishimoto's writings from the 1940s? To begin with, Nishimoto is perhaps the most frequently cited author of Japanese descent who was among those subject to mass incarceration by the federal government during World War II and who also wrote on the subject. His prominence came from the fact that, with University of California demographer and sociologist Dorothy S. Thomas, he is listed as a co-author of *The Spoilage*, published in 1946.[1] Despite initial criticism in reviews in professional journals, for many years *The Spoilage* was the only detailed study of the "resegregation" phase of Tule Lake, a War Relocation Authority (WRA) camp in northern California where Japanese Americans who had requested "repatriation" back to Japan or whose loyalties were otherwise deemed suspicious by the federal government were sent in 1943.[2] This fact, along with the book's general examination of the politics and policies that led to the mass incarceration of people of Japanese descent, guaranteed that *The Spoilage* would become a classic text. Not only was it used in more traditional history, civics, and law classes, some twenty-five years after it was published it was also adopted in nascent Asian American Studies courses at campuses like San Francisco State and the University of California, Berkeley, to illustrate a hidden heritage of resistance.[3]

Beyond this, Richard Nishimoto's writings provide an especially keen and insightful portrait of daily life at Poston, the popular name of the Colorado River War Relocation Center, located near Parker, Arizona. Moreover, the three studies that appear below describe work, leisure (focusing on the popular pastime of gambling), and Japanese Americans' responses to WRA policies—aspects of daily life about which little has been published, especially from a Japanese American perspective.[4]

Nishimoto's ability to produce detailed studies of daily life in Poston from an insider's point of view was a product of his personal background and the nature of the Japanese American Evacuation and Resettlement Study (JERS), which employed him as a field researcher. Nishimoto was able to draw from his immigrant roots, bicultural and bilingual background, occupational experiences, and political proclivities, all of which are described below. According to Yuji Ichioka, the goals of JERS under the directorship of Dorothy Swaine Thomas of the University of California at Berkeley were primarily empirical and revolved around constructing a sociohistorical record of "enforced mass migration." For most of the Nisei, or second-generation, graduate students employed by Thomas as fieldworkers, Thomas's reluctance to specify any theoretical or conceptual guidelines for their data collection was frustrating.[5] Nishimoto, however, seemed to revel in the production of the kinds of descriptive materials that Thomas desired. In short, all of Nishimoto's reports on Poston, his sociological journal, and his personal correspondence, none of which have been published, were written while he was himself incarcerated at the camp. His writings thus retain a freshness, an intimacy, and a level of detail that is especially useful for researchers. Given this situation, what I also find very significant about the Nishimoto corpus is that, although he certainly did not set out to do this, his research describes numerous acts of popular resistance by the Japanese Americans in the course of a wide range of daily activities.[6]

As historian Gary Y. Okihiro indicates, the Japanese in America faced oppression fairly early in the twentieth century aimed at the "control and exploitation [of] individuals or groups," but the record also reveals the Japanese Americans' continuing resistance, in which they sought to secure the right to self-determination.[7] Okihiro posits that the assertion of human dignity and human rights on the part of Issei laborers can be seen, for example, in the fact that they responded to the denigration of Japanese culture by creating institutions such as Japanese language schools and ethnic churches, and to labor exploitation by conducting demonstrations, protests, and strikes. Mass incarceration generated much the same response.

One of the most obvious outcomes of mass removal and mass incarceration was the racialization of the Japanese Americans so treated.[8] All pre–World War II distinctions—whether of region, occupation, class, religion, or creed—were essentially erased because all persons of Japanese descent, whether or not they were U.S. citizens, were subject to basically the same regulations that characterized their institutionalization in a racially segregated setting operated by agencies of the federal government.

Open resistance was impossible under such circumstances, of course. Nonetheless, if popular resistance can be defined as protest that is "the collective expression of a group or social class's interests or perspectives about the nature of its position within the social, political, economic, and/or cultural institutions of society," Nishimoto's writings are rich with subtle and overt examples of actions taken by ordinary people in the day-to-day settings of camp life at Poston.[9] The diversity of such examples is one of the most important reasons to read Nishimoto today.

My intention is to examine the man and his work, and the work's strengths and weaknesses for increasing our understanding of the World War II era so that the value of Nishimoto's writings, and those of others who labored under similarly difficult circumstances to carry out firsthand research on the Japanese American experience during the 1940s, will be more widely recognized and appreciated.

The Pivotal Role of Nishimoto in JERS

Given Nishimoto's long working relationship with Dorothy Thomas, it is surprising that relatively little has been written about him. Indeed, before the late 1980s no account or assessment of Nishimoto's life, his multiple roles within Poston, his intellectual orientation, and his political commitments had ever been published.[10] This is a serious oversight, considering how frequently the Thomas and Nishimoto study has been cited as an authoritative source and used as a textbook in academic settings.

Nishimoto became an official member of the project in early 1943 on the recommendation of JERS staff member (and Poston resident) Tamie Tsuchiyama. His initial task was to assist Tsuchiyama with her study of the situation in Poston.[11] After receiving Nishimoto's materials for half a year, Thomas was clearly impressed by his potential. In a letter dated September 22, 1943, she wrote: "Dear X [as Nishimoto initially insisted he be called in all JERS correspondence]: This, I believe, is the first time I have written to you directly. . . . I feel very strongly that you are one of the most valuable observers on our study, and I certainly look forward to your further contributions."[12]

By 1944 the scope of Nishimoto's tasks had expanded. Even though he still lived at Poston, Nishimoto was able to work closely with Thomas via an active correspondence. His duties included what he described in his résumé as the "coordination and evaluation of field reports," and the "compilation and analysis of statistical data."

After being forced to leave Poston in July 1945 (under circumstances discussed below), Nishimoto was retained on the project and went to Berkeley, California, to continue his work. That same year Thomas decided to retain Nishimoto on her staff as her only postwar research assistant.[13] He remained on the JERS staff until 1948.

Among his various accomplishments, Nishimoto wrote hundreds of pages of material about Japanese Americans and camp life at Poston in the form of historical and demographic surveys, ethnographic studies, a sociological journal, and reflections captured in his personal correspondence.[14] He also became the only person of Japanese descent on the JERS staff to co-author a publication with the director. The publication was, of course, *The Spoilage.*

According to his own account, in 1947 and 1948 Nishimoto "visited the libraries of all major universities on the coast and scrutinized all the doctorate [*sic*] dissertations and MA theses pertaining to the subject."[15] During this same period he reportedly wrote a book-length manuscript focusing on the prewar economic situation of Japanese Americans entitled "The Economic History of Japanese on the Pacific Coast, 1885–1941." Most of the manuscript, however, has been either lost or destroyed; only scattered chapters from it appear in the JERS collection. Thomas apparently used some of Nishimoto's research in a companion text to *The Spoilage* called *The Salvage* (1952). Leonard Broom and Ruth Riemer apparently did the same in *Removal and Return* (1949), as Nishimoto privately complained that their use of his data was insufficiently acknowledged.[16]

Even after he officially left the project, at Dorothy Thomas's direct request Nishimoto agreed in 1952 to work as a consultant on yet another JERS-related publication. Three of Thomas's Berkeley colleagues—Jacobus tenBroek, Edward Barnhart, and Floyd Matson—were revising a draft of what would eventually become the third volume of the so-called JERS trilogy: *Prejudice, War and the Constitution.* Upon reading this draft in 1952, Thomas, she later wrote, "recommended to Dr. Barnhart that he have it read critically by someone who was thoroughly familiar with the sources and had access to all of the data, prior to revision. I suggested Richard S. Nishimoto, for whom, as you know, I have the highest possible regard."[17]

For Nishimoto's efforts, when *Prejudice, War and the Constitution* was published in 1954 the authors' preface noted: "Richard S. Nishimoto, who is as informed about the Japanese in America as any living person, has meticulously read the manuscript; he has corrected many errors, supplied many facts, and suggested many interpretive hypotheses."[18] Thus Nishimoto played a significant role in all three official publications resulting from the Japanese American Evacuation and Resettlement Study. His name also appears in the acknowledgments of other key studies of the period, including Leighton's *The Governing of Men* (1945) and Broom and Riemers's *Removal and Return*. Examining how Nishimoto established his reputation as an authoritative source on the Poston component of the JERS project even though he had been trained as an engineer, not an anthropologist, allows us to explore the combination of factors that made him especially valuable to Thomas.[19]

Nishimoto's Background

Nishimoto was born on August 23, 1904, in Tokyo and was given the name Nishimoto Shigeaki. He received an elementary school education between the ages of six and twelve and subsequently studied in the intermediate school (or *chugaku-ko*) of an American Episcopalian endowment in Tokyo, Rikkyo Middle School, where he graduated in 1921. Nishimoto wrote that because he had lived in school dormitories since he was ten, he basically grew up apart from his parents, "in a large group of boys of similar age." Nishimoto believed that his childhood and school experiences made him want always to "get to the top."[20]

At the age of seventeen, Nishimoto emigrated to the United States in 1921, where he joined his parents, who were living and working in San Francisco.[21] At that time Nishimoto's father was running an export business. Nishimoto helped out and also enrolled in San Francisco's Lowell High School. He completed his studies there between 1921 and 1925. He then immediately enrolled at Stanford University, studying there between 1925 and 1929. He earned a bachelor's degree from the School of Engineering but also completed introductory courses in sociology, economics, psychology, and political science.[22]

During his summer vacations, and for a quarter when he took a leave of absence from the university to save enough for his expenses, Nishimoto worked on a large fruit orchard in the Sacramento Valley. Eventually he managed the orchard for a while, and he once wrote: "There I gained

Looking confident and upbeat, Nishimoto was an undergraduate engineering major at Stanford University when this photograph was taken in about 1925. (Yae Nishimoto Collection, Japanese American National Museum)

valuable experience in associating with and handling thirty to one hundred-and-fifty resident and migrant farm laborers—Japanese, Portuguese, Spanish Filipino, etc."[23]

In 1929, when Nishimoto graduated in engineering, it was already the custom for businesses and corporations to come to Stanford to interview members of the senior class. One associate of Nishimoto's recalled that all of the class members received job offers after the interviews except for Nishimoto. When he asked the reason, he was reportedly told: "Look at your face. It's Oriental. No one will hire you."[24] This experience angered and hurt him very deeply at both a professional and a personal level. Despite his strong scholastic record, he never tried to apply for employment as an engineer again, although after he left the JERS project in 1948 he did work at a greenhouse in San Leandro, where some of his training as an engineer came into play.

After finishing at Stanford, Nishimoto moved to Los Angeles, where he engaged in a number of different occupations between 1929 and 1934. According to his résumé, his principal means of livelihood was running an insurance brokerage firm, although he also offered income tax services on the side. Until civil service status was required, Nishimoto was also "on call" as a Japanese-English interpreter for the municipal and superior courts of Los Angeles.

While visiting in Los Angeles in 1926, when Nishimoto was a sophomore at Stanford, his younger brother had introduced him to Yae Imai, a Nisei woman born in San Francisco who was only a few years younger than him. Nishimoto got to know her and began taking her to dances. They were married in San Francisco on August 22, 1931, and subsequently returned to Los Angeles to live.

By 1934 the couple was living in Gardena, California, with their two-year-old daughter, Roberta.[25] Nishimoto started out as a partner in a Japanese grocery store, but within a year and a half he had become the owner and operator of a fruit and vegetable market of his own in Gardena. Nishimoto commented: "People often wondered why I, a college engineering graduate, was in such a 'low down business.' To that I used to say 'I just learned the art of "bull session" at the expense of [a] hard earned $5,000.'"[26]

When Nishimoto and his family were incarcerated at Poston in 1942, Nishimoto was thirty-eight years old. He had two daughters, Marcia and Roberta, who were eight and ten years old. That same year he wrote of himself: "My friends tell me that I have the appearance of a Nisei, and act like one, yet my thoughts are typically those of intelligent Issei."[27]

Richard S. and Yae Nishimoto, an Issei-Nisei couple, on their wedding day in San Francisco on August 22, 1931. (Courtesy of Roberta Shiroma)

Poston

The Colorado River War Relocation Center was located in Arizona about midway along the border with California and seventeen miles south of the town of Parker.[28] The second largest of the ten WRA camps, it housed almost 18,000 residents at its peak and was in existence from May 1942 through November 1945. Poston was different from the nine other WRA camps in that it was divided into three subunits that were about three miles apart on a north-south axis.[29] Nishimoto lived in the largest of the three, Unit I.

The army selected the site because it intended to make the project as self-sufficient as possible, and a water supply and irrigable land were available there. The camp was named after Col. Charles Poston, the superintendent of Indian affairs in Arizona Territory during the 1860s, who reportedly believed that the valley could eventually be converted into productive farmland. It would be a mistake to think that water was plentiful at the Poston camp, however. Most of the water came from the Colorado River, which ran along the western perimeter of the project's boundary and which was close enough to be diverted to the agricultural fields surrounding the camp. The land around Poston was actually dry and desertlike. Temperatures ranged from a low of 20 degrees in the winter to a high of 125 degrees in the summer. Given that the area registered only three and a half inches of rainfall annually, loose desert soil fed major dust storms when the wind rose. The observations of Robert N. Parnell (the acting chief of operations in the engineering section) concerning the arriving Japanese Americans' reaction to Poston's environment are worth quoting in this regard:

> The people[,] with one look at this dry, barren desert, with its bleak tar papered barracks that were bare and dirty with sawdust still on its floors, were very disappointed. Each morning these people washed out their plain one room apartments with water and hose if they could get one, if not they brought bucketsful of water from the end of the barrack, perhaps one hundred feet away, trying their best to overcome the dust that had a tendency to settle on everything.[30]

Except for being divided into three distinct camps, or units, Poston was set up essentially like the nine other WRA camps. The layout of Unit I, the oldest and largest of the three, followed the standard arrangement. Extending over almost a square mile of cleared ground, Unit I was divided into thirty-six residential blocks. Each block had twenty buildings, or barracks, fourteen of which were used as living quarters for the 250 to 300 Japanese Americans residing in

The three units of the Colorado River War Relocation Center, or Poston. (Based on a map in Alexander H. Leighton, *The Governing of Men: General Principles and Recommendations Based on Experience at a Japanese Relocation Camp* [Princeton, N.J.: Princeton University Press, 1945], 57)

the block. Each of the barracks was divided into between four and seven family units. Each block also had a set of service buildings, which included a communal mess hall for meals, communal toilet and shower facilities for men and women, a recreation hall, and laundry and ironing rooms. No individual facilities for any of these purposes was made available, so in effect the design of the barracks and the block was essentially the same as that provided for young, single soldiers in the armed forces.

The majority of Japanese Americans who wound up in one of the ten WRA camps by the end of 1942 were processed through an "assembly center." This was the case with 3,459 Japanese Americans who originally resided in California and who came to Poston via the Salinas assembly center and another 1,573 who came via the one at the Santa Anita racetrack. The vast majority of Poston's inhabitants, however (some 11,738 persons), were sent directly to the camp.

Readers will recall that this last fact represents an exception to the general processes of mass incarceration. For most Japanese Americans, the initial phase of mass removal was handled by the U.S. military through the Wartime Civil Control Administration (WCCA), and it involved a stay in one of fifteen temporary "assembly centers." On March 18, 1942, the War Relocation Authority was created and was charged with administering the ten more permanent camps to which the Japanese Americans were transferred by the early fall of 1942. Two of the camps, Manzanar and Poston, were exceptions to the rule. Manzanar was a WCCA camp that was converted to a WRA camp. Poston, which was on the Colorado River Indian Reservation, was originally placed under the direction of the Office of Indian Affairs (OIA) and was run by the OIA (under contract to the WRA) until December 31, 1943.[31] The army contracted with the OIA because—in the confusion generated by the enormous logistical tasks that arose before the plan for the WRA was fully developed—the army apparently concluded that John Collier, Sr., and his staff had the necessary expertise to set up and run a camp designed to confine enemy aliens and their children, the vast majority of whom were U.S. citizens.

As one result of this setup, politics in Poston were especially complex. In addition to the usual split between the national WRA policy makers and the men and women in charge of day-to-day operations in a specific camp like Poston, there were distinct WRA and OIA factions within Poston's Euro-American administrative staff. The JERS reports (including reports and letters by Nishimoto, Tsuchiyama and Thomas) devote much attention to the latter

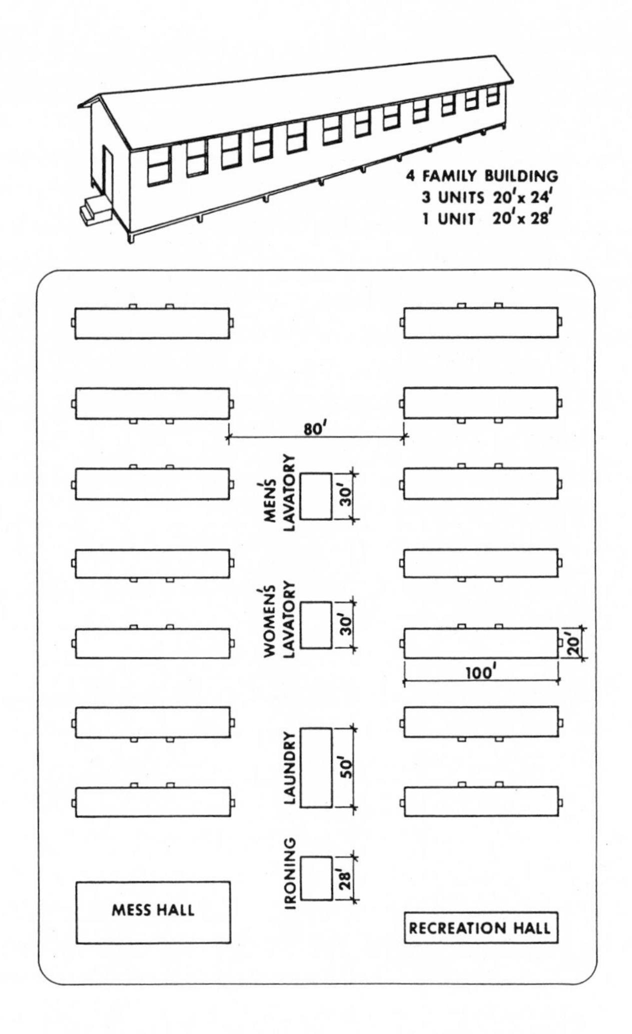

The plan of a typical block at Poston. (From Edward Spicer et al., *Impounded People: Japanese-Americans in the Relocation Centers* [Tucson: University of Arizona Press, 1969], 70)

split because of the constant tension it produced: each faction had its own views about the aims and proper administration of Poston.[32]

In addition, because of this unusual setup, Poston was the only camp to be the site of three different research projects: the Bureau of Sociological Research (BSR), which ran from June 1942 through September 1943; the Japanese American Evacuation and Resettlement Study, an independent University of California project whose Poston phase lasted from the fall of 1942 (when Tamie Tsuchiyama began her fieldwork) to the summer of 1945 (when Nishimoto was forced to leave Poston); and the WRA's Community Analysis Section, which was modeled directly after the BSR and which was represented at Poston by anthropologist and "community analyst" David H. French.[33]

Third, Poston was unusual in that its key administrator, Wade Head, tried to maximize self-governance in an effort to lessen the effects of alienation.[34] Some of Head's efforts, in fact, were viewed with suspicion by the WRA administrators, who concluded that he might be deviating from official policy. In any case, Poston's residents—like the residents of the other WRA camps—became seriously divided. Intracommunity conflict was, in fact, a major theme in Nishimoto's field journals. Such conflict was reflected in a major strike in November 1942, which was triggered by the arrest of two men accused of beating a suspected *inu*, or informer. Because it was an early and major manifestation of popular discontent, the Poston strike has been one of the major focuses of the published literature on the camp.[35]

Because the political organization of the Japanese Americans confined in Poston was complex and continually evolving, I will offer here only a brief overview, outlined in the accompanying diagram and intended mainly as a means of clarifying Nishimoto's references to the government of Poston.

The administrative design employed by the Office of Indian Affairs was originally developed by anthropologist Solon T. Kimball, but it generally followed the design specified by the WRA. Under the project director, Wade Head, there was a project attorney, the Department of Development and Services (which organized and ran physical operations, businesses, and community services for Poston), and the Community Management Department (which included Euro-American administrators for each of the three units). Beyond this, at the core of the administrative relationship between the OIA/WRA staff and the Japanese Americans was the block system (depicted on the left side of the diagram).

The role of the block system evolved in the following way. Because logistical organization was imperative from day one, many of the Japanese Americans (primarily Nisei) who volunteered to come early to Poston to help set up the camp were appointed as block managers. Each block manager supervised a small staff, whose activities revolved around cleaning and maintaining the block. Through the block managers' council, made up of all thirty-six managers, and the Japanese American supervisor of the block managers, block-level

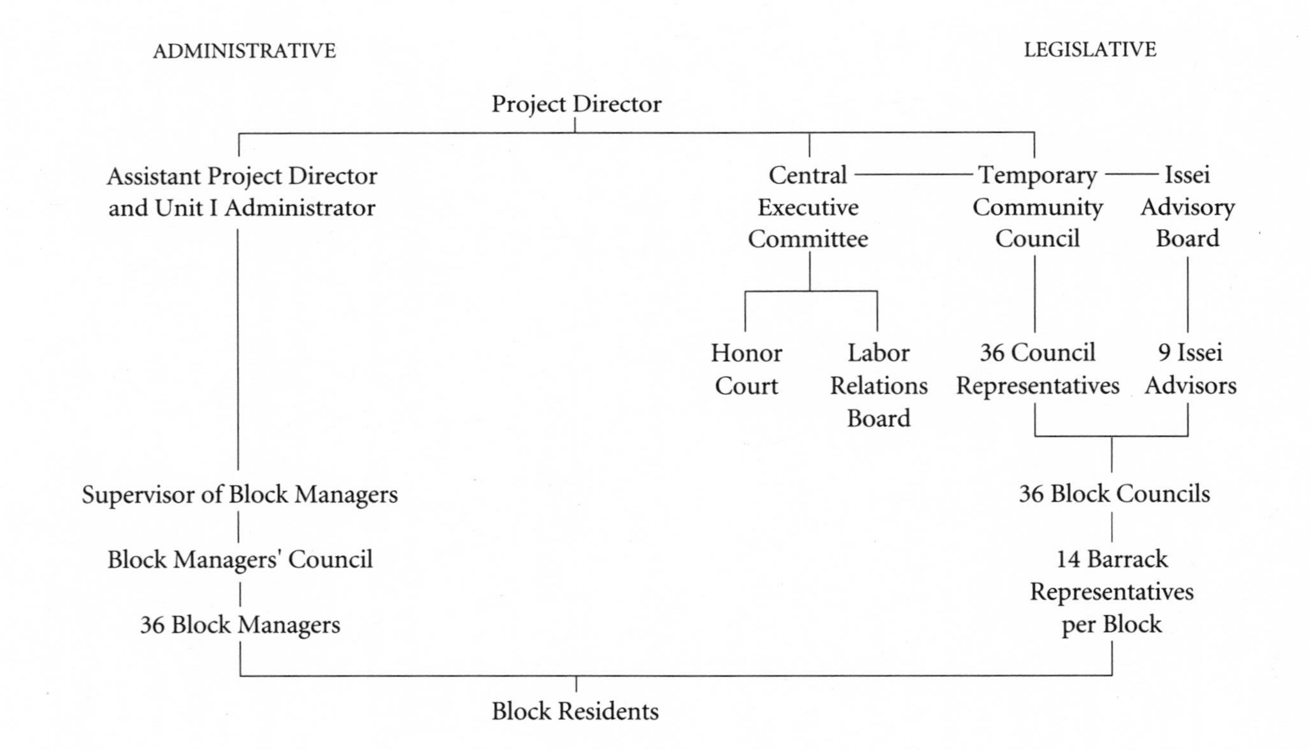

The poststrike power structure of Unit I at Poston.

concerns could be transmitted upward through the hierarchy to the assistant project director, John Evans (who was also initially the Unit I administrator). Evans could, in turn, relay matters to the project director. The same hierarchy served to disseminate information about administrative policy downward to the block managers and ultimately to the 250 or so residents of each block. The block manager system, then, was a hierarchical administrative order with the Euro-American administrators on the top. It was what the administration used to run the day-to-day affairs of the camp.

The right side of the diagram depicts the "legislative" setup of Poston. Since one of the general aims of the WRA was to make the Japanese American experience in the WRA camps an education in American democracy, from the beginning it emphasized that the Japanese Americans should exercise a degree of self-governance. This policy became the focus of intense controversy in Poston because in early June 1942 the WRA banned the first-generation Issei, who had been the undisputed leaders of the prewar Japanese American community, from holding elective office in Poston's government because of their status as Japanese nationals. So, while each block could establish a block council made up of fourteen representatives (often one person from each barrack), only Nisei were allowed to become council representatives, and thus only Nisei could play a formal role in Unit I's Temporary Community Council (also known as the Local Community Council), composed of thirty-six members, one from each block. Because this policy gave power to Nisei "kids," who were generally regarded as lacking in both the experience and knowledge to be effective leaders, it was unacceptable to the Issei leadership and proved to be one of the key stimuli behind the famed Poston strike of November 1942.

After the strike was settled, the Euro-American administration sought to remedy the situation by permitting the Japanese Americans to establish various Issei advisory boards and committees. These were designed to supplement existing bodies like the Temporary Community Council. As Nishimoto's reports on gambling and the All Center Conference indicate, from this point the Issei began to wield a great deal of power in Poston via their participation in the newly created Central Executive Committee (or Central Executive Board), their virtual control over the Labor Relations Board (which had the power to fire any Japanese American who held an appointed position), and their influence over Poston's "City Council" (the bureaucratic name for the Temporary Community Council and the Issei Advisory Board together).

The Issei sometimes used their new positions as a platform for debate and ultimately as means of influencing popular opinion in regard to the central issues facing Poston's residents. Much debate occurred, for example, on the question of whether the residents should return to the West Coast as the war wound down. Nishimoto's All Center Conference report records the various voices in this key debate and also indicates his efforts to weaken the influence of those Issei leaders who advocated staying in Poston for the duration, largely because he believed that Poston, as a racially segregated city under the control of a civilian agency of the federal government, was an anomalous and therefore basically unhealthy environment.

In addition, although the supervisor of the block managers was initially appointed by Poston's Euro-American administrators, later this became an elected position, and Nishimoto eventually held it. Similarly, although the unit administrators were exclusively Euro-American OIA personnel, Japanese Americans eventually took over the position of city manager.

Little has been published about the political organization of Units II and III, but they too were governed by a similar, constantly evolving set of committees.

Nishimoto in Poston

A review of Nishimoto's activities at Poston demonstrates how multifaceted his roles were within the camp. As soon as he and his family arrived in May 1942, Nishimoto took on a variety of jobs in Unit I. Between June and September 1942, he was the foreman of the "firebreak gang," a work group of Japanese American laborers who were responsible for clearing the grounds of construction debris and completing other menial tasks.[36] By February 1943, Nishimoto had been elected as the manager of Block 45. Later he became a block councilman for the same block. By resolving a variety of personnel problems in each of these positions, Nishimoto quickly established his skill at administration.[37]

In assessing Nishimoto's rise as a community leader, it should be remembered here that his educational background probably had a favorable influence on his social status. The Issei valued education, so educated men had prestige. Because he had been educated in Japan at a higher level than most Issei and because he was older and better educated than most of the Kibei Nisei (who had been born in the United States but had been educated in Japan) Nishimoto had one of the necessary prerequisites in this subculture to assume a leadership role. Although he spoke English with an accent, his degree from Stanford meant that he was also better educated than most of the Nisei, even by their own American educational standards. Furthermore, although Nishimoto was among the younger Issei, his age cohorts were Issei, not the younger Nisei, which is significant in a subculture in which generational age grading was a significant dimension of the social structure.

Although he served in official and semiofficial capacities, Nishimoto was also an active participant in camp protests from the very beginning.[38] On November 18, 1942, for example, as the momentum for protest began to build, Nishimoto was well enough regarded to be selected as the leader of a demonstration outside Ward 7 of the camp hospital, where John Evans (the assistant director of Poston and the chief administrative officer of Unit I) was scheduled to address the city council. Although the demonstration was canceled, Nishimoto was clearly willing to carry out his charge.

Not long afterward, Nishimoto talked the block managers of Unit I into resigning as a group. In doing so he is said to have argued: "Don't kid yourselves. The job [of negotiating with the WRA] is too big for us. We have elected representatives whose duty it is to negotiate with Mr. Evans. What we should do is resign and join the movement."[39]

His colleague Tamie Tsuchiyama reported that Nishimoto told several "young Nisei intellectuals," who felt uncomfortable about the block flags, which looked suspiciously like Japanese flags to them:

> That is a sign of defiance. For example, when you scold a child, he sticks his tongue out at you. If you kick a dog around several times eventually he will bite you. . . . This fight against the administration is a result of their incompetency and inefficiency added to the suffering caused by evacuation. We've got to let off our steam sometime. . . . [The flags are] just made up by a few crackpots with mischievous notions. If they really wanted to signify their allegiance they would have instead put up real flags. They are trying to tease the Caucasians as they have been teased by them so often.[40]

As the archival record reveals, Nishimoto also used his position as block manager to influence residents to support the strike, albeit in a way he considered appropriate. An excellent example is included in a report by Tamie Tsuchiyama. Her account illustrates the manipulative nature of Nishimoto's leadership style:

> In other blocks the intimidation was more subtle. Thus in block 45 "X" [Nishimoto] told me that by adroit handling on the first day he was able to bring his indifferent block into line and steer its course the way he wanted without any overt expression of dissatisfaction emerging throughout the incident. He began

> his experiment by calling a block meeting on Thursday morning at seven o'clock—the breakfast hour—so that the turn out would be as nearly 100% as possible. At that time he explained that the City Council, the Issei Advisory Board, and the block managers had all resigned the day before and that a general strike had been called by the Emergency Council. He informed them that block 45 had certain commitments to fulfill *along with every block in camp*, one of them being supporting the strike 100% and furnishing pickets in front of the police station at all hours of the day and night. He then read off the names of the block people who had participated in the demonstration the day before and asked the audience to show their appreciation of them by clapping. He next assigned pickets to certain shifts and when he arrived at the graveyard shift (midnight to 8:00 A.M.) he stopped momentarily and then resumed quietly: "Now let me read the names of people who *volunteered* for these hours." There were fourteen of them and when he added an extra seven there was no opposition from that quarter. Then cleverly he approached two older men—one, a confirmed invalid, the other a cripple—and requested their cooperation in picketing. When these two acquiesced there was no other recourse for any one but to fall in line and support his program. Only one individual was not approached—Reverend Kitano [pseudonym], the blind Evangelist. But when he came on his own accord, and when X spied him on the highway, [Nishimoto] went out to meet him and melodramatically led him to the proper campfire to the surprise of fellow block pickets. Through clever intimidation he had no difficulty in securing the fullest cooperation of his block throughout the strike or in suppressing any overt action, e.g., the hoisting of a Japanese flag or the reciting of loud banzais. Their standard was simply a large white banner with 45 in red letters. [Emphasis in original.][41]

Clearly, Nishimoto was very good at using popular issues to establish his leadership skills and consolidate his power base.

According to Nishimoto, in the year following the Poston strike he was involved in a series of political maneuvers that led him to assume a leadership position in the camp as a whole. As he subsequently explained to his JERS colleagues at a staff conference in Salt Lake City in 1944, he was able to win political battles and consolidate his power base because, he said,

> [I] held no official position, but had good influence over pre-evacuation leaders who returned from internment camp or who were afraid to take part in the movement of the extremists. They didn't hold official positions. Orange County blocks, for instance, were controlled by a man named Murata. . . . [I] contacted about five of these men. [I] controlled the Orange County, Salinas, Imperial and Los Angeles groups. [I] knew how the pre-evacuation politics worked.[42]

By 1943, many of Poston's residents simply wanted peace and order. Responding to this mood, Nishimoto maneuvered to gain as much power as possible for the block managers. He believed that since the block managers had intimate ties to the residents and because the executive committee of the block managers was in turn selected by the block managers themselves, the managers constituted a fair and representative system of self-government. In the same 1944 report Nishimoto commented: "The residents want to bring their problems where it is most effective. By bringing problems to the block managers their problems are being solved."[43] By comparison, other formal and informal political bodies in Poston were ineffectual or divided. Therefore, because he led the block managers, Nishimoto was able to influence the city council, successfully challenge competing Issei and Kibei leaders, and become a formidable power broker within the camp. Nishimoto's "sociological" journal entries indicate that his assistance and counsel were widely sought throughout the camp by Japanese Americans and Euro-American WRA employees alike.

Nishimoto eventually became the official supervisor of the block managers of Unit I and what he described as a "personal advisor" to Poston's project director. For example, at an unusual conference of JERS personnel that was held in Salt Lake City in early December 1944 and that included both Euro-American and key Japanese American fieldworkers for the project, Nishimoto boasted to his colleagues that the Poston project director "does not act on important matters without consulting [me]. The assistant project directors come to [me]. It creates pressures on the Caucasian hierarchy. When any emergency arises, Caucasians are placed under [me]."[44] Although it has not been possible to fully corroborate Nishimoto's claims, it does appear that he had gained a tremendous amount of influence within Poston by 1944.

Nishimoto's Research Activities

By June 1942, just a month after he arrived in camp, Nishimoto was already working as an assistant for the Bureau of Sociological Research (BSR). Presumably he obtained employment because, as an educated and fully bilingual and bicultural individual, the bureau's administrators considered him especially well qualified to record the impact of relocation. In this capacity Nishimoto received an important measure of training and was also put in touch with a range of student and professional researchers from whom he continued to draw information during his stay at Poston. At any rate, Nishimoto disliked Alexander Leighton, the director of the bureau, so he quit relatively quickly (in October according to Nishimoto; in December according to Tamie Tsuchiyama).[45]

Tamie Tsuchiyama was also initially an employee of the bureau. A Nisei born in Kauai County, Hawaii, in 1915, Tsuchiyama had been a graduate student in the Department of Anthropology at the University of California, Berkeley, before the war. After President Roosevelt signed Executive Order 9066 on February 19, 1942, and after Dorothy Thomas was put in charge of the JERS project in the spring of 1942, Thomas and her fellow professors began to identify Japanese American undergraduate and graduate students who would be in a good position to document the impact of forced removal on the community because of their educational background and, of course, because they were going to be directly involved and impacted anyway. Tsuchiyama apparently could have escaped mass incarceration by returning to Hawaii to rejoin her parents. Nevertheless, on the recommendation of Robert H. Lowie, one of her anthropology professors at Berkeley, she decided to accompany her mainland compatriots to the camp, primarily in order to study the situation as a JERS fieldworker. What is more, archival documents make it clear that the Poston authorities were notified in writing in advance as to Tsuchiyama's status in the camp as a JERS researcher officially employed by the University of California.[46]

After beginning as a fieldworker for the Bureau of Sociological Research, Tsuchiyama quit at around the same time as Nishimoto because she found Leighton hard to relate to. Since she had already been recruited by the JERS project, when she quit the BSR she simply moved over into the other research project full-time. During her stint with the BSR, however, Tsuchiyama, who had met Nishimoto socially before the war, had gotten to know him as a colleague and had come to appreciate his knowledge and keen insights.[47]

In early January 1943, Tsuchiyama wrote to Thomas: "Since the strike I have gained the confidence of X [Nishimoto], one of the two most powerful figures in camp. . . . [He] supplies me with all the political intrigues behind the scenes so that I am at present in a better position to analyze camp politics. Frequently he gives me advance notices of certain movements on foot so that I shall more fully appreciate them when they happen."[48] Nishimoto also allowed Tsuchiyama access to his journal, which she cut up and filed in order to make it available as data for JERS.

In early April 1943, Tsuchiyama was staggering under her fieldwork and writing agenda. She wrote to Thomas, wondering

> whether there were sufficient funds in the Study to permit me to take X as an Issei observer, just as Bob [Robert Spencer] has Abe [pseudonym] and Hayano [pseudonym] for his assistants. I sounded out X . . . in a round about way and gathered that he would be perfectly willing. . . . One of the advantages in "hiring" X is that I can have access to all the official memos sent out by the administration to the blocks. Furthermore he comes in daily contact with a great number of Issei and a certain type of Nisei that it will permit me to focus my attention on that type of Nisei he does not touch. So far I have found his material very reliable.[49]

Thomas formally hired Nishimoto in early 1943, largely on Tsuchiyama's recommendation and with an initial assignment of acting as Tsuchiyama's assistant and helping her prepare her JERS reports on the daily events in Poston. In fact, throughout the years from 1942 to 1945 Nishimoto served as a clandestine researcher in Poston for the JERS project, and he made every effort to conceal this fact at the time.[50] Because he realized that he would have no access to information should his role as a JERS researcher be known, Nishimoto asked that all references to him in JERS materials be coded as "X" to avoid identifying him by name. Apparently he believed that mail at Poston could be too easily searched or seized by the WRA staff or fellow inmates. Although Nishimoto seldom mentioned any fear for his personal safety, it is clear from his notes that other "researchers" were suspected of being *inu*, or informers, and that such a reputation could put them in physical jeopardy.[51]

When Nishimoto was first hired as Tsuchiyama's "Issei assistant," he was paid fifteen dollars a month.[52] Thomas pointed out that although California did not allow direct payments to Issei, "we are allowed to buy their 'product.'" Two months later, after assessing his contributions to the JERS project, Thomas raised Nishimoto's salary to fifty and then eighty dollars a month. It is worth remembering, for the record, that salaries for the Japanese Americans who chose to work at Poston ranged from twelve dollars a month for menial labor to nineteen for highly trained personnel, including dentists and doctors. In this light, an extra sixty dollars a month was no mean sum.

The Bases of Nishimoto's Authority in JERS

Now that Nishimoto's personal background, his public roles at Poston, and his various research activities have been outlined, the issue of Nishimoto's position as an authoritative source for the JERS project can be delineated.

We have seen how, coming from a family of some means, Nishimoto had received the benefit of a good education. He had more schooling in Japan than the average immigrant Issei, and his education was probably of a higher quality: it was more recent, and all of Nishimoto's schools were located in the capital city of Tokyo.

By the time he emigrated, Nishimoto was old enough to have become quite familiar with Japanese culture and society. At the same time, his middle-school experience in Japan, sponsored by the Episcopalians, implies some exposure to the English language and American values and culture. This exposure, along with the fact that he knew he was to join his parents in America, probably resulted in his having a degree of preadaptation, which would partly account for Nishimoto's success in completing coursework at Lowell High School in four years even though he was a recent immigrant. Subsequently it took him only four years (not counting the quarter he worked in an orchard in order to earn money for his tuition and expenses) to earn his baccalaureate degree in engineering from Stanford. In short, Nishimoto, because of his bicultural background and education in Japan and the United States, had unique qualities that made him a suitable candidate to record the impact of removal and incarceration.

Regarding his apparent lack of training for his work as a field researcher, it should be noted that before World War II even graduate coursework in anthropology did not include systematic or comprehensive instruction in ethnographic field methods.[53] Nishimoto was, however, exposed to intensive training in Poston via classes set up under the auspices of the Bureau of Sociological Research—classes that the bureau originated primarily to train select Japanese Americans in Poston to be BSR research assistants and fieldworkers. Transcriptions of BSR sessions suggest that Nishimoto's exposure to field methods and the fundamental tools of sociocultural analysis were probably as advanced, if not more advanced, than many of the formally trained graduate students of the day.[54] Nishimoto's instructors at the BSR were, after all, well-known anthropologists like Professors Alexander H. Leighton and Edward Spicer. Subsequently, as a JERS employee, Nishimoto continued to have extensive contacts with Spicer, a lively correspondence with Dorothy Thomas, and various collegial relationships with other formally trained "graduate student" researchers at Poston, including anthropologists Tsuchiyama; Elizabeth Colson, whom Leighton hired as a BSR staff member; David French, who was the WRA-appointed "community analyst" at Poston; and Rosalie Wax, another JERS fieldworker whom Nishimoto and Tsuchiyama visited briefly in the Gila River WRA camp, also in Arizona, in September 1943.[55] In short, as a member of both the BSR and JERS, Nishimoto gained instruction in the goals and methods of both projects, had contact with both directors, and attended BSR and JERS staff meetings and seminars. In addition, he studied and learned as he went along. His own notes and his associates' correspondence suggest that he bought and read the latest literature in order to keep up with the social science theories and methods of his day.[56]

Given such experiences, it is really not surprising that his BSR and JERS reports indicate that Nishimoto was able to record data systematically and that he could be a careful and thorough observer. His early "Firebreak Gang" study, reproduced below, clearly indicates that Nishimoto had the ability to arrange data into a thematic report that included his own sociocultural analysis.

The same educational and linguistic skills that made Nishimoto attractive as a research assistant put him in a good position to achieve a prominent leadership position in Poston. Also, Nishimoto had had the opportunity to gain experience as a manager in the course of supervising a multi-ethnic labor force in the agricultural setting of Vacaville long before he entered Poston. Further, by the time the war broke out, he had the added advantage of close contact with many individuals and institutions in the two areas that had been the heart of mainland Japanese America since early in the century: the San Francisco Bay area and Los Angeles. His various occupational endeavors during the 1920s in northern California and the 1930s in southern California gave him exposure to rural and urban populations, settings, and communities, and also a wide range of personal contacts. At the same time, his English-language skills, gained via his education at Lowell and Stanford and his exposure to employment in other dominant-society institutions ranging from the southern California insurance industry to the Los Angeles County court system gave him a certain style and flair that not many of his fellow Issei could boast of. For all of these reasons, Nishimoto was clearly more familiar with and more comfortable relating to dominant society institutions and bureaucracies than most Issei and many Nisei—a fact that he would put to good use during the war years.

In his various administrative posts, largely tied to the block managers group, Nishimoto was in an excellent position to carry out his BSR and JERS research duties, especially because of the access to information such positions gave him. He had a legitimate reason, that is, to know about everything that was going on in Poston, so he was able to ask questions without exciting suspicion. His role among the block managers also gave him extensive access to the Euro-American staff at Poston. Especially in his role as the head of the executive committee of Unit I's block managers, he could again manage to speak with a wide range of Poston's staff members without exciting attention or suspicion. It is not surprising, then, that Nishimoto's journals are rich in data: they contain information that would probably have been denied to Euro-American ethnographers or researchers and that would not have been available to many of Poston's residents.

Nishimoto's language skills, education, and temperament also enabled him to become an able mediator between Poston's various interest groups. He was able to communicate with and understand both the Issei and the Nisei. Further, because of his experience in bureaucratic institutions in the dominant society, and with his interest in management theory, he was also able to understand and deal with WRA administrators and researchers.[57] For these same reasons, Nishimoto was consulted by many people within Poston—Japanese American and Euro-American alike. Nishimoto's advice was valued because he had extensive knowledge of the operation of the camp, and he also knew quite a bit about WRA bureaucracy and policy. He could frame his counsel in terms of both viewpoints.[58]

At the same time, as a credible witness and a key informant who was able to produce page upon page of description, commentary, and analysis, Nishimoto impressed Dorothy Thomas as an energetic, informed fieldworker even though he was much more active and involved than a social science participant-observer would normally be. Nishimoto was, in short, perfectly positioned to be a researcher in Poston for the JERS project:

1. He was an Issei subject to incarceration.
2. He was educated, had both Japanese and English language skills, and was bicultural.
3. He had been exposed to Japanese Americans in a range of community and occupational settings throughout California.
4. He had extensive experience in dominant-society educational, business, and judicial institutions.
5. He was a careful observer when he chose to be, able to record data,

systematically assess evidence, and arrange the materials he collected and processed into effective reports.

6. He knew all of the key leaders at Poston—both Euro-American and Japanese American—and as revealed in his sociological journal, he had assessed their basic motives and intentions based on research data collected for such purposes.
7. As supervisor of the block managers, he had access to diverse kinds of information, and the right to pursue information with either Euro-Americans or Japanese Americans.
8. Finally, he had the political knowledge, skills, and savvy to play the role of an effective mediator and a broker between the Japanese Americans and the administrators.

These same attributes also go far toward explaining why Dorothy Thomas came to rely so heavily on Nishimoto.[59] While Thomas was a highly trained professional, she did not speak or read Japanese; she was not familiar with the details of the internal relationships of the Japanese American community, its leaders, or its politics; and she did not live or engage in extensive participant observation in any of the camps. In all these areas, Nishimoto's experience, skills, and insights fully complemented those of his boss. Further, it is clear that Thomas herself fully recognized Nishimoto's value in this regard. In a letter fragment (written in about 1952 or 1953 to Edward Barnhart) Thomas commented on the inconsistencies between a draft copy of what was to become *Prejudice, War and the Constitution* and her own two books, noting that

> In some instances, I felt that these inconsistencies were due merely to the fact that complete documentation was not available in secondary sources, or in our files, and that gaps would have to be filled in by having an informed, intelligent "insider" review these sections. In this respect, I thought and continue to think that Nishimoto has unique value. I am therefore deeply gratified that he has turned up at this crucial moment.[60]

For all of these reasons, then, Nishimoto's writings are a very valuable resource for social scientists and historians who seek to understand the long- and short-term significance of mass incarceration for Japanese Americans and for American history as a whole.

Notes

1. It is interesting to note how Thomas and Nishimoto were characterized on the dust jacket of the original edition of *The Spoilage:* "Authors of this volume are Dorothy Swaine Thomas, noted sociologist, and Richard S. Nishimoto, Tokyo-born, long-time resident of California, himself an evacuee and a participant-observer of this mass displacement of people."

2. See, for example, Marvin K. Opler's review of *The Spoilage* in *American Anthropologist* 50 (1948): 307–31.

3. See the findings of Lowell Chun-Hoon and his colleagues at the Asian American Studies Center, UCLA, who conducted a survey that revealed that, out of seventy-two required texts in Asian American courses, *The Spoilage* ranked number four in overall popularity, although it was included to document popular resistance in a way that the authors did not necessarily intend; Lowell Chun-Hoon et al., "Curriculum Development in Asian American Studies: A Working Paper," in *Proceedings of National Asian American Studies Conference II*, ed. George Kagiwada et al. (Davis, Calif.: University of California, Davis, Department of Applied Behavioral Sciences, Asian American Studies Center, 1973), 85.

4. I would like to acknowledge the support of the University of Arizona Press in realizing the importance of making available a variety of points of view on mass incarceration. Having already published books that represent the perspective of anthropologists involved as WRA "community analysts" in Edward Spicer et al., *Impounded People: Japanese-Americans in the Relocation Centers* (1969), and a WRA director's experiences in Dillon S. Myer's *Uprooted Americans* (1971), the press agreed that it was fitting to add Nishimoto's voice to the record.

5. The Issei were people born in Japan but residing in the United States as legal resident aliens. They were ineligible for naturalization before 1952. The Nisei were second-generation Japanese Americans who were U.S. citizens by virtue of being born on U.S. soil (or in the Territory of Hawaii after 1900). The Kibei (a subset of the Nisei) were Nisei who, after being born in the United States, were sent back to Japan and received socialization and all or part of their formal education there. According to Toshio Yatsushiro, the War Relocation Authority estimated that Kibei made up on the order of 13 percent of the second generation; see *Politics and Cultural Values: The World War II Japanese Relocation Centers and the United States Government* (Ph.D. diss., Cornell University, 1954; reprint, New York: Arno Press, 1978), 305–7.

6. In this sense, I have selected and interpreted Nishimoto's work in ways that he might not necessarily have agreed with. For more information on JERS, see Yuji Ichioka, "JERS Revisited: Introduction," in *Views from Within: The Japanese American Evacuation and Resettlement Study*, ed. Yuji Ichioka (Los Angeles: Asian American Studies Center, 1989), 3–27. For an assessment of Dorothy Thomas's intellectual leadership as

the director of JERS by a former employee of the Japanese American Evacuation and Resettlement Study, see S. Frank Miyamoto, "Dorothy Swaine Thomas as Director of JERS: Some Personal Observations," in Ichioka, *Views from Within*, 40–41.

7. Timothy Lukes and Gary Y. Okihiro, *Japanese Legacy: Farming and Community Life in California's Santa Clara Valley* (Cupertino: California History Center, 1985), 2–3.

8. The concept of "racialization" that I draw from here is presented in Michael Omi and Howard Winant, *Racial Formation in the United States* (New York: Routledge, 1986), and in Howard Winant, "Contesting the Meaning of Race in the Post-Civil Rights Period," in his book *Racial Conditions* (New York: Routledge, 1994), 57–68.

9. The quote is taken from an unpublished manuscript by Manning Marable, "Contemporary Black Protest Movements" in the editor's possession. Popular resistance in the camps is a revisionist historical theme pioneered by Gary Y. Okihiro. See his essay "Japanese Resistance in America's Concentration Camps," *Amerasia Journal* 2 (1973): 20–34. Also, see Arthur A. Hansen and David A. Hacker, "The Manzanar Riot: An Ethnic Perspective," *Amerasia Journal* 2 (1974): 112–57; Arthur A. Hansen, "Cultural Politics in the Gila River Relocation Center, 1942–1943," *Arizona and the West* 27 (1985): 327–62; and Michie Weglyn, *Years of Infamy: The Untold Story of America's Concentration Camps* (New York: William Morrow, 1976), all of which contributed to the conceptualization offered here.

10. The major exception is Richard Drinnon's brief but incisive comments about Nishimoto in *Keeper of Concentration Camps: Dillon S. Myer and American Racism* (Berkeley: University of California Press, 1987), 48–49, 169–70, 282.

11. Tsuchiyama to Thomas, April 6, 1943, Bancroft Library, University of California, Berkeley, Japanese American Evacuation and Resettlement Study (JERS), J 6.32.

12. Thomas to Nishimoto, September 22, 1943, JERS W 1.25A.

13. Yuji Ichioka, "JERS Revisited: Introduction" in Ichioka, *Views From Within*, 17. Details of Nishimoto's life in the four years following his departure from the project are also detailed in a letter from Nishimoto to Thomas of March 5, 1952; "Unpublished manuscripts," Dorothy S. Thomas, Papers Regarding Japanese Relocation, 78/53c, Bancroft Library (hereafter cited as the Thomas Papers).

14. The bulk of Nishimoto's research materials, all of which are unpublished, are held in the Bancroft Library at the University of California, Berkeley, although archives at both the University of Arizona and the University of California, Los Angeles, hold reports and correspondence by Nishimoto as well.

15. Nishimoto to Thomas, March 5, 1952; Thomas Papers.

16. Leonard Broom and Ruth Riemer, *Removal and Return: The Socio-Economic Effects of the War on Japanese Americans* (Berkeley: University of California Press, 1949). Nishimoto's research has been drawn on by many different scholars of the camps, some of whom have acknowledged this fact; see Audrie Girdner and Anne Loftis, *The Great*

Betrayal: The Evacuation of the Japanese-Americans during World War II (London: Macmillan, 1969), 221–23; and Isami Arifuku Waugh, "Hidden Crime and Deviance in the Japanese-American Community" (Ph.D. dissertation., University of California, Berkeley, 1978). Others apparently drew from Nishimoto's work but did not, for whatever reason, choose to acknowledge this fact; see, for example, Alexander H. Leighton, *The Governing of Men: General Principles and Recommendations Based on Experience at a Japanese Relocation Camp* (1945; reprint, New York: Octagon, 1964), 131–32; Edward H. Spicer et al., *Impounded People*, 219. Some seem not to have understood exactly who Nishimoto really was; see, for example, Thomas James, *Exile Within: The Schooling of Japanese Americans, 1942–1945* (Cambridge, Mass.: Harvard University Press, 1987), 96, 193n. 17.

17. Thomas to August Fruge, March 25, 1953.

18. Jacobus tenBroek et al., *Prejudice, War and the Constitution* (Berkeley: University of California Press, 1954), xii–xiii.

19. This was a question that puzzled some of the JERS researchers even some forty years after the fact; see Robert Spencer's queries to Arthur A. Hansen along these lines in "An Interview with Robert F. Spencer" in *Japanese American World War Two Evacuation Oral History Project*, ed. Arthur A. Hansen, pt. 3: *Analysts* (Munich: K. G. Saur, 1994), 211, 271–72, and passim.

20. Leighton interview with Nishimoto, November 28, 1942, JERS J 6.15. Some twenty-one years later Nishimoto observed of his religious orientation that "I'm registered as a Episcopalian but it doesn't mean a thing"; transcript, Bureau of Sociological Research staff meeting, November 3, 1942, p. 3, Japanese American Relocation Papers, #3830, Department of Manuscripts and Archives, Cornell University Library.

Nishimoto, like many Issei, took on a Western name after he came to the United States. Roberta Shiroma, Nishimoto's eldest daughter, supplied some of the biographical data concerning her father, including a copy of his résumé. Some points are also discussed in chapters 1 and 2 below.

21. This made Nishimoto an *oya no yobiyose*, a first-generation immigrant child who was left in Japan when the parents went overseas but who "was called" to join them once they had become established.

22. Nishimoto's undergraduate training is described in Dorothy S. Thomas and Richard Nishimoto, *The Spoilage*, Japanese American Evacuation and Resettlement series (Berkeley: University of California Press, 1946), viii. The information is also available in Nishimoto's transcript in the Thomas Papers.

23. From his "Firebreak Gang" report, below.

24. Interview by the editor, August 27, 1987. Interviewee prefers to remain anonymous.

25. For a study of the Japanese American community in Gardena, see Lane Ryo Hirabayashi and George Tanaka, "The Issei Community in Moneta and the Gardena Valley," *Southern California Quarterly* 70 (1988): 127–58.

26. From "Firebreak Gang" below.

27. From "Letter to Alexander Leighton" below.

28. A number of studies focus specifically on Poston, including Alexander H. Leighton, *The Governing of Men*, and Paul Bailey, *City in the Sun: The Japanese Concentration Camp at Poston, Arizona* (Los Angeles: Westernlore Press, 1971).

29. I have been told but have been unable to independently document the point that Poston was divided in this fashion because experts who had set up camps for the Civilian Conservation Corps advised that the size of any given residential unit be kept below 10,000 persons; Mr. Dean Yabuki, personal communication, 1991. Reference to CCC participation in the early construction of Poston can be found in Robert N. Parnell, "Final Report: Operations Division," JERS J 3.96.

30. Robert N. Parnell, "Final Report: Operations Division," JERS J 3.96.

31. Leighton, *The Governing of Men*, 48–52.

32. Tamie Tsuchiyama, "The Poston Strike: A Chronological Account," JERS J 6.24; Leighton, *The Governing of Men*, 91–92, 151. The administrative factions are discussed in the report to the JERS staff at the JERS Chicago conference in December 1943; JERS W 1.10, 43 and passim.

33. Orin Starn, "Engineering Internment: Anthropologists and the War Relocation Authority," *American Ethnologist* 13 (1986): 700–720.

34. Leighton, *The Governing of Men*, 82, 208–9; Nishimoto to Thomas, January 24, 1944, Thomas Papers.

35. In addition to the books by Leighton and Bailey, see the comparative analyses of the Poston strike of November 1942 offered by Gary Y. Okihiro in "Japanese Resistance in America's Concentration Camps: A Re-Evaluation," *Amerasia Journal* 2 (1973): 20–34; and Toshio Yatsushiro in *Politics and Cultural Values* (New York: Arno Press, 1978).

36. This experience is described in detail in "Firebreak Gang" below.

37. This information is found in Nishimoto's own account, presented in JERS W 1.15, December 4, 1944, 1–20; and his JERS journals, which are filled with references to specific cases.

38. The account of Nishimoto's protest activities is synthesized from his statement "Richard Nishimoto on the Political Organization of Poston," December 4, 1944, JERS W 1.1.5; and Tamie Tsuchiyama's report "The Poston Strike," JERS J 6.24. I was also able to confirm the general thrust of both documents in a series of interviews in 1987 and 1988 with a former Poston resident who was a close friend of Nishimoto's after the war and who asked to remain anonymous.

39. Tsuchiyama, "The Poston Strike." This information was probably given to Tsuchiyama by Nishimoto himself; see "An Interview with Robert F. Spencer" in Hansen, *Evacuation Oral History Project*, pt. 3, pp. 210–11.

40. Tsuchiyama, "The Poston Strike."

41. Ibid. Tsuchiyama clearly believed that Nishimoto was an important community leader, although he was working behind the scenes (as he noted he liked to do; see his

"Letter to Alexander Leighton" below). At any rate, although Nishimoto was not yet employed by JERS as Tsuchiyama's assistant, information thus obtained and presented must be handled critically. On occasion Nishimoto had a tendency to dramatize when discussing his own thoughts and actions (see, for example, his statement to his colleagues in December 1944; JERS W 1.15). At his worst, he even appears to have exaggerated and overinflated the importance of his contributions.

42. Nishimoto, "Political Organization of Poston," 9.

43. Ibid., passim.

44. Ibid., p. 20. Throughout this document, Nishimoto uses the pseudonym *Sawada* for himself.

45. Nishimoto to Thomas, October 22, 1943, Thomas Papers. In this letter Nishimoto wrote that, ultimately, "I didn't trust Leighton, nor did I have faith in what he could do." See also Tsuchiyama to Thomas, November 2, 1943, JERS J 6.32.

46. Tsuchiyama to Robert H. Lowie, August 24, 1942, JERS J 6.32.

47. The letters deposited in the JERS collection often provide a rich set of insights into the personalities of the JERS staff, as well as the development of their interpersonal relationships. There is, for example, an amazing correspondence between Tsuchiyama and Thomas (JERS J 6.32) that begins with great cordiality and progresses to complete acrimony immediately before Tsuchiyama's resignation from the project. Although Tsuchiyama went on to finish her Ph.D. dissertation ("A Comparison of the Folklore of the Northern, Southern and Pacific Athabaskans: A Study in Stability of Folklore within a Linguistic Stock" [University of California, Berkeley, 1947]), she apparently never contacted her JERS colleagues again before she died in May 1984. These personal letters may nonetheless eventually provide the basis for a more detailed understanding of the complex relationship between these two social scientists.

48. Tsuchiyama to Thomas, January 3, 1943, JERS J 6.32.

49. Tsuchiyama to Thomas, April 6, 1943, JERS J 6.32. Although I have not been able to verify this, rumor has it that Nishimoto and Tsuchiyama became more than just colleagues while both were at Poston working as JERS staff. See, for example, Robert Spencer's commentary "An Interview with Robert F. Spencer" in Hansen, *Evacuation Oral History Project*, pt. 3, pp. 210, 255. As far as I can determine, however, this relationship and its termination did not impinge on Nishimoto's work for JERS, although it may in fact have affected Tsuchiyama's scholarship. Her correspondence indicates that in July 1943 Tsuchiyama decided to leave Poston for a writing stint in Chicago that began around November 1943 and lasted through July 1944. She was on the JERS payroll and was supposed to be focusing solely on writing up her research, but according to Thomas's letter of July 28, 1944, she did not make any tangible progress during the eight-month period. Clearly smarting from Thomas's sharp, condescending remarks, Tsuchiyama resigned from the JERS project three days later. Interested readers should note that S. Frank Miyamoto concluded that Dorothy Thomas's proprietary attitude toward her staff members' field notes caused a great deal of conflict within the project;

see S. Frank Miyamoto, "Dorothy Swaine Thomas as Director of JERS: Some Personal Observations," in Ichioka, *Views from Within*, 41–43.

50. Ordinarily there is a world of difference between an informant, who is generally a knowledgeable member of a sociocultural group who is retained in a fairly public fashion by a social scientist in order to provide an insider's point of view on a given society and culture, and an informer, who passes along information to someone else covertly. Some argue that in cases like Nishimoto's this line was blurred and that Nishimoto may even have acted unethically because, at least while he was in camp, he chose not to reveal his role as a researcher. This raises some ethical issues, and my position on them is as follows. First, Nishimoto was not a professionally trained social scientist but entered the JERS project via his insider's knowledge, bilingual abilities, and undergraduate academic skills, among other attributes. Second, it does not seem reasonable to hold Nishimoto to today's standards of ethical conduct, including the practice of obtaining the informed consent of those being studied. Third, according to Richard Drinnon, once WRA head Dillon S. Myer became convinced that Nishimoto was indeed a JERS staff member, he ordered that Nishimoto be put on "permanent leave" status from Poston. It seems unlikely that Myer would have taken this step if Nishimoto was in fact an intelligence agent or operative working on behalf of the U.S. government. Finally, once out of Poston, Nishimoto did not appear to have any reservations about being known publicly as a JERS staff member.

51. Nishimoto to Thomas, February 14 and September 26, 1944, JERS W 1.25. For one example of an *inu* being in danger, see Nishimoto's journal entry for March 13, 1943; JERS J 6.13C, 7.

52. Thomas to Tsuchiyama, April 8 and June 23, 1943, JERS J 6.32.

53. As Prof. George M. Foster once noted, when his teacher, the eminent American anthropologist A. L. Kroeber, sent him to the field in 1937 to study the Yuki Indians of California, the only guidance and advice concerning fieldwork that Foster received from his mentor was "to buy a pencil and a stenographer's notebook" (George M. Foster; lecture to Ph.D. candidates in the first-year graduate seminar Foundations of Socio-cultural Anthropology, University of California, Berkeley, October 1974). More general evidence is provided in Rose H. Wax's aptly named study *Doing Fieldwork: Warnings and Advice* (Chicago: University of Chicago Press, 1971).

54. Important BSR staff meetings, in which lectures were given by and to the BSR staff, have been transcribed and deposited in the collection Japanese American Relocation Papers, #3830, Department of Manuscripts and Archives, Cornell University Library. Offerings in October 1942, for example, included lectures by Japanese American and Euro-American staff members and discussions with those in attendance on such topics as the political situation of Poston agriculture and the Second Annual Meeting of the Society for Applied Anthropology. On October 30, Alexander Leighton lectured on the overall program at Poston, especially in terms of self-government. On November 6, 1942, Dr. Edward Spicer gave the first in a series of lectures to the BSR staff on the

influences of "clique and class" in Poston. Leighton followed up, on November 27, 1942, with a lecture on general field techniques. I hope eventually to work through these materials and develop an analysis of the day-to-day operations of the BSR and of how the production of knowledge there ultimately informed the creation of studies such as Leighton's classic monograph *The Governing of Men.*

55. Nishimoto's personal correspondence (as appears, for example, in JERS W 1.25, files A and B) and his sociological journals (JERS J 6.13, A–E) are filled with entries documenting his interactions with the above-mentioned colleagues and with Poston's Euro-American staff members.

56. Evidence to this effect can be found Nishimoto's previously cited journal entry of October 1, 1943, JERS J 6.13A, 1–3; and Tsuchiyama to Thomas, March 4, 1943, JERS J 6.32, 4.

57. Nishimoto's journal contains numerous examples of his communications with the staff. His entries for the month of March 1944 alone cite conversations with Edward Spicer, David French, and John Powell; JERS J 6.13C.

58. Again, Nishimoto's journal lists so many instances that they would be difficult to enumerate; see JERS J 6.13, A–E.

59. Nishimoto's attributes also answer Robert F. Spencer's important query as to why—given that she had access to large pool of talented, professionally trained anthropologists, sociologists, and other social scientists—Thomas ultimately privileged Nishimoto's contributions and collaboration; see "An Interview with Robert F. Spencer" in Hansen, *Evacuation Oral History Project,* pt. 3, pp. 271–72.

60. Letter fragment courtesy of Roberta Shiroma.

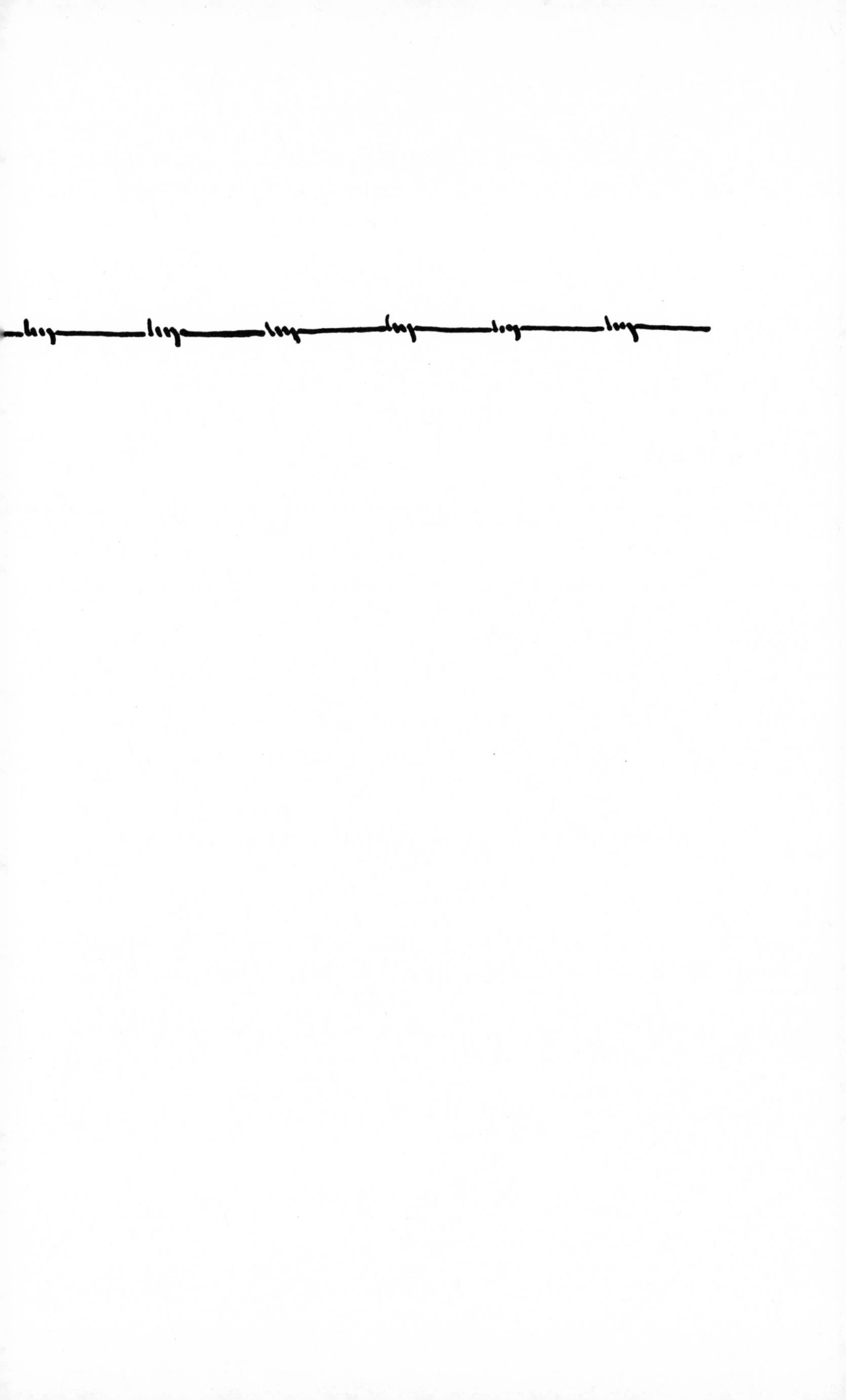

INSIDE AN AMERICAN CONCENTRATION CAMP

AUTOBIOGRAPHY

Nishimoto's Letter to Dr. Alexander M. Leighton, November 1, 1942

Introduction

To explain why Nishimoto wrote this letter, a bit of background on how the Nishimotos arrived in Arizona is in order. Unlike the other Japanese Americans living in and around Gardena, a farming community south of Los Angeles, when the Nishimotos were removed from the coast they were not taken to the Tulare Assembly Center. Instead, according to Roberta Shiroma, Nishimoto's eldest daughter, their landlord came to see them two or three days after the Japanese attack on Pearl Harbor and asked them to move out.[1] The landlord was evidently concerned that hostile parties might burn his property if it became known that the house was occupied by "Japanese." In response, the Nishimotos asked the Reverend Herbert V. Nicholson (who spoke Japanese fluently and who became famous in the Japanese American community for his work on their behalf during World War II) to persuade the landlord to let them stay long enough to dispose of their household and business property.[2]

In the meantime, Nishimoto's wife's sister, who owned a house in East Los Angeles, learned of the situation. She invited the Nishimotos to come and stay with her until the evacuation order was issued, partly because in this fashion the family would be moved as a unit and could therefore stay together. This is how the Nishimoto family joined a Los Angeles Japanese American contingent that was sent directly to Poston without being processed through one of the so-called assembly centers.

Once settled in Poston, Nishimoto was quickly tapped as a researcher for the Bureau of Sociological Research (BSR). The BSR had been set up by the commissioner of the Office of Indian Affairs, John Collier, Sr., as an integral part of Poston's administrative offices.[3] Collier, who was knowledgeable about the applied uses of anthropology,[4] wanted to set up an institute whose researchers could help Poston's administrators monitor the pulse of the community and provide advice regarding policy options. The BSR was headed by Dr. Alexander H. Leighton, who held a bachelor's degree from Princeton (1932), a master's degree from Cambridge (1934), and an M.D. degree from Johns Hopkins (1936). Leighton was essentially a psychiatrist who was interested in comparative psychological and cultural studies, and on this basis he had carried out prior fieldwork among Navajo and Eskimo communities.[5] Partly because of the BSR's perceived success in quieting the crisis during the Poston strike in November 1942, the BSR became a model for the Community Analysis research teams set up in the War Relocation Authority (WRA) to carry out similar functions in a variety of WRA camps.[6]

Leighton's abiding interest in culture and personality, a focus characteristic of North American anthropology of the day, was at the heart of the BSR research.[7] As part of his ethnographic research, Leighton collected information pertaining to the lives and personalities of a surprising number of Poston residents.[8] Nishimoto apparently wrote the letter to Leighton reproduced below at Leighton's request, and it essentially presents Nishimoto's autobiography through 1940. The account is chronological, focusing on his self-development and covering the classic bases of family background, education, influence of peer groups, growth as an individual, and the formation of his career and family.[9]

Insofar as his autobiography pivots around the epiphany (or key life event) of mass incarceration,[10] it is evident that Nishimoto offers witness concerning his life and seeks to protest certain events in it. We get a sense of a man and a community at the crossroads. The experiences of both were marked by challenges, with the resulting failures and accomplishments. By 1942, however, everything—both past accomplishments and future prospects—is totally up in the air. In this sense, Nishimoto's epiphany is homologous with the larger community's epiphany. To be more precise, in his letters, field diary, field notes, and research reports, Nishimoto used reflection about his life and situation as a mirror that he could use to become more fully conscious of both himself and the larger community.

To take one example, in the closing section of his letter Nishimoto returns

Richard, Yae, Marcia, and Roberta Nishimoto in front of Block 45, Barrack 2, Apartment C, which is where they lived while they were at Poston. (Courtesy of Roberta Shiroma)

to the theater setting with which he began it in order to sketch the impact of the war and the impending mass incarceration on his two young daughters. This passage is perhaps one of the most poignant moments in Nishimoto's writing. He expanded on it in comments Edward Spicer recorded on December 29, 1942, in Poston following a discussion with Nishimoto about the economic losses Japanese Americans had sustained as a result of mass incarceration. At the conclusion of this discussion Nishimoto said:

> Now you can understand what I mean when I say I am loyal to both Japan and the U.S. That's what I am. If anything came up where I had to make a decision between the two, I would commit suicide. But I lean in one direction. Can you understand this? A year ago, I was not quite this way. Now I am more on the Japanese side than before. But I was going that way for a long time. I hated Japan when I left there. I hated her. Evacuation finished what was going on with me. If my girls were babies, I would indoctrinate them for Japan and go back to

> Japan as soon as I could. Now I know that they will stay here. I feel that I am obligated to U.S. for some things. My girls grew up here. They have to be Americans. But I know what I am now. I am [an] enemy alien . . . here.[11]

Thus, although Nishimoto was a Japanese national, and although he came to realize during the 1930s and 1940s that he would always be seen as such, it is evident that he fully understood his young American daughters' situation and sentiments.

In sum, the autobiographical letter is vintage Nishimoto: humorous, frank, manipulative, sarcastic, and sassy. Throughout, one feels the presence of an unusual man, at least in terms of the Japanese American community of the time, whose observations are framed and tempered by both Japanese and North American values and sensibilities.

To what extent can or should we believe what Nishimoto tells us about himself? I propose that, beyond a certain point, it is not worthwhile to interrogate Nishimoto's autobiography along these lines. It is crucial to keep in mind that Nishimoto's autobiography, like all autobiographies, is best thought of as a construct entailing his thoughts at a given moment in time (late 1942) in what was certainly a continuous, lifelong process of reflection and self-realization.[12]

The fact that Nishimoto's 1942 letter is punctuated by a somewhat facetious tone suggests to me that he was fully conscious that he was producing this autobiographical document for Leighton's collection of profiles. Nishimoto sometimes even pokes fun at Leighton, especially in the letter's dramatized introduction. Nonetheless, certain passages are deeply revealing, and as I point out in the introduction to this book, they deserve our attention because Nishimoto's self-described personal characteristics and values are in accord with and can be used to interpret his multifaceted career at, and writings about, Poston.

It is fascinating and instructive to juxtapose the letter with the various notes and studies that Nishimoto generated between 1942 and 1945. In fact, this is partly why I have included the letter in conjunction with Nishimoto's reports on labor, leisure, and popular resistance presented below. From this vantage point, it is quite evident from his letter to Leighton that many of the interests, abilities, and values that would characterize Nishimoto's life and work in Poston were already well in place by the time he and his family arrived in Arizona.

Notes

1. Personal communication from Roberta Shiroma, February 16, 1994.

2. Nicholson's own account of the war years is available in his paper "Notes on the Evacuation of Japanese during World War II: Being the Personal Experience of H. V. Nicholson," held in the Japanese American Research Project collection, University Library, University of California, Los Angeles, box 160, folder 18. Also, see *Valiant Odyssey: Herbert Nicholson in and out of America's Concentration Camps*, ed. Michi Weglyn and Betty E. Mitson (Upland, Calif.: Privately printed, 1978).

3. A readily available description of the organization and goals of the Bureau of Sociological Research is available in the study "Applied Anthropology in a Dislocated Community," by Alexander H. Leighton and Edward H. Spicer, which appears as an appendix in Leighton's *The Governing of Men: General Principles and Recommendations Based on Experience at a Japanese Relocation Camp* (1945; reprint, New York: Octagon, 1964), 371–97.

4. An interesting biography of John Collier, Sr., with special emphasis on his role in helping to pass the Indian Reorganization Act of 1934, is available in Lawrence C. Kelly, *The Assault on Assimilation: John Collier and the Origins of Indian Policy Reform* (Albuquerque: University of New Mexico Press, 1983). Richard Drinnon also offers some important insights into Collier's role vis-à-vis Poston, including the "Poston Incident," in which Collier's public comments about the long-term status of Poston were immediately refuted by Dillon Myer on the basis of WRA policy; see Richard Drinnon, *Keeper of Concentration Camps: Dillon S. Myer and American Racism* (Berkeley: University of California Press, 1987), 40–42 and passim.

5. A biographical interview with Leighton that touches on the war years and that includes a comprehensive list of his publications is presented in Jerome Barkow, "Interview with Alex Leighton," *Anthropologica* 31 (1989): 237–61.

6. See Leighton and Spicer, "Applied Anthropology in a Dislocated Community," 374, and Spicer's reflections on the BSR in his article "Early Applications of Anthropology in North America" in *Perspectives on Anthropology, 1976*, ed. Anthony F. C. Wallace et al. (Washington, D.C.: American Anthropological Association, 1977), 116–41. Although no one has yet attempted a critical evaluation of the BSR, interested readers can consult two thought-provoking reviews of the role of anthropologists in the WRA: Peter T. Suzuki, "Anthropologists in the Wartime Camps for Japanese Americans: A Documentary Study," *Dialectical Anthropology* 6 (1981): 23–60; and Orin Starn, "Engineering Internment: Anthropologists and the War Relocation Authority," *American Ethnologist* 13 (1986): 700–720.

7. Leighton briefly describes the methodological importance of collecting personality studies in Leighton and Spicer, "Applied Anthropology in a Dislocated Community,"

389–94. He also indicates that a similar methodology was employed in his field research among the Navajo (ibid., n. 10).

8. The personality studies of Poston residents that Leighton collected for the BSR are held in the Department of Manuscripts and University Archives in the Cornell University Library, although currently their use is restricted.

9. Philippe Lejeune defines autobiography as a "[r]etrospective prose narrative written by a real person concerning his own existence, where the focus is his individual life, in particular the story of his personality"; Philippe Lejeune, *On Autobiography* (Minneapolis, University of Minnesota Press, 1989), 4 and passim. In terms of this definition, then, Nishimoto's letter is fully autobiographical.

10. Sociologist Norman K. Denzin introduced the concept and use of *epiphany* for the interpretive analysis of life experiences; see "The Art and Politics of Interpretation" in *The Handbook of Qualitative Sociology*, Norman K. Denzin and Yvonna S. Lincoln, eds. (Thousand Oaks, Calif.: Sage, 1994), 510–11.

11. Edward H. Spicer, "Nishimoto, R.S.," Japanese American Evacuation and Resettlement Study Collection, Bancroft Library, University of California, Berkeley, J 6.15, 1.

12. Two excellent sources have shaped my view of autobiography as (1) a construct shaped by the experiential and intellectual context of the writer, and (2) a work predicated on certain assumptions held by both the writer and the reader. They are Norman K. Denzin, *Interpretive Biography* (Newbury Park, Calif.: Sage, 1989), and Philippe Lejeune, *On Autobiography*.

On the uses of autobiographical writing for reconfiguring the meaning and significance of ethnic history in the United States, see Genaro M. Padilla, *My History, Not Yours: The Formation of Mexican American Autobiography* (Madison: University of Wisconsin Press, 1993).

Finally, it is notable that, despite the fact that commentators such as Norman K. Denzin, Louis M. Smith ("Biographical Method," *Handbook of Qualitative Sociology*, 286–305), and others have written about the role and place of biography and autobiography in the social sciences, no one, to my knowledge, has fully discussed their methodological or theoretical importance for the critical interpretation of a given author's ethnographic research and writings. One of the few sources that begins to address what is at stake is *Fieldnotes: The Makings of Anthropology*, Roger Sanjek, ed. (Ithaca, N.Y.: Cornell University Press, 1990). Three chapters that are very useful in this regard are Nancy Lutkehaus's "Refractions of Reality: On the Use of Other Ethnographers' Fieldnotes," 303–23; Roger Sanjek, 'Fieldnotes and Others," 324–40; and Robert J. Smith, "Hearing Voices, Joining the Chorus: Appropriating Someone Else's Fieldnotes," 356–70.

November 1, 1942

Dr. A. H. Leighton,[1]
Bureau of Sociological Research,
The Colorado River War Relocation Project,
Poston, Arizona

Dear Sir:

Well, doctor! Don't you think we better go in now? The overture for the second act has begun, you know. Oh, yes, I know you have been studying the personality traits of the lady standing over there. But don't you think you have been looking at her long enough? You have been glaring at her for the last fifteen minutes, you know. Yes, yes. I know she is beautiful, glamorous, and all that, but I think the leading character of the drama is more interesting.

Look, doctor! The stage setting is peculiar, isn't it? It looks like a little room in a bunk house, doesn't it? Look! It's raining, too. May I see the program you have: Let me see now. Here it is. It says, "Bunk house at a Colusa rice field—November, 1920."[2] It says, "The characters in order of appearance—Richard S. Nishimoto, and so on." There is a man, sitting in front of the desk! That must be Nishimoto. He certainly looks unhappy and depressed, doesn't he?

Thus, I found myself in a rice field at Colusa, California. As soon as I had landed at San Francisco on August 26, 1920, I was shipped to the ranch, where a distant relative of our family was managing. My father told me to observe what an immigrant's life was like. He said that it was essential to feel and to act as an immigrant by working among such a group, because every Japanese in America had gone through the experience sometime or other during the pioneering days. As I mingle with these men from now on, I must know them. He said that the idea of working as a laborer was not shameful, unlike in Japan; in fact, sons of the plutocratic class in America were too eager to work in order to earn their own spending money during their summer vacations. When I left my parents behind in San Francisco, where I stayed only for six days without having a chance to shake off sea legs, my father's parting words were, "It's going to be a wonderful experience for you."

To this day, I do not know what this "wonderful experience" meant. The

---

1. Japanese American Evacuation and Resettlement Study Collection, Bancroft Library, University of California, Berkeley, J 6.25.
2. Colusa, California, is an agricultural community north of Sacramento.

experience there was everything else but wonderful. The first day I arrived there, I was supplied with a shovel to irrigate the rice field and this was the first time that I saw a shovel, let alone to handle it with my tender hands. I was terrified that I was to dig ditches like the "coolies" whom I had seen in Japan and had been contemptuous of. It was horrifying that now I was to act as a "coolie;" I, who was born with silver spoons in my mouth. I was reconciled to the idea of manipulating the shovel, as all the people around me were strangers and my protests were of no avail. I began to dig ditches with other Japanese laborers in the scorching sun of 110 degrees F. The way I handled the implement was too funny to others that they constantly ridiculed me and giggled imitating my predicament. I resented such "courtesies" to the new comer; and the resentment found a consolation in a feeling that my father had intended to torture me unnecessarily. I thought that my father was so greedy with money that he did not wish to feed me in our home. He was not interested enough in me that he had shoved me off to a strange place among strange people, I reflected. I worked until the end of the day, checking my tears with pugnacious determination. My shoulder was aching, my back was cracking, and my muscles were sore.

In the evening I protested to the relative-manager that I was not fit for this type of "low-down" labor and that I should be transferred to some easier work. This protest was turned down by him, as he was afraid to show any favoritism toward me, thinking of its effect upon other workers.

The next day I dug more ditches. The next more ditches and so on. It took many, many days to go from one end of the ranch to the other, as it covered about 2500 acres of land, growing rice for the consumption by the Japanese people in California. Meanwhile, the art of handling the shovel was improving, but far from perfection. But the soreness of my shoulder, of my back, and of my hips were aggravating. The bitterness toward my father was increasing.

About the middle of October, the rice crop was ready to be harvested. For the harvest, many Caucasian laborers came into the camp to handle the binders and the thrashing machines. The increase of the population in the camp brought gayety to the locale. For their mess, five Chinese were employed; of them three addicts of morphine, who acted peculiarly on numerous occasions. They acted as if they had lost all the meaning of life. They were depressed with forlorn expressions on their faces. When I inquired [of] some Japanese about their appearances, I was told that the Chinese were bothered with diarrhea, because they had run out of the supply of morphine. Thus, a new association of thoughts—Chinese–morphine–diarrhea—was formed in me.

The increased population increased the trading activities in the camp and a new commissary was opened. And to this store I was transferred after much coaxing [by] my relative. Now I stood behind the counter, selling tobaccos, gloves, candies, etc. But this selling was entirely confined to the Japanese customers, as I was afraid to talk to and impossible to understand the Caucasians. Whenever the white men came in, I rushed out of the store and called my relatives. Among them there was one Englishman who always chatted with my relative for a great length of time in the store. He was always "careful" to interpose the word "God dam" every three or four words he uttered, while chewing a cube of tobacco he had bought. This was the beginning of my education in use of profanity. I did not know what "God dam" meant as the relative could not give me a clear conception of the words. Yet I felt smart when I interposed the words between broken English I spoke. Soon afterward I felt a soothing consolation whenever I had interjected "God damn" while I was mad.

The rice was thrashed and sacked. The sacks were then loaded on trucks and shipped to a warehouse in a nearby town. When about one thousand sacks of rice had been sacked and stored, rain began to fall. Torrential rains. Gales and thunders accompanying. It did not let up. If it did, it was only for a day or two, then torrential storms revisited. The fields were drenched and inundated; the rice on the field was drenched and rot. The crop was ruined completely now when the rain stopped for four days at the beginning of November. There was no way to retrieve the harvest beyond the thousand sacks which had been stored. Yet the payroll to the laborers must be met; and to cover this there was no cash on hand. The operating cash had been expended when the equipments were bought for the harvest. In order to raise the fund, my relative left for Oakland to see a banker for loans; he had to leave the ranch on horse back, because the roads were quagmires and automobiles were not usable. After he had left, the rainy weather continued again. There was no indication when the rain would stop. The workers were getting restless and wanted to leave the isolated ranch for towns, for which it was necessary to pay off their wages, but no one [was] there to pay off nor the money. They, sensing that my relative was not returning soon, began to leave by fours and fives, threatening a foreman indignantly that they would sue for the wages as soon as they would reach the town. This was the first observation of the industrious relationship [that] existed in America.

I could not leave the camp, because I did not know how to return to San Francisco nor did I feel sure about my English speaking ability for making such a trip alone. There were no mails coming in on account of the bad weather; I brought no books to read. All I could do were either to meditate alone or watch other Japanese play poker or Japanese flower games,[3] which I did not understand and even if I had understood them I had no money to play among the men. The gayety and loud laughters of the players, soon, began to irritate me and [I] found refuge in a little haven in the commissary, sitting alone in front of a desk, sometimes looking at the rain falling outside of a little window, other times covering my head with my hands on the desk top, plying through the unfathomable mysteries of life. The same routines continued for days and days as the rain did not let up. I was depressed and unhappy. I was homesick. But yearning for what home? I was certain then by self determination, that I was not welcome in the house of my parents in San Francisco. For the orphan of the destiny there was one companion—a terrier, in whom I often confided my sorrows. With the dog I sometimes went for rabbit hunting, lamenting my own troubles. Often I was irritated when I failed to find sympathetic audience in the dog, the irritation sometimes taking the form of kicking the dog with my leg. Yet the dog followed the master faithfully, as they trod through mud and puddles.

When my relative returned to the ranch it was already in December. He had lost all his friendly manners, constantly mumbling to himself unintelligible words. He was worried from the financial failure due to the act of God; he was worried about the future, the future of the enterprise and the future of himself. He had been successful in his trip only to the extent of a few hundred dollars from his personal friends and not from the banker, who had closed all the doors of credit. With such a nominal fund and no new source available, it was necessary now to close the ranch and liquidate. His words of the decision were conveyed to the still remaining workers in the camp, bringing much resentments and scathing accusations. Some went to the extreme, saying that my relative was amorous and had some ambitious female companion in the city, to whom all of the cash of the project had been drained secretly and illegally.

It was now necessary for the manager to consult a lawyer for the final liquidation. He left again for San Francisco and this time I accompanied him with fifteen dollars, which had been paid as a prorated compensation for my service for the past four months. It was December 26, 1920, a day after Christmas. The colored lamps of Christmas trees were seen through windows as I passed

3. Also known as *hana*, a popular Japanese card game. See below, p. 97.

through the dark streets of Sacramento in a train coach on my way back to the city.

It was at the beginning of the term in January, 1921, when my father ordered me to attend a high school. He told me that it was "no good" to stay at home and to remain idle. For this, I went to see a Y.M.C.A. secretary, who wrote me letter of introduction to the principal of Lowell High School. The next morning I opened the first page of my career as a school boy in an American school, when I took the letter to the principal alone. I stood in his office blank, without understanding a single word he said, the only means of exchanging our ideas being with various manipulations of our hands. Then another Japanese boy was brought into his office, who obligingly took me to a classroom, where I found all the boys and girls with brown hair and hazel eyes. As I remember now, there was one Japanese girl in the room, but she turned her face away as soon as I looked at her.

It was the same thing repeated in the classroom. I could not understand what was going on; I could not make out what the teacher was saying nor what the pupils said. Once I asked the Japanese girl for some information in Japanese, but she stared at me a little while and walked away without answering my question. I felt cheap, yet I was mad to see this Japanese girl who ignored the boy in distress. I never spoke to her after this incident; never again during the four years together in the same class. Incidentally, she turned out to be a brilliant doctor, known widely and respected in the bay region. Nevertheless, another association of thoughts was formed in me—a Nisei–a brilliant doctor–inhuman and unkind.

The state of being dumb and mute in the school continued for the next six months. Only language of exchanging views was the acrobatic use of our hands, to which method many Caucasian pupils showed impatience and aversion. However, there was one boy, who was always willing to lead my way, going into details of teaching me to pronounce English words correctly and to hear them intelligibly. He tried to train my mouth, lips, and ears, as he knew that I had a vocabulary of about 300 English words, a souvenir of the Japanese educational system. He spent all his spare time with me, often inviting me to his home for lunches and dinners on Saturdays and Sundays. To this boy, I owe a great deal of bridging over the gap in me between the Japanese background and the new American way of life. This lasted for all four years of our high school career until we parted after the graduation; he going to Berkeley campus of University of California and I to Stanford. Yes, you will nod your head if I tell you that he was a tow-headed, freckle-faced Jewish boy.

About the middle of my Sophomore year, I began to understand the classroom proceedings, and my scholastic grades were improving. Up to this time, the grades were A's and C's and D's; A's in mathematics and Latin, C's in science courses and D's in History and English courses. Now the C's improved to B's and D's to C's. As the time went on the discrepancies in the grade disappeared, being a recipient of A grades during the senior year, except one F in the "Shakespearean Drama." I flunked in it, because I could not make out head or tail what the bard was saying. Yes, I tried to understand the passages, reading them over and over, but the rereadings did not bring any progressive clearness in my mind, Shakespeare's words being just as incomprehensive as at the beginning when I had opened the book. Soon this state brought despair to me; that is to say, I no longer opened his books. If I had flunked in it, I had to take the course over again. The result was not any better, except that the same teacher had pity in me and passed me with a grade of C. This is the origin of my current sentiment, "Shakespeare is a crackpot. He is trying to overtax our brain." Every time someone quotes his passage I try to close my nerve paths from the auditory organ; I am irritated and want to offend the speaker with some sarcastic remarks. This is exactly what happened when you quoted a passage from "Macbeth" (or was it from "The Merchant of Venice?") one day in the staff conference. I was irritated and felt ticklish in checking within myself words of sarcasm. Ah, doctor, a confession is good for one's soul.

It was also during my senior year that I had a little altercation with the principal and made him apologize to me after much arguments. I shall not go into the detail of this incident. Nor shall I describe my constant arguments within the "Civics" teacher in regard to then pending Exclusion Act aimed at the Japanese. Thinking retrospectively, it is interesting that I was already championing the Californian Japanese cause then. Anyway, the teacher was sport enough to give me an A for the course, and about him I say now, "He was a very nice fellow."

About this time, I was acquainted with a noted author, a Japanese, who was a political refugee from Japan because of his Socialistic idealism, which he had advocated to the populace contrary to the principles propagated by the Japanese government. During his thirty years in America he toned down in his accusation of the Japanese political system and his view was much milder towards the end, which in turn elicited criticisms from the other end this time, from men such as Arthur Brisbane, Edgar Snow, etc., accusing him of being a paid Japanese propagandist. This author's specialty, as you imagined, was in the field of the Japanese immigration problems in the United States and the diplomatic relations between the two countries, America and Japan. These books he loaned to me to give me a better perspective of the Japanese as a minority race, not only in California, but also in the world. He presented the Japanese side of the view along with the American side. These opinions, I thought were fair and based on the facts, although not acceptable in the popular mind. I admire him, because he was not afraid to present what he thought without weighing its personal disadvantages. On one side, his criticism was more or less of common place variety, accusing the American public of being ignorant of the realities in the Far East. He accused them that the American public was prone to be misled by livelihood-earning race baiters, to whom a presentation of facts is source of their economic insecurity. His attack, on the other hand, against the Japanese government was more specific and vigorous. Once he accused the Manchurian invasion by Japanese of being "foolhardy," headstrong, and unnecessary, which naturally created an uproar in Japan. When I asked him if he was worried about the criticism against him both in his native country and in his adopted country, he said, "If you are afraid of criticisms which may result from what you have written, don't write it at all. If you write, the truth above all. A presentation of falsified facts is the death sentence to that writer." The name of the courageous author is K. K. Kawakami.[4]

In 1924 Kawakami left for Washington, D.C., with his family to act as a foreign correspondent for the leading newspaper in Japan. Even then, he was not afraid to say to the laymen public of Japan what he wanted to say. His audacity in presenting the truthful facts and his fearless conclusions brought him many embarrassing remarks and unhappy accusations in the ensuing years, resulting finally in his editor's request for his resignation in 1937. It is ironical to find him now in a detention camp near Washington as a potentially dangerous enemy alien.

Another sentiment which I held for a long time is also traceable to this Kawakami. By that is meant, a sentiment, "Don't marry a Caucasian girl. She is a fine companion, but not an ideal wife. Inter-marriage has many draw-

4. Karl Kiyoshi Kawakami was born in 1879 and was one of the founders of Japan's Social Democratic Party. Coming to America after the party was disbanded, Kawakami studied political science and received an M.A. degree from the University of Iowa. A prolific author, Kawakami defended Japan and Issei immigrants in the United States in many of his books; see the entry on Kawakami in *Japanese American History: An A-to-Z Reference from 1868 to the Present*, Brian Niiya, ed. (New York: Facts on File, 1993), 197–98.

backs." He was qualified to make this statement as he was married to an elegant Caucasian lady of the New England stock, an accomplished artist in oil paintings.

As he said, Mrs. Kawakami was a wonderful companion, even to a boy of the high school age. She always welcomed me in her household, trying to familiarize me with a decent American family. The first thing she undertook with me was to correct my habit of saying "God damn" now and then. Her advice on this subject was, "Say it within yourself. Don't make articulate sound." She was a lady of even temperament, rather unusual for an artist, I dare say. She was an expert in use of subtle humors, about which she gave me numerous lessons. While we were conversing, she often stopped the discourse in the middle and said, "Now can you think of some humorous comment, relevant to the subject we are discussing?" When I offered my contribution, she said, "Now you are getting the technique." Thinking of this, I chuckle now and then, saying to myself, "How I was ignorant of a little psychological technique of "a little assurance from time to time["]!

As we approached the graduation from the high school, there was a question of what college we were to go. Many of my friends were headed for Berkeley and I thought that was the best place to go. When I consulted my Jewish pal concerning this selection, he said, "Well, you are a foreigner, and that means that you have to pay an enormous amount of money for tuition. And for the same amount of money, you can go through Stanford. Say, why don't you go to Stanford, instead?" And this was the index finger directing me to Stanford.

One day I brought the subject of going to the college to my father. He was interested in my ambition and said in cold calculated way, "That's fine. I will give you $100 as a present when you enroll at Stanford. But after that, you must work through the college yourself. Don't expect any support from me." Then he asked me what I was going to take up. I said, "I want to be a lawyer, but that's no good in this country, being an alien. The second choice will be the engineering course, as I am pretty sure I can make good in it." And this is the clue to my social maladjustment in my later years, being the source of many frustrations.

The generous donation of $100 from my father would not be enough even to pass through the comptroller's window at Stanford. More money was needed to defray the living expenses on the campus. For that purpose, I obtained an employment in a little curio shop in the San Francisco Chinatown. I worked there until April, 1925, as a salesman, waiting on people from the

East, the Middle West, and the South. As I earned money for the academic education, I acquired a practical education, besides an appreciation of the differences between the people from different sections of the country. Of the customers I always made it my point to ask, beginning with "How do you like San Francisco?" and leading to an ultimate question, "Where are you from, by the way?" To the tourists from the South I was more inquisitive regarding the Negroes, keeping the customers more than one hour frequently. This "extra-curricular" activity was, of course, taboo and unpopular with the proprietor of the store that he was more than glad, I suspected, when I left for the institution of higher learning in the spring.

On April 1, the April Fool day, I found myself in the Japanese Student Club on the Stanford campus, where my tenure of four years began. That morning I took an Entrance Aptitude test, so-called Thorndyke Intelligence test, among a group of sixty. I still remember a director of the test standing on the stage of the auditorium, barking at us, "Time is up. Turn your page now." The time was certainly up too soon, as I had not finished any more than two or three lines from the top on some pages when a new page was reeled into my sight. When the test was completed at noon, I was sick worrying from the anticipated pronouncement of failure in the result. I thought that I must go back to the "old grind" in San Francisco if I had failed, and the probability of failing was very great.

I spent the next two days in torture and anxiety; one of the longest two days in my life. On the third day when I tore open an envelope from the Registrar in a great excitement, I found a card with a X mark at the bottom of the list composed of six or seven classifications. In addition to this, there was a scribbled statement, "The result disregarded due to the foreign student status." By this special consideration I was completely relieved, yet I said to my friend, "Hell, why didn't they tell me so from the beginning?" Nevertheless, I felt silly tinged with defiance, "Intelligence? That doesn't mean a thing. I will show 'em that I am good."

I made good for the Spring Quarter of 1925, my grade card showing "A's" without variance. And I laughed up my sleeve, "See! The intelligence test doesn't mean a thing."

As soon as the term was over in June, I packed my suitcase and left for Vacaville, a little town near Sacramento, California. It was a good year for the fruit industry throughout the state of California and the labor supply was scarce. Due to the scarcity, employers were compelled to hire workers haphazardly. Before I had waited two hours in an employment office in Vacaville, a

Japanese fruit orchardist approached to me and said, "You look awfully frail to me. Are you sure you can stand hard work?" I replied with enthusiasm, "Yes, sir! I have an experience of having worked on a rice field near Colusa. I did lots of shovel work in the scorching sun there and I don't see how the work around here would be any harder than that." It was a slightly colored presentation of a fact, but one could not accuse me of distorting it. The man immediately replied, "Let's go. You are going to work for me from tomorrow morning."

From the next morning I started a new life as a picker of fruits, apricots, plums, peaches, and pears. And this routine was repeated every summer during my college career.

On October 1, 1925, I returned to the Stanford campus, all set financially for the academic year to come, together with a scholarship which had been granted by the university. This time I really began to bathe in the college life; parties, meetings, rallies, football games, etc. Of the meetings I attended, there was one which made it possible for me to see a great figure in the American cultural history for the first time. The great scientist, David Starr Jordan, presided over informal conference every Thursday evenings. Some of his conferences I attended, although his voice was hardly audible, as he was already beyond 75 years of age and in ill health. He spoke in low, slow tone, but his personality radiated from his large stature in contrast to his fading vitality. He spoke often about simple life of fishermen in an isolated village in Japan, where he had spent some months. He had lived among them and had felt their primitive culture. Those fishing folks, he used to say, were the real Japanese, unspoiled by the half-baked adaptation of the western civilization. "That little village in the northeastern part of Hondo is the place where you must visit," he fervently advised a Caucasian graduate, who was leaving for Japan with a teaching appointment.

His conferences were sporadically held toward the end of the year and were suspended entirely when he was failing in health, finally passing away in February, 1926. To this man I owe a great deal. It was the first time that I appreciated the true sincerity in a man, understanding and feeling its significance and observing its far reaching effect. His subject matter itself was common, not novel in its aspect nor in timeliness, but the great difference was its treatment and presentation. It was his uncolored discourse with delicate emotion that drew respect and reverence from me. I was simply awed in his presence.

To Dr. David Starr Jordan, I must thank for another trait imbued in me. To help helpless, weak people. To aid persons suffering. To guide men in trouble.

Not only give assistance, but fight for them. All these instructions I value to this day.

Besides the meetings presided [over] by Dr. Jordan, I attended meetings of Caucasian students and among them I felt natural and comfortable. "Bull sessions" were more congenial with me and I thought time well spent listening and arguing. Some arguments I thought were well presented and endeavored to remember, others I thought were loathsome and naive to which I often made sarcastic retorts. About the latter attitude, i.e., the attitude of giving sarcastic remarks, I soon began to sense a feeling of regret and remorse, as soon as I had uttered offensive words. In order to inhibit a desire of aggressive retaliation, I closed my eyes completely with vigor and shut my thinking from the outside world, at first; then in a later training period, I was able to keep my eyes open and listen to any statement without saying anything. Instead I learned, this time, to chuckle within myself. The negative cultivation is a difficult process, as even today I am not a complete master, the desire manifesting itself either in a sneer or in a caustic remark. Give me another five years, doctor; then I may be skillful in hiding the obnoxious trait by keeping a placid facial expression.

With such offending character, you would think that I had difficulty in getting along with other students. On the contrary, I found many friends easily among Caucasians and Japanese. The latter, however, being constantly occupied with their studies or with their part time employment, I found myself oftener among Caucasians. With them I spent many weekends on hiking or motoring trips. By the end of my junior year, I thought, I was reacting [in] Caucasian ways.

One Thanksgiving vacation, I spent in a students' conference of the Institute of Pacific Relations in a mountain retreat. I say a conference, but it was more of "bull sessions" than an organized meeting. Here I met many students of both sexes from the foreign countries as well as from the native land. Among these students representing colleges and universities, I was educated on the existing questions of the racial minorities. The conference being held in California, the agenda was usually filled with the Japanese problems on the Pacific coast, on which I acted as an information dispenser. This experience was valuable in later years in giving me the extent to which the intellectuals could understand and beyond which progressive explanations only aggravated mysteries to them. I was shocked by the paucity of their knowledge and their incapacity to appreciate the Oriental way of thinking. Therefore, my axiom is, "The racial minority problems they can understand so much and no more, unless you yourself are in the midst." Some students who had historical training were able to appreciate a little better than the others, yet their attitude was that of patronizing desire, which was as guilty and offensive as that of ignorance.

Among my Japanese friends there was one man with whom I associated very closely; "closely" in the superlative term, as I lived with him in a small room for three years. This man, K. Kawai, was a son of the pastor of the Japanese Christian Church in Los Angeles, who had transferred from the southern branch of University of California after his sophomore year.[5] He came to Stanford with brilliant scholastic record, well versed in subjects of social science, especially in his chosen field of history. (Incidentally, he is a professor of History at U.C.L.A. before the evacuation.) He could rattle off answers on a snap of fingers whenever he was asked for assistance on history and its affiliated subjects. But there was a catch. I could not tolerate his company at first, as he came to the club house as a "small town big shot." He was cocky, showy, and pedantic. His ideas were "cute." He insisted on propagating the fundamentalistic conception of "sins," to smoke, to drink, to blaspheme, to gamble, to dance, and thousand others. He insisted on going to church service on Sundays, as if it was a vital commitment of the human subsistence process; and not satisfied with his own religious behaviorism, he initiated a propaganda activity anxious to impart the pattern in me. Thus a tug of war began between us. I sneered, jeered, ridiculed, and laughed at him. I insulted him one minute and ignored him the next. And he was not less aggressive either. It was a give and take proposition all the way.

The first thing I undertook with him was the "sin" of smoking. I puffed cigarettes, filling the room with gray smoke. To this he objected, saying, "Can't you smoke outside the room?" I was waiting for the protest with a preframed answer, "Whatta hell! Can't you take it? Don't be such goody-goody. . . . Boy. This is good."

It was not necessary to repeat the process too often, as he finally came around to say, "For Christ sake, . . . " Ah, he was giving an inch of his ground.

---

5. Like Nishimoto, Kasuo Kawai was born in Japan. He came to the United States in 1910 and started school at the age of six. Kawai became a professor and, as a member of the Department of Political Science at Washington University in Saint Louis, published the scholarly book *Japan's American Interlude* (Chicago: University of Chicago Press, 1960). For an overview of his education and the development of his views of the Nisei role as a bridge between the United States and Japan, see Jerrold Haruo Takahashi, "Japanese American Responses to Race Relations: The Formation of Nisei Perspectives," *Amerasia Journal* 9 (1982): 32–35.

Afterward, his reaction was meeker, "Let me try a cigarette;" and finally a little stronger later, "Hell, where is a weed."

Now the "sin" of smoking having been taken care of, it was necessary to solicit a few conspirators to tackle the problem of drinking, as we were still in the "speakeasy" period. First, some pure alcohol was requisitioned from a pre-medical student and was mixed with apple cider. With the supply prepared, we invited a few confederates together with Kawai to gobble the liquid down, as his primary desire by this time was to act like one of "us."

Thus his dogmatically conceived "superegos" were destroyed one by one, turning out eventually to be one of the most popular boys on the campus. However, among the "sins," there was one which was restore[d] in his repertoire of conscience after it had once been destroyed. That was the idea of gambling. The gambling techniques were taught in minute details with numerous practical applications, especially with respect to dice throwing and stud poker. In spite of our detailed instructions, he was slow to acquire the skill, his investment running high; finally resulting in our advice for prohibition of his participation in such recreation. We, the confederates, informed him that he was very low in "gambling I.Q.," to which he readily acquiesced.

Eventually Kawai was one of the "moral revolutionists," engaging actively in "reform" campaigns. He was an energetic worker when we acquired another "guinea pig" from Santa Barbara, a small town boy wonder who had starred on a baseball team. This boy, Asakura, was one of us after our "disintegration and integration" process and was a participating instructor on someone else. It is interesting to add here that Asakura was the administrator in the Tulare Assembly Center and was well liked there according to the reports I have.

In the spring of 1927, K. Kawai and I left Stanford University temporarily, Kawai to Harvard University and I to a college of "hard knocks" at Vacaville.[6] I returned to Vacaville by necessity as I had run out of fund to go on at Stanford and I must replenish my treasury. I returned to the same orchard where I had worked two previous summer vacations and this time I was entrusted with the managership. I not only saved all the money I had earned, but also I gained priceless experience in acquainting myself with farm migratory laborers. I intermingled with seasonal laborers of many races; Japanese, Filipinos,

6. The date here does not agree with Nishimoto's Stanford University transcript, which indicates that he did in fact attend classes during the spring quarter of 1927. Nishimoto was absent during the spring quarter of 1926, which is probably the period of his work at Vacaville.

Spaniards[7], Portuguese, etc. sometimes over 100 in number. To manage these people successfully I had to observe them more closely than I had been doing in the previous years, especially because I was interested in maintaining high efficiency, a great degree of their satisfaction in their work, and harmony among them. It was not difficult to attain these purposes once I had rationalized their prevailing characteristics, finding common denominators of personalities. These characteristics were numerous. They were hardly educated, none of them going beyond an elementary education. They were aggressive, whenever they were slightly provoked. They were secretive and seclusive, having tendency to keep among themselves, often openly suspicious and distrustful of others. Even within the group as small as this, there was a clear cut demarcation along the racial differences, being proud and boastful of their own race, sometimes resulting in inter-racial jealousies. It was, therefore, difficult to keep all these workers together engaged in one place and was found more feasible to separate them assigning them with a separate task at a different locality. Higher efficiency was maintained creating rivalry among them, and for harmony we had several parties after the working hours, although thorough conversations were difficult among them due to poor command of the English language. Thus, I learned an advanced lesson in human relationship, how to manage a group of persons, by practicing with this complex conglomerate of races. The lesson was useful in knowing how to trade with Mexican laborers in a store which I operated some years later, as they behaved very similarly as a whole.

With the cash which I had earned during the six months since April, 1927, I returned to Stanford and continued on with my studies in the engineering school, fully realized a bright future ahead of me. The realization was incentive for study with zeal, enabling me to maintain "A" average. Yet I did not forget to intermingle with the Japanese and Caucasian students. From these intellectuals I began to realize the scarcity of vocational opportunities for me in America after my graduation. The sense of future insecurity increased gradually as I advanced in my Junior year. In addition to this fear, there was another, i.e. I was not fit nor qualified to be an engineer.

The realization was more vivid and acute as days and months passed by. I was fully aware by the spring of 1928 that I could not be a scientist nor a

7. This is probably a mistake; Nishimoto was most likely referring here to Mexicans or Mexican Americans (who spoke Spanish but who were not Spaniards).

technical expert who confined himself in complicated experiments. I was not a type to seclude myself in a small laboratory for researches. The two fears, the paucity of opportunity in America and my ineptitude, were interrelated and resulted in a concrete realization that if I were to remain an engineer, I must seek my future in Japan. The corporations here had its door closed to the Orientals and in Japan only there was an opening which welcome me. But I felt great antipathy in accepting this verdict of returning to Japan, as my childhood memories were nothing but detestable there. In fact, there was no solution for my problems and I spent days in anxiety and dilemma. Sometimes, I had a firm conviction to remain in America and forget about my engineering career; other times, I had an adventurous ambition to go to China to seek a new fortune. Yet at no time was the idea of repatriating to the homeland accepted in my mind. The debate between these conflicting ideas kept me depressed and uncertain, never to be solved until my marriage, when I was reconciled to let the nature take its course. Ah, the clash of motives within the individual!

The fear of unfitness to become a highly technical engineer was sometimes carried a little too far. Once when I was taking a course in Applied Psychology from Dr. E. K. Strong, I filled out a questionnaire for the Vocational Guidance Test.[8] Although the professor's request was to come to his office individually and to discuss the findings of the test, I shrank away from the opportunity. I was afraid to hear his pronouncement that I would be a common place engineer, who would not get anywhere. To this day I do not know what Dr. Strong found out about me and he never mentioned the subject, although I met him several times after my graduation. I am curious now to the extent that I may write to him for the result soon.

---

8. Among his many publications, Professor Edward Kellogg Strong wrote two books on Japanese Americans: *Japanese in California* (Stanford, Calif.: Stanford University Press, 1933); and *The Second-Generation Japanese Problem* (Stanford, Calif.: Stanford University Press, 1934). In the latter volume Strong wrestled with the fact that, although the Nisei generation had high educational and occupational aspirations, he believed that they were not really going to be able to realize the latter because of racial prejudice and discrimination. In regard to its graduates of Chinese descent, for example, Stanford University's placement office noted as late as 1926 that "it was almost impossible to place a Chinese of either the first or second generation in *any* kind of position: engineering, manufacturing, or business. Many firms had regulations against employing them; others objected on the ground that other men employed in their firms did not care to work with them"; Pao-Min Chang, *Continuity and Change: A Profile of Chinese Americans* (New York: Vantage Press, 1983), 97 (thanks to Professor Michael Chang, De Anza Community College, for sharing this reference with me). We will never know, but perhaps, based on such evidence, Strong was planning to warn Nishimoto that his aspiration to become a working engineer in the United States was not very realistic.

In passing, I must mention that this is the only training I had in the psychology department. It is stated here in the interest and in defense of the high quality of the department at Stanford, so that whatever I may say or do in your class should not reflect upon its reputation. Incidentally, I pulled a "D" in the course and the only memory remaining at present are two: the word "fatigue" and the fact that I sat in front of a mirror and drew a continuous line in the same pattern of maze twenty times on twenty separated sheets of paper. Nevertheless, in order to laugh away the "D" grade for the course, it is necessary to state that the hour of the class being at 11 A.M. and his delivery of lecture in dry low monotone was not conducive to awake my mental drowsiness.

My financial status was no more secure than the mental state, which I have stated. Due to the dwindling fund, I negotiated and obtained a loan from the university on tuition note. And this practice was easy to repeat once that ice had been broken. I borrowed from the university comptroller every quarter thereafter, finally totaling about four hundred dollars at the time of my graduation.

The summer of 1928 I spent in Vacaville again with a heterogeneous group of workers and saved all the money I earned for the living expense on the campus.

The fall quarter which opened on October 1, 1928, was an eventful chapter not only in my life but also in the history of Stanford University. Herbert Hoover, an alumnus, was campaigning as a Presidential candidate throughout the country; the progress of his retinue and his speeches we followed closely in daily newspapers. When he returned to his estate on the campus, which was adjoining our clubhouse, after the strenuous trip across the continent, the student body was enthusiastic and proud in anticipation that we were to produce the highest executive official from our school. I, too, felt the general excitement about me, assuming a role of a political campaign worker, carrying my conversations in political parlance.

The political fervor reached the climax on the night of the national election, as the returns were pouring in from the four corners of the country. We assembled in cold chilly air in front of Mr. Hoover's residence and paid vociferous homage to the President elect. Mr. and Mrs. Hoover stood on a veranda for hours acknowledging clamorous felicitations from thousands in front of them. Among them assembled, there was John Phillip Sousa serenading with his band. I stood next to him watching his facial expressions and the choppy angular motion of his right forearm, which held the baton. As the finale, he played

"The Star Spangled Banner," with more zeal and more vigor. I cannot forget that I had difficulty in checking tears choking up in me. Since then every time the national anthem is played the vibrant image of Mr. Sousa moving his forearm vigorously comes back to me, followed by feeling of tears crawling up in me. This association was, however, weakened, after the fatal December 7th, as the anthem was played over and over on every radio program.

I saw Mr. Hoover many times after the election. On two occasions, I spoke to him. I met him when he was walking between two secret service men on the narrow paved path of the "fraternity row" and I coming in the opposite direction. As the path was so narrow that I had to step aside and let the Presidential party go [by]. I stood there watching him with reverence. As he passed me, he took his hand out of a pocket of his thick overcoat and said, tipping his hat, "Good morning." I answered him in awe, "Good morning, Mr. President." The same procedure was repeated on another cold windy day. Since then, I have a belief that all the high officials in Washington are considerate and thoughtful as Mr. Hoover or Mr. Ray L. Wilbur, his Secretary of Interior, whom I met several times. When you spoke of Mr. Roosevelt and Mr. Ickes the other day, the memory of these great men was recalled in my mind.

The fall quarter of 1928 brought not only the new President to Stanford, but also Kawai back from Harvard. He returned to my room after a year in the east and began life with me as a finished product in suavity and sophistication. On my questioning upon his return, he said, "Well, I was so lonesome without your mug that I had to come back." He was so good in passing out subtle statements now that I could not tell whether he meant it genuinely or otherwise.

In harmony with the campus atmosphere inundated with the national politics, I campaigned for Kawai for the presidency of the Japanese Students' house. And having succeeded in electing him to the office, I began to pull a wire behind him. The satisfaction of being the "power behind the throne" was immense; the fascination of ability to run the house affairs in my own way without actually taking the leadership was enormous. During his tenure for one year, I was intoxicated with the satisfaction and the fascination. As the result, I was no longer willing to take leadership in any activity, always endeavoring to thrive behind a curtain. I still consider it the best method in attaining one's end.

In June, 1929, I graduated with a little better than "B" average from Stanford University, which conferred me [a] Bachelor of Art degree and entered into the complex, unfathomable world. Upon graduation I filed applications to many manufacturing corporations; General Electric, Westinghouse, Otis Elevator. The applications, were, however, of no avail, as their answer invariable mentioned my drawback of being a foreigner, especially of Japanese race. My Caucasian classmates, who could not approach anywhere near my scholastic record, were accepted without trouble, whereas I was left behind without any definite future—the greatest humiliation of my life because I belonged to a racial minority. I was mad and furious, vehemently attacking the social injustice. But the anger would not bring a successful solution of the problem. What could one do under the circumstance?

My friends, Caucasian and Japanese, advised me to continue to the graduate school, saying that a higher degree might bring me a desirous employment from the companies, which had rejected me. By this time, I was disappointed and had lost faith in life to believe in the word "might." Nor did I have fund to go on with the advanced study. Let alone the fund, there was that debt to the university in the amount of about $400 which must be repaid promptly. Urgency of raising money immediately was imminent. With the thought, "Hell with engineering," "Hell with the Bachelor of Art," and "Hell with everything," I packed my belongings and ran down to Los Angeles in August, 1929.

My arrival in Los Angeles was the beginning of the third cycle of my life. Although I had no plan in advance of what to do for my living, it did not take more than one week in a boarding house before I embarked on the third base. I was taken in by a friend of mine into an insurance firm as a junior partner. The firm specialized in the casualty field, i.e., automobile insurance, tenant liability insurance, workmen's compensation, accident and health insurance, etc. I sold these policies to the Japanese people all over the Los Angeles County, contacting prospects every day. I also participated in adjustment of claims arising therefrom with adjusters from the companies, of which our firm acted as an agent. Soon the routine was set in such a way that I was selling insurance policies at night and I was investigating claims during daytime. Often I investigated automobile accidents alone and made out detailed reports to the respective company, from which I was commended for the conciseness and the thoroughness of the findings. I was proud to receive these sincere praises and felt a little more confident in what I was doing. My participation in the investigations necessarily required my presence in law courts on many occasions. Sometimes I was on the witness stand myself either as a direct witness or as a rebuttal witness; other times I assisted our lawyers in presenting our cases. Among these lawyers, there were many noted and respected ones in the city of Los Angeles, such as Jerry Geisler, Leonard Wilson, S. Hahn, etc. With one of them

I became closely attached as a warm confidential friend. He was a young Jewish barrister. He was brilliant and sharp, especially adept in questioning the witnesses and in final arguments to juries. In examinations of witnesses, he was shrewd in reframing questions, which had been objected [to] by the opposing attorney, and was successful by circumvention in getting answers he wanted in the record. In presentation of the final arguments, he was careful to pick out in advance two or three jurors, who might turn in a contrary verdict. Among these two or three jurors he invariably included a man whom he judged would be most "wind baggy," as this juror would in most cases be elected to be the foreman subsequently in the jury room. In arguing, the Jewish attorney paid his especial attention upon these pre-selected persons, pointing out one of them sometime and saying, "Of course, you would appreciate the situation wouldn't you?" or some such form of questioning to which the juror addressed could not do anything but to nod. He usually began his speech with an anecdote, then difficult terminology with incomprehensive vocabulary, then he sneered at his own words caustically, finally presenting the main theme in the level of these laymen, flattering them subtly as occasions demanded. I memorized these techniques and rehearsed them again and again in my mind. I was envious and wanted to myself these rare qualities of bringing around other people to one's point of view. There were many days assuming the role of this genius, as I sat in front of the counsel's table.

Having studied how he practiced in law, I soon worked as an apprentice. Whenever he was handling a Japanese case, he called me in. I participated in impaneling of jury, telling him to challenge this man or to accept that woman. During the course of the trial, I used to say to him, "Watch No. 2 there," "That No. 7 is shifting to our side," or "No. 10 has made up his mind against us." I was instructed to watch the jurors and gave a signal to my colleague, whenever the line of questioning was over their head. During his final argument, I was ordered to check each of the twelve jurors with "for" and "against" our side, as the estimate was important especially in framing a rebuttal. After a few practices, my estimate of "for" and "against" were pretty accurate, when it was checked with the polling of the jurors as the verdict was read.

My Jewish friend had another excelled capacity, that is his great capacity in storing a vast amount of legal knowledge in his head. He was sharp and to the point when he was arguing with a judge on points of law, rattling off either a legal code or cases pertaining to the particular question. I don't know how he did that extemporaneously. Without a moment of hesitation and without aid of any note, he could cite, "In 26 Cal 453, in the case of John Doe vs. R. Roe, the point in question was decided, your honor, in this manner: . . . " Very often, his arguments were over the knowledge of some of the jurists, [the] more honest of them remarking, "I never heard of case like that. Tell me the whole case." When I complimented him he advised me, "Don't accept any statement until you have examined it thoroughly. Look for fallibility of the statement. If you think it is fallacious, look for an authority to back your belief. Then speak up. It is not difficult." He said it was not difficult, but after many years of practice I still find it difficult to find the authority to back up my argument instantaneously.

About this time, I worked part time as an official interpreter on call in the Los Angeles courts. I don't remember how I happened to embark upon this career. The only thing I remember now is that I was thoroughly disgusted with the interpretations given by a man permanently employed. I saw some witnesses placed at disadvantage because the interpreter had translated erroneously. A probable explanation for my new career is that I might have said, "Hell, let me try it. I can't do any worse than that guy." However, this experience was valuable in two aspect. First, I learned to value in translating the strength and force of a statement with its connotations, minimizing the idea of direct translation. Second, I learned to evaluate the credibility and veracity of a witness while I was addressing him.

As a court interpreter, I worked for two years off and on, until the chief of interpreters ordered that I must relinquish my job, because I did not have citizenship and was not eligible for the civil service status. This was another occasion when I was ostracized because of racial limitation and not because of incompetency.

Meanwhile, in March, 1930, I moved to Gardena, a town of 2000, about 20 miles southwest of the city hall of Los Angeles. I selected this town, because it was a hub about which there were about 2000 Japanese families located within 15 miles radius. I was able to cover the territory more easily in the evenings to sell insurance policies.

Within the week after I had settled down in the new house, my father passed away due to sudden illness, which was diagnosed as bronchial pneumonia. For his funeral, I returned to San Francisco and came south again to resume the daily routine.

In the summer of 1931, I was married to a Nisei girl from San Francisco. I took the fatal last step with my eyes wide open. Yet to all inquirers, I say, "Every woman wants to believe that her husband was deeply and blindly in love when he married her. Let it go as so. Why should we disillusion any one?" Ah, doctor, you are a famous psychiatrist, who knows thousands when he is told of one thing. You are to elaborate from here on. Anyway, the end of the last chapter of "My Marriage" narrates, "I was happy ever after, still happily married in 1942, eleven years after the Lohengrin's march."

In June 1932, a daughter was born whom we named Roberta Akiko. We were proud of her; proud of her so much that she might have looked to others as if she was a guinea pig for our physiological and psychological experiments. We, my wife, and I, often argued mildly in the technique of raising the child. When she had colics, we hurriedly and excitedly turned the pages of a book on infant cures, anxious to find immediate relief for her. Snapshots of the girl were taken at a regular interval and each new development was recorded in a book. We even saved her hairs when we cut her tresses the first time.

She and another girl, who was born in May, 1934, and was named Marcia Chizuko, are the center of our attraction at present, their future being our primary concern and our future being secondary. We are always planning so that our daughters would not go through the hard life which I had gone through.

In 1933, we had the bank holiday and the New Deal came in. As I kept on in the insurance business, my territory was strictly confined by expediency to the agricultural and the suburban district southwest of Los Angeles. The farmers and merchants, all Isseis, came often to my house, instead of going to my office in Los Angeles, to consult me on their business and personal matters, not pertaining to the insurance. I was glad to give all necessary aids to them, always willing to go out of my way, resulting eventually in good will toward my family and my business. The business flourished and my family was satisfied and well established. Do good things keep on forever?

The years 1929–1933 were too satisfactory and too comfortable for my pattern of life which the nature bestowed upon me. During this time, I was working steadily, having paid off the university debt, having married, and having been blessed with two daughters. I was happy as a member of a contented family. The state of equilibrium did not continue in this manner. Since the beginning of 1934, the farming area began to feel the depression of the Post Hoover period. A crate of carrots was sold for 15 cents, a lug of summer squash was sold for 5 cents and so on. The merchants in the district, too, felt decline in prosperity. In conformity with this financial condition, my business began to fall in volume; even if there was a good volume remaining, collection of the premiums were getting more difficult each day, as each day brought more grief and newer disappointment to the Japanese people. Having realized that there was no immediate improvement of the agricultural situation in sight, I decided to sell my share of the business and to get out of it quickly. I believe that I was fortunate in liquidating the business in January, 1935, as the agricultural prices did not regain the profitable operational margin until 1941, the acreage of each enterprise decreasing gradually, the use of outside labor eventually eliminated, confining the supply of labor within one's family in most cases. The Japanese commercial firms were suffering as well, because their business were dependent upon these farmers. Thus, I felt and experienced the low economic cycle in the rural and semi-rural districts, suffering with these Japanese farmers and merchants.

In the spring of 1935, I opened a retail produce market in Gardena. Instead of selling Caucasian goods to Japanese as in the insurance business, I began to sell products of the Japanese to Caucasian people. I bought vegetables directly from the Japanese farmers in the district, supplementing with fruits and out of season vegetables from the Los Angeles wholesale market. Our business improved day by day and soon reached a prosperous stage with a steady clientele, many coming from distant towns regularly. There were many Caucasian people who came not only to trade but to talk to me. These people ranged in their social status, varying from a retired lieutenant commander of the U.S. Navy or a trustee of University of Southern California to high school teachers; from a chemical engineer of the Port of Los Angeles, originally of Texas, to a W.P.A. worker, formerly of Oklahoma; from a Jehovah's Witness worker to a Townsendite.[9] My friends were numerous and with them I spent many hours exchanging our ideas and conversing about our personal experiences. They gave me cross-sectional sentiments of the American Public, whereas I gave them my knowledge of then shifting public opinions in Japan, in which they were immensely interested. I was well informed on the contemporary conditions of Japan as they had appeared in print, for I was as a hobby making a comparative study of changing public opinions in the two countries; for this study I used Tokyo newspapers and magazines published in Japan. My convic-

9. Townsendites were supporters of Francis W. Townsend's plan for old-age pensions, which became very popular during the Depression; see Abraham Holtzman, *The Townsend Movement* (New York: Brookman Associates, 1963), 28–46.

tion as early as in 1937 was that the war between America and Japan was inevitable, as Japan was preparing to that end, whereas the public in this country was ignorant of the actual conditions of the Far East and of the Japanese reactions to American diplomatic policies. I believed that the general public was misled by braggers and wishful-thinkers. The people were misled by newspapers to fear the Japanese people in San Pedro instead of realizing what was actually happening in the Orient. By June of 1941, I was certain that the war would come soon and told so to my friends, both Caucasian and Japanese.

In spite of my unwelcome convictions, the Caucasian friends continued to trade with us, even after December 7, although other less friendly customers dropped out of sight gradually. My Japanese friends, who were more concerned with the progressively worsening situation, frequented our store and home increasing, asking for personal advises. These advises were more in demand when the evacuation was in order, although at first they could not believe that such a stupendous task would be undertaken by the American government. As early as on December 10, I told them that all Isseis would be ordered away from the coast and by December 20, I advised Nisei to prepare to come along with us. These Japanese could not accept what I pronounced as their fate and accused me of being a "crack-pot." But when the first evacuation step was announced, I expanded my chest and said silently, "I told you so." I regret that I could not join these Japanese people of the Gardena Valley in their evacuation trip to the Tulare Assembly Center in spite of their persistent imploring.

The evacuation of the Japanese from the Pacific Coast was the beginning of the fourth cycle of my life, whose description must necessarily wait until a further date, at which time I could see the things which had taken place retrospectively in better perspective. However, there is one incident I wish to record here. That is, it happened on or about January 15th, when the question of the Japanese mass migration was discussed widely pro and con among the Caucasian populace. The newspapers all over the coast were handling its necessity and its urgency as of the primary importance at that time. The scene of the incident took place in the parlor of my home in Gardena. It was about 8 p. m. We, my wife, Roberta, Marcia, and I, were in the parlor, sitting on the floor around a gas stove. Marcia, nicknamed Cheeko, was drawing a picture with crayons; Roberta, commonly called Peepo, was reading a story book. My wife was working on her quilt and I was reading an evening newspaper. The radio was going at full blast, carrying Dvorak's "New World Symphony" on its waves.

Cheeko soon finished her drawing and passed it to Peepo, who, in turn, returned the paper after she had written a line on it. Yae, my wife, took notice of what was happening between the children and said,

Yae: Cheeko, may I see the paper?

Cheeko passes the paper to her mother and Yae looks at it. She smiles.

Yae: Look, dad. Isn't this a nice picture?

Then Yae passes the picture to her husband, Dick. He looks at it and smiles. He looks at Yae and both smile and nod understandingly. (Cheeko drew a red circle on a white background, representing a Japanese flag. Above the flag she wrote, "The flag I hate." Peepo wrote on the same paper, "Me, too.")

Dick: (To Yae, in whisper) Don't say anything (to the children). This is a nice drawing. (Returning the paper to Cheeko.) Thank you.

Silence. The radio is playing a classical music.

At the end of the number, there is a station identification. Then a news broadcast.

Radio: The evacuation of all the Japanese from the Pacific Coast must be undertaken. . . .

Yae: Peepo, turn the radio off.

Peepo gets up from her sitting position on the floor and turns the knob. Silence for about a minute.

Cheeko: Daddy, do I have to go, too?

Dick: Yes, we all have to go.

Cheeko: But I am an American citizen, though. Where is my birth certificate, Mama?

Yae: We have to get yours from the city hall.

Cheeko: Let's go and get it from the city hall. If I show my birth certificate, I bet I don't have to move.

Peepo is smiling. She winks to Dick and then to Yae.

Yae: Yes, you are an American citizen, but your face is Japanese. Everyone with Japanese face must go. Do you want to stay alone, when your daddy and mamma are gone?

Cheeko: Why don't you show our birth certificates. Maybe they will let you stay, too.

Peepo still smiling interrupts.

Peepo: Cheeko, it's about time to go to bed. Come on.

Peepo and Cheeko: (leaving the room hand in hand.) Good night.

Yae: Good night, Peepo and Cheeko.

Dick: Good night, girls.

Dick and Yae look at each other and smile. Yae resumes her needle work and Dick goes back to his newspaper.

Silence.

[Curtain]

Very truly yours,

Richard S. Nishimoto

LABOR

Nishimoto's Report on the Firebreak Gang

Introduction

In this second selection, Nishimoto describes his experiences as the supervisor of a work crew of men from the Unit I facility during Poston's first year of operation. This report, which provides extensive detail about the day-to-day work experiences of ordinary men, is unique in the published literature about life in the camps.[1]

When planning the camps, the War Relocation Authority determined that it would provide opportunities to work for all those adults who wished to do so. This policy was evidence of the WRA's concern with idleness, which might exacerbate frustration and popular discontent, but it was also in accord with its view that the camps should be made as economically and materially self-sufficient as possible.[2] When Poston opened, in fact, there was still much to be done in order to make the primitive facilities fully operational, let alone prepare them for the cold, damp Arizona winter.

Upon entering Poston, Japanese Americans were asked to sign an oath promising that they would pursue work in the camp and thus be productive members of the community. Because of its rather harsh, authoritarian provisions, the oath is worth quoting here at length:

> I swear loyalty to the United States and enlist in the War Relocation Work Corps for the duration of the war and 14 days thereafter in order to contribute to the

> needs of the nation and in order to earn a livelihood for myself and my dependents. I will accept whatever pay, unspecified at the present time, the War Relocation Authority determines, and I will observe all rules and regulations.
>
> In doing this I understand that I shall not be entitled to any cash or allowances beyond the wages due me at the time of discharge from the work corps; that I may be transferred from one relocation center to another by the War Relocation Authority; that medical care will be provided, but that I cannot make a claim against the United States for any injury or disease acquired by me while in the Work Corps; that I shall be subject to special assessments for educational, medical and other community service as may be provided for in the support of any dependents who reside in a relocation center; that I shall be financially responsible for the full value of any government property that I use while in the work corps; and that the infraction of any regulations of the War Relocation Authority will render me liable to trial and suitable punishment. So help me God.[3]

Salaries for unskilled laborers of Japanese descent were set at twelve dollars a month,[4] but they were not actually paid even this much, although they carried out demanding physical work. Sometimes, as Nishimoto notes, the WRA officials were not willing to pay them their wages at all. While the basic necessities of life were provided by the federal government, the heavier clothes and boots that were badly needed during the winter months, while available through mail-order catalogs, were often out of the Japanese Americans' financial reach because of their low wages.

Wives, single women, and teenagers could earn the same basic salaries. Before the war, as Nishimoto described in his letter to Alexander Leighton, discriminatory hiring practices in the larger society had blocked even the American-born second-generation men and women who had education, degrees, and the necessary credentials to practice a profession or livelihood. Now, occupational opportunities, albeit circumscribed, actually opened up for women and young people. As a result, the male heads of households lost their position as the main providers for the Japanese American family, since even those who refused to work were eligible to feed their families three times a day in the camp mess hall. The federal government had become the provider.

When reading about the incidents of recalcitrance and even outright anger among Nishimoto's crew, we need to remember that work per se had lost most of its prewar meaning for adult men. The dissatisfaction expressed by the members of the firebreak gang represents many of the Japanese Americans' discontent with work in the Poston setting over such issues as confusing administrative regulations and plans, the make-work atmosphere that sometimes

When they entered Poston, Japanese Americans were required to swear their loyalty to the United States and promise that they would work for the duration of the war plus fourteen days, accepting whatever wages the federal government offered for their labor. (Courtesy of the Bancroft Library)

Unit I firemen and volunteers work to extinguish a blaze that broke out in Block 6 on November 16, 1943. The wooden barracks and the very hot, dry Arizona summers made fire a constant concern at Poston. To reduce the threat, Nishimoto's firebreak gang worked to clear away brush and the remaining construction debris. (Courtesy of the Bancroft Library)

surrounded tasks in camp, wage scales, pressure from supervisors to work harder, delays in paying wages, indications of corruption on the part of the Euro-American staff, and the allocation of the best jobs, which were often given to Nisei who had arrived early to help set up the camp. All of these issues generated controversy over working conditions and helped to undergird protests and strikes at Poston and at other camps, including Tule Lake and Manzanar.

Beyond the descriptions of the day-to-day challenges of heavy labor in a climate where in the summer the temperature could easily soar to 110 degrees in the shade, the "Firebreak Gang" report captures the tensions of camp life in Poston that were already surfacing by the fall of 1942. In particular, Nishimoto notes various instances in which labor issues became a medium for the expression of complaints about Euro-American staff and their Nisei "assistants." The report also clearly documents the belligerent responses on the part of Nishimoto's crew when Euro-Americans assaulted their dignity and efforts by trying to lecture them about how to do their work.

Further, the text indicates that Nishimoto faithfully recorded the conversations of the crew, revealing a range of political, gender, and racial attitudes among the members of the firebreak gang as they conversed with each other while carrying on their daily routine. Such attitudes, especially the shape they took in ordinary work settings, should be the subject of ethnographic description if only as an index of popular consciousness. Thus Nishimoto's documentation of the thoughts and offhand comments of the Issei and Nisei men seems true to life, even though hostility toward "others" may have served as an emotional displacement for the men who labored under the conditions of incarceration and, indeed, under the blazing Arizona sun with little recognition and with little in the way of monetary reward for their efforts.

Finally, Nishimoto's report illustrates his early attempts to utilize his cultural and communication skills to manage the Japanese Americans under his supervision—an effort that in fact continued throughout Nishimoto's career at Poston, as we will see in the fourth selection, on the All Center Conference.

It is relevant to note here that Nishimoto, even more than the applied anthropologists who set up and helped to run Poston, deeply appreciated how maintaining solidarity and morale among the members of the firebreak gang was a means of insuring their sense of basic human dignity. Beyond his analytic interest in management issues, then, many of Nishimoto's efforts on behalf of his crew were directed toward creating an atmosphere in which the travails of incarceration might be at least partially overcome by pride in their work.

Notes

1. Edward Spicer's essay "Reluctant Cotton-Pickers: Incentive to Work in a Japanese Relocation Center," which reports on an experiment in applied anthropology, is one of the few longer works available that focuses specifically on workers and working conditions. It is a somewhat specialized study, however, because it focuses on the issue of how, as applied anthropologists, Spicer and his colleagues sought to motivate Japanese Americans to go out of camp on "work leave" in order to help local Euro-American farmers harvest their crops. It is included in *Human Problems in Technological Change: A Casebook*, ed. Edward H. Spicer (New York: Russell Sage Foundation, 1952), 41–52.

2. The WRA also hoped that Japanese Americans in confinement would even be able to contribute to the war effort. Projects to grow guayule for rubber and to produce

camouflage nets were initiated in a number of the camps, including Poston. An historical overview of the WRA's efforts to formulate an official policy on work for the camps is available in a study of the President's Commission on the Wartime Relocation and Internment of Citizens (CWRIC), *Personal Justice Denied* (Washington, D.C.: Government Printing Office, 1982), 146, 165–69.

3. As quoted in Alexander H. Leighton, *The Governing of Men: General Principles and Recommendations Based on Experience at a Japanese Relocation Camp* (1945; reprint, New York: Octagon, 1964), 64–65.

4. Skilled laborers could earn as much as sixteen dollars a month, although the highest salaries—nineteen dollars a month—were reserved for highly trained professionals like doctors and dentists. Even so, Japanese Americans, including doctors, felt resentment when the Euro-Americans working side-by-side with them earned wages that were many times their own. In one example, cited in the CWRIC report, a "WRA librarian received $167 a month, while her evacuee staff received $16 a month"; CWRIC, *Personal Justice Denied*, 167. Evidently, one of the reasons for the lower salaries for people of Japanese descent was that administrators believed that it was inappropriate for the latter to earn more than the twenty-one dollars a month paid to privates in the army; see CWRIC, *Personal Justice Denied*, 166. It is interesting to note that, although the base pay of privates rose to fifty dollars per month shortly after this rate went into effect, wages at the WRA camps remained at nineteen dollars; see John H. Provinse and Solon T. Kimball, "Building New Communities during War Time," *American Sociological Review* 11 (1946): 398.

FIREBREAK GANG

Preface

The mass evacuation and migration of the Japanese were a novel and extraordinary adventure of the American government.[1] The exodus in its scope and its circumstance was unprecedented and was such remarkable and unusual nature as to be recorded on pages of the American political and economical history. It was a compulsory migration against free will, enforced and administered by the governmental agencies. The people, under the extraordinary circumstance and in a new unaccustomed environment, presented an interesting study to many students.

The writer desired to write stories in Japanese, depicting such exodus and life at a relocation camp for his pleasure. The materials used in this report were originally collected and intended for such purposes—jotted down on little pieces of paper from time to time. Some expressions were kept verbatim in Japanese and filed under the speaker's name. Often the thoughts and the sentiments of the writer were recorded. Therefore, in making this report available for research workers, it was necessary to interview each individual to obtain the statistical information. This report was written by reconstructing the

1. Japanese American Evacuation and Resettlement Study Collection, Bancroft Library, University of California, Berkeley, J 6.07.

events in chronological order, with which the recorded reactions and the statistical data were correlated.

In translating Japanese expressions, the writer adhered to the technique he used while he was acting as a court interpreter. He attempted to preserve the speaker's intent above all, evaluating the force and strength of the statement—for example, free translation rather than direct.[1]

To John G. Evans [the assistant director of Poston and the administrator of Unit I], the writer makes grateful acknowledgment, not only for valuable advice and assistance while he was in charge of the crew, but for his unfailing trust and encouragement.

[Richard S. Nishimoto]
Poston, Arizona.
September, 1942.

Introduction

This is a report of a group of thirty odd men, commonly referred to as "firebreak gang," who were engaged in cleaning and subjugation work of land in Camp I of the Colorado River War Relocation Project at Poston, Arizona. It is a chronicle of the hectic early days, depicting the confused state of affairs prevailing. The subject covers a period of eighty days, beginning on June 27, 1942, and ending on September 14.

It is a typical group of men who were engaged in the outdoor labor of unskilled variety in this project.[2] It is my presumption that the characteristics found in the "firebreak gang" were either similar or identical with those of other outdoor labor groups such as the poultry crew, the fish culture crew, the farm gang, etc.

I acted as the foreman of this group of men, supervising and directing them on the field, having full responsibility for maintaining order and harmony among them and keeping in contact with the administrative branches or the Engineering Department for coordination.

I took a part in its organization and was responsible for its disbandment. It is noteworthy that there was neither friction nor quarrel among them. There was neither antagonistic feeling nor open defiance against the foreman, except at its inception. They were willing to cooperate with each other and to be obedient to the leader. There was neither a trace of sentiment nor an occasion to resort to such a concerted collective action as a strike, even at the time when labor disputes were frequent and grievances of the dissatisfied workers were widely discussed and gossiped in the camp.[3] They were, indeed, well satisfied and contented in what they were doing as days went on.[4] The Caucasians who had supervised or who had knowledge of what we were doing were also well satisfied and expressed their commendation and appreciation.[5] It is my belief that we had one happy family, having complete harmony and trust among us. I am afraid, therefore, that this report might give the reader an impression of being a "success story." However, I decided to exercise no restraint and to report as I saw, as I heard, and as I felt.

Myself

At the outset, I believe it is helpful for the reader to understand this report if I presented a brief sketch of my life. I am a male of 38 years of age, born in Tokio, Japan. I married a Nisei girl and have two daughters of ten and eight years old respectively. While in Japan, I entered an elementary school at six and graduated at twelve. At the age of seventeen I completed my education in an intermediate school (*chugaku-ko*) of American Episcopalian endowment in Tokio. I grew up in a large group of boys of similar age, as I have lived in school dormitories since ten.

At the age of seventeen, I came to the United States to join my parents and entered a high school in San Francisco. At twenty-one I enrolled in Stanford University and five years later I graduated from the School of Engineering. During the summer vacations and one year of leave of absence, I worked on, and later managed, a fruit orchard, about 300 acres in size, in Sacramento Valley, California. There I gained valuable experiences in associating with and handling 30–150 resident and migratory farm laborers—Japanese, Portuguese, Spaniards, Filipinos, etc.

After graduation I came to Los Angeles and operated an insurance brokerage firm until 1934. Concurrently, I served in law courts as an interpreter on call, until the civil service status was strictly required. Since then I owned and operated a small retail produce market in the southwestern suburban section of Los Angeles, where Japanese truck gardeners were heavily concentrated. People often wondered why I a college engineering graduate, was in such a "low-down business." To them I used to say, "I learned just the art of 'bull session' at the expense of hard earned $5,000." Beyond that I had no desire to elaborate.

My friends tell me that I have the appearance of a Nisei and act like one, yet my thoughts and reactions are typically those of intelligent Isseis.[6]

The Work

The work, attended and accomplished by the "firebreak gang" during June 27–September 14, 1942, is separated into two categories: one, to segregate and clean piles of scrap lumber in various areas in Camp 1, which were remnants of the materials used by a construction company in building barracks for living and other accessory purposes. In other words, segregation and cleaning mean[t] to separate usable lumber from scraps and trash, to haul away usable lumber, [and] to burn the remaining scraps and trash.

These lumber piles were located in the following areas:[7] the firebreak and recreational area between Block 36 and Block 45 on one side and Block 37 and Block 44 on the other—about 5 acres of ground covered densely with the remnants. At some places the heaps were as high as 4 feet from the ground; the Firebreak area east of Block 53 and Block 60—about 3 acres; the area immediately west of Block 22—about 1 acre; the firebreak area between Block 38 and Block 39—3 acres of medium density, about 2 feet deep; the warehouse area west of "E" Street—about 3 acres of medium density; and other small areas. (The areas are listed in the chronological order.)

[Second,] to prepare land preliminary to the leveling by heavy equipments.[8] [This involved work] to assemble and gather into small piles trunks, branches and brushes of mesquites and cottonwood trees, which were previously knocked down or dragged out by heavy duty tractors; to dig and cut the residual stumps with shovels and axes; to burn the piles.

The tools and equipments used were as follows: Fordson tractors attached with small Ferguson trailers, which were of stake body type of 2-ton capacity. They were also used in transporting the workers to and from the work. Later, the tractors, detached of the trailers, were chained with heavy cables and were employed in dragging stumps. [Tools also included] axes, shovels, rakes, pitchforks, etc.

The Chaotic Beginning

The request of cleaning the lumber piles was first made by the Engineering Department to John G. Evans.[9] It was necessary to remove them so that a lateral system for farm irrigation and for dust control could be constructed. It was originally suggested to employ at least 250 Japanese residents in Camp 1 and clean up the Firebreak and recreational area (marked as A and B), where the canal was to run lengthwise, in three or four days. It was suggested and was stressed by Mr. Barbour that this was very important preparatory work which must by undertaken quickly and accomplished in the shortest possible time, as "rigs" were ready to come into the field. The Associate Engineer thought that the recruiting of 250 workers should not be difficult and that with all these men the work would be accomplished in no time, if enough trucks and trailer-tractors were pooled from various departments. But as the thing turned out later, Barbour was over-optimistic and was wishful-thinking, and his desire and expectation were shattered.[10]

According to Evans, the following steps were taken to recruit workers. In their meeting Evans instructed all the Block Managers to get all the idle men out. Block Managers contacted the men without employment and persuaded them. They pointed out as persuasive arguments, I was told, several points such as the whole community would be benefited by it; sooner we have the canal, quicker we will have water for our vegetable gardens and for dust control. If water was brought into Block, it would have cooling effect and we would not be suffering from heat. They would be compensated for their public-spirited service.

Tomo Ito,[[2]] Evans' assistant, with whom I was acquainted in my college days, asked me to "help the country"; inasmuch as I was unemployed, I should come out and supervise the men.

On the morning of June 27, I reported to the area immediately east of Block 44—area (A). The entire place was in a turmoil—one big mess. One hundred

---

2. In a transcription of an oral report given to his JERS colleagues in Salt Lake City on December 4, 1944, Nishimoto comments that Ito attended Stanford University between 1926 and 1930. Ito was reported to have avoided contact with Japanese American students at Stanford, as well as the larger Japanese American community after graduation. In addition, Ito was one of the Nisei volunteers who elected to go to Poston early to help set up the camp. Because he was well liked by the Euro-American staff, Ito was selected as the first supervisor of the block managers, although he lost this position later in 1942. See "Richard Nishimoto on the Political Organization of Poston," Bancroft Library, University of California, Berkeley, Japanese American Evacuation and Resettlement Study Collection, W 1.15, pp. 3–5.

men, almost entirely of elderly Isseis, were excitedly picking up lumber off the ground and were energetically throwing it on trucks and trailers scattered all over.[11] Loaded tractors were speeding down dusty, dirty roads with droning hums, kicking up smoke high into the air. Tractors were rushing back to the field unloaded, as if they were in a great hurry to get somewhere. Some men were raking up trash into small heaps with great enthusiasm. There was commotion and confusion all over the field. In this atmosphere I was told by F. Evans' other assistant, who had been directing the operations, to take charge of the men and to keep them constantly busy. He said, "Don't let them ease up. Keep 'em busy."

So I kept them busy all the time, keeping the vehicles scattered here, there, and all over, in order to keep all the men busy all the time. Whenever a car was not available to load, I made them clean up the trash into small piles with rakes. The work was progressing fast for about two hours. Then about 10 A.M., I began to hear grumbling and complaints here and there in Japanese. One man said, "How do they expect us to work without any drinking water around."

A few shouted, "Who do they think we are? Hell, we're no slaves. We don't have to work, if we don't want to."

Some in another part were talking aloud, "It's too hot. No use working! We're getting only six cents an hour anyway." I breathed ominous, ugly air. Some men were leaving the field already for home. I thought that something must be done immediately and quickly, otherwise all of them would quit the work and would go home. Yet the only idea that came to my mind at the moment was to talk to these men. I moved swiftly among them. I said in polite Japanese, "I am sorry. I didn't realize how difficult it is for you to work in this heat. If you would suggest to me what changes can be made, I am more than willing to listen. I am not here to 'slave drive' you. On the contrary, I am here to serve for you."

My pleading had little effect, although no one has left since. I realized that it was too late to retrieve the situation. The damage was done. They felt and resented that I was trying to get the most out of them in the shortest time. I could sense uneasiness and unrest among the men. I knew that they resented my "slave driving." They hated to be "suckers." They were not like the Isseis I had known before the evacuation. The Isseis I had known were all industrious, diligent, obedient and courteous people. These men were not like them. They were suspicious, ill-humored, discourteous, irritable people. I calculated that they were under severe strain and in abnormal state of mind resulting from the evacuation, as they had not fully conceived the meaning of the war and had not adjusted themselves to the new environment. They were skeptical and suspicious of me, of anything and of everything. They were oversensitive, yet they were inconsiderate of my feeling when they grumbled and complained. I knew that they thought of me as a white-man's "stooge." I also suspected that they were not working there entirely from their free will, but instead, some kind of pressure or coercion was exercised upon them.[12] Consequently, I decided to take some immediate corrective measures. I sent some young boys to the near-by kitchens for pails of drinking water. I ordered the men not to rake the trash and rest between loadings. I ordered them to load in much slower tempo. In other words, I tried to salvage whatever I could out of this "wreckage." I called the noon recess and decided to wait for further development.

After the lunch, I reported to the field at 1 P.M. and saw a few people coming in slowly from all directions, but I did not see one hundred men coming back. When a roll was called a little later, I found that there were only forty-four men present including ten young truck and tractor drivers. I said to myself, "I knew this would happen. I bet those guys—meaning those who failed to return—are sore now. I bet they think I am 'apple polishing' white guys. I must be more careful from now on."

I again instructed the men to pick up lumber in a more comfortable speed, to sit down and rest while the tractors are away, [and that] no raking is necessary.

As the result grumblings were less and far in between. I ran to this and that part of the field continually in the afternoon, worried and sick over the dissatisfied men, in order to eliminate complaints entirely.

As I called the recess for the day [at] 4:30, a middle aged man, while walking away from me, said sarcastically and defiantly, "You mean to say we can't go home unless you say so?" I understood the meaning and I was hurt. I was tired, too. I was so tired and worried that I did not know whether I wanted to continue on with the job. I was disappointed and disgusted as well. On my way home, I said to myself, "I have two strikes on me, before I even get started. I am having a hell of a time and I don't deserve it."

It was fortunate that the next day was Sunday. The day gave me quiet hours to reflect upon what had taken place. I pondered, "The job is much bigger than I've anticipated. But I can't quit now. I can't fail. If I fail now, I am just rotten and no good."

I kept on in my thought, "These men are sick mentally, because they are in an unusual place under extraordinary circumstances. My past experiences of managing men of an orchard aren't quite enough to cope with the special situation. Something more must be figured. Here is a priceless chance to utilize understanding and knowledge of Isseis. Let's see what I can do."

As a tentative formula in treating the workers, who were almost entirely Isseis, I decided on the following procedures: to show respect and treat them as my superiors. Never to show cockiness or discourtesy. Never to be pedantic. Always to be willing to consult them as if their advices are needed and valued. To increase their faith and trust in Democracy. To help them forget unhappy experiences and unfortunate losses resulted from the evacuation. To increase the spirit of cooperation among themselves and to the community. To equalize by some lawful method on the field the wage differential. (These men were to receive $12.00 a month.)

In order to obtain the above objectives, I intended to try out, at first, the following steps: to appoint two assistant foremen who would direct and supervise the operation, so that I might be free to move about among the men. To carry all my conversation in Japanese, strictly in the more polite form.[13] To disregard the idea of efficiency. To forget about the amount of work to be done in a day. To let them establish their own speed. To make them rest and relax as much as they need.

Thus, on June 30, I started the morning with fresh vigor and new ambition. First, I called on two men at their apartments, who particularly attracted my attention on the first day, and asked them to act as my assistants. One was a Nisei of 22 years of age and the other an Issei of 37. I gave them explicit instructions as to what they were to do and told them what I was intending to do; and we were all set to go. As I look back retrospectively now, the selection was a happy one. They stuck with me to the end and gave me valuable assistance in carrying out all the tedious and routine duties. They were loyal to me throughout placing their faith and confidence in my sincerity and integrity. Indeed, to them much of our success is attributable.

About ten minutes before 8 A.M., two assistants and I reported to the field and waited for the people to arrive. As they began to come, I met them with a smile and "*Ohayo gozaimasu.*" Only a few returned me a greeting friendlily. The majority were still antagonistic and sullen. Some ignored me completely. I told myself, "For Christ sake, can't they see that I am trying to be their friend. Can't they see that I am going to do everything possible for their benefit."

The assistants began moving to take charge as the tractors were coming in. I was told that for the day no truck was available and instead seven tractors were assigned. "Good!" I thought, "Now the men can take it easy today."

One Fordson left with three-quarter capacity load. Another followed with a half load. All the drivers were fidgety and did not wait until the trailer was loaded to the capacity. They were anxious to get going and to keep moving. They found great enjoyment and thrill in riding tractors, as if they were newly possessed toys. Two were going down the road with the throttles wide open. They were racing the rough road, bouncing up and down, a part of the load falling out, scattering all over. I said to myself, "Bunch of young fools! That's Nisei for you. They are just trying to have a good time. Don't they realize that they are working for money? Why doesn't someone who is in charge of these kids bawl them out? The Fordsons won't last much longer, if they keep on treating them like that."

A roll call that morning revealed that there were thirty-two men and seven young drivers. The assistants were busy directing the drivers where to park their vehicles. They were also helping in loading. I walked around the field and tried to be friendly with the men. Here and there I initiated conversation. I felt that I was still avoided. I suspected that they still considered me as a "stooge." When they talked to me their tone was not friendly, but peevish and glum.

Soon a tractor came back unloaded. As soon as the driver backed the trailer into a designated place, he ran to me and reported excitedly, "Hey, those guys are plenty sore."

"What guys?" I asked.

"You know, those guys unloading out there. Only two guys out there this morning!" said he.

"Yeah? I didn't know where you fellows were taking the loads. All right! I will go down there and will find out what the trouble is," I replied.

More trouble! I hopped on the first tractor going out of the field.

This was the first time I learned that the lumber was unloaded west of proposed "L" Street, approximately one quarter of a mile due west of Block 42.[14] As I arrived there, I saw two men frantically unloading—perspiration running down their faces and their shirts dripping wet. Moreover, there were two tractors waiting in line for unloading. When I stopped them and asked, they were too eager to expound their grievances. Those were as follows. [First,] there were some 15 men working on the first day. They were from Block 43. They believed it was useless to return to the work, as there was no one to take their attendance. [Second,] there was no drinking water available.

As a reply, I informed these men that I had no idea that I was to take charge of the unloading crew. I was under the impression that I was responsible only for the loading men. In fact, F told me to do just that.

From now on, I would be around regularly to check their attendance. I would see to it that the due credit would be given to the men who worked on the first day. I would see the manager of Block 43 and would ask him to get the men back. Meanwhile, they should pass the word around that we need more men. Second, they should set their own pace or speed of work, ignoring the tractors waiting in line. Third, they would be supplied with drinking water immediately. Accordingly, on the way back, I arranged for more men and drinking water.

When I returned to the loading field, the Boyle Height[3] Isseis of Block 45 about five in number, were complaining that the weather was "Too hot to suit" them and that they had never "intended to stoop down to this low-down labor."

One of them said, "This is a kind of work for the Mexicans."

About fifteen men, all elderly Isseis from a "bachelors' barrack" in Block 37, were talking aloud in a group to themselves, working entirely apart from the others. As soon as I approached them, their conversation ceased. I felt insulted; I felt like revolting. Yet I was curious and wanted to find out what they had been discussing. By some roundabout inquiries, I learned from others, who were in the vicinity, that the topics of their conversation were as follows: they were involuntary evacuees. No one could compel them to work. They doubted if they would be paid for their service. Their manager told them that this work was to last only a day or two. On the contrary, they had observed and calculated that they could not possibly finish it even in ten days. They resented the idea that they had been tricked into this work by some premeditated scheming. They expressed that if it was for one day or two, they would not mind, but not for ten days. It was too hot to suit them. (It was about 10:30 A.M. The temperature was about 110 degrees F.)[15]

I knew then that I had lost these men—the city people and the bachelors. I was disappointed that they would not give me a chance. On the other hand, I was contemptuous and scornful of them. I thought that they were unduly susceptible and provocative. I was determined now to go on without them.

3. Boyle Heights is a district just east of downtown Los Angeles where, before the war, there was a large concentration of Japanese Americans.

Just before the noon, a Nisei driver reported that a sharply pointed scrap pierced through one of the rear traction tires of his Fordson. As I did not know where to report the puncture, I said to him, "Go and find the fellow who gave the key to you."

In the afternoon only fourteen men reported to the work. I wondered if I were to lose everyone of them by the next morning. The Issei assistant was worried, too, and said, "Did you notice few men were resting, although you told them to take it easy? You know what's the trouble? They say that they can't sit down and rest while others are working busily nearby. They feel out of place. They don't feel 'right' to sit down just themselves. Why don't you give all of them rest at the same time. Usually the fellows who don't sit down and keep on working are ones who gamble the most."

"All right. I will try anything once," I said to him, "Give them 15 minutes rest every hour on the hour. Take them to a shady place and let them relax."

We tried the new system and we soon found out that the men liked it.[16]

If it was not one thing, it was always something else. One tractor was disabled on account of distributor trouble caused by excessive dust.

Another tractor was gone due to a punctured rear tire, again from the same cause.

About 4 o'clock Frasier[17] drove down to the field and inquired of a man as to the whereabouts of his foreman, who, in turn, pointed me out and called me.

"You have to take care of the tractors more carefully. Each puncture costs the government more than $60; besides, the tire must be sent all the way to Los Angeles for repair," said he excitedly.

I said, "Who are you anyway? And what do you mean by that I must take care of the tractors. I have no authority over the drivers. They are sent by somebody I don't know."

"I am in charge of all the equipment in the camp and those tractors were assigned to you," said he.

"But I've never seen you before. Why didn't you tell me at the beginning. Then I could have told those boys a few things," I retorted.

After a little consultation over the existing condition, Frasier and I agreed on the following points. The driver is to be warned. If the warning is not heeded, he must be discharged.

I warned all the drivers to handle their tractors more carefully. I warned them that reckless driving would not be tolerated and that the speed limit of 10 miles per hour should be strictly observed. I added that if they should disobey the regulations, they would be placed on the blacklist, which would bar them from any position involving driving of vehicles.

About fifteen minutes later, another Caucasian appeared in a coupe. This time a fat, chubby, red-faced old man. (This was my first meeting with Mr. Barbour.) "Now, what does he want?" I wondered.

"Well, how many men you got here working?" he asked.

"Nineteen, sir."

"Nineteen? Why don't you get more men? There are lots of men sitting on their asses all over the camp. Why don't you get 'em? You should have at least a couple of hundred out here," said he optimistically.

"A couple of hundred? Like hell! Just try and get those guys sitting on their asses, and see how far you can get with that," I thought.

Instead, I said to him, "I certainly would be glad to have more men, but I am kept busy here and can't get around to that. Will you see if you can get some more men for me?"

"All right. I will see what I can do for you," said Mr. Barbour.

I did not know what happened subsequently, but that was the last time the subject of getting more men was brought up by Barbour. I did not get even a single man through his effort.

That night, I met Evans at the intake station and received his assurance that the work was officially recognized and the men would be paid for their service. As to recruiting more men, I was advised to contact various Block Managers.

On June 30, I found a little encouragement in finding 21 men and five drivers. I could sense that the situation was eased on the field. I could hear laughter now and then for the first time. The men were rested on the hour as the day before, as this procedure was bringing in the result desired.

When I went to the unloading ground, there were eight men present, an increase of three. They were busily building a shanty hut under a big mesquite tree, utilizing scrap lumber and torn roofing paper. They told me that they divided themselves into three units; and each unit was to take turn in unloading. They were to rest between the unloading operations under the shade. (The hut was enlarged from time to time, and at the end it was large enough to house forty people.) I was amused to observe the method, which I had tried with the loading crew and failed, was more acceptable here.

I thought this was a good opening to talk to those men. I commended them for their idea and added, "We don't need to work any more than we are physically able. We don't need [to] exhaust ourselves. The white men in this project are not our enemies. On the contrary, they are trying everything possible for our benefit. They want to see that we are willing to cooperate with them."

This was one of my favorite themes and was repeated to them often in the ensuing days.

Late in the afternoon, when the men were resting in a shady place, Frasier was coming down the road. They noticed him and began to get up. I said to them, "Never mind the white man. Just keep on resting. I am the one responsible for you people."

When I walked up to him, Frasier asked me, "Say, how come those men are sitting down?"

"Well, they are fagged out. They need rest," I replied.

"Yes, but it doesn't look so good. Looks as if they are on a 'sit-down' strike. Why don't you rest them a few at a time?" said the overseer.

"All right," I answered reluctantly.

And to myself I said, "Hell with looks! Suppose it looks like a sit-down strike. So what?"

This was one of the orders I intentionally disobeyed. I was convinced by this time that it was better to rest the loading crew as a body. Moreover, I wanted to sit with them and talk to them all at one time.

Then Frasier brought up the subject of tractors. He told me that two young Niseis of another crew were racing with their tractors and collided with each other. The extent of damage was one smashed radiator one bent axle and two torn front tires. Second, that as soon as my drivers got out of my sight, they were driving too fast and recklessly. [He informed me that] the Engineering Department was seriously considering taking all tractors away from the Japanese, as evidence of careless and negligent handling were mounting and avoidable and unnecessary damages were piling up. [Since this was the case], some immediate steps should be taken in addition to warnings.

We agreed that the best solution would be to hire a foreman to take charge of the tractors and drivers. I told him that I knew just the man.

That evening, I sought out a Nisei of 22 years of age, who had considerable experience in operating such equipment on his farm and had knowledge of the mechanism. I knew him as a serious minded young man, to whom such responsibilities could be entrusted. After a lengthy discussion on the state of affairs, we decided to take the following steps as remedies: to assign a tractor to each driver and to let him be responsible for the same machine every day; to order every driver to take the same route between the two points; the tractor foreman would ride with different drivers constantly and would check the movements of others; we should discharge the boys of ages 15–17 and should substitute with older men. This meant that we must discharge 3 boys.

The young foreman reported to me the next morning and began to put the above steps into practice. Thanks to his ceaseless efforts, we were free from accidents and damages since then, except for three minor repairs.

About two days later, when I met in the Administration Building Mr. Rupkey, Chief Engineer, he threatened vehemently that the department had decided upon taking all equipment away from Japanese and substituting with Caucasian workers. Knowing the alarming condition then existed, I did not think he was bluffing. I thought he meant what he said. I explained to him the measures I had taken and advised him that we should be given a chance to prove that we could cope with it. I recommended to him that the similar steps should be taken with other crews. I told him that we were in the weeding-out process. It was impossible then to distinguish capable drivers from incapable ones until one actually had seen them in operation. I promised him that we would soon see calmer, settled days after this transitional period. Mr. Rupkey was impressed and said that he would wait and see.

Since that day condition improved gradually. The alarming situation was corrected and all the tractors, including heavy-duty types, are operated by Japanese at present.

On July 4, the Firebreak and Recreational Area (area marked as 'A' on the map) was finally raked up and cleaned. Now it was the question of burning the trash. But it was too dangerous for a small group of men to undertake [for a number of different reasons]. Huge quantities of highly inflammable dry trash were scattered all over the area; in some parts densely heaped up, in another part too close (20 feet) to the combustible barracks fabricated with tar paper. Gale and whirl wind, which were of daily occurrence, complicated the question of burning.

I thought, "If we only had the assistance from the boys of the Recreation Department and the firemen. Why not? This area belongs to the Recreation Department, anyway. They have about 150 boys, who aren't doing anything. Firemen? Sure! All they do is play baseball."

POSTON UNIT I

The pattern of blocks in Unit I, with the areas cleared by Nishimoto's firebreak gang marked *A* through *G*. (Based on a map in the appendix to the "Firebreak Gang" report; JERS J 6.07)

Bureaucracy

The "firebreak gang" dwindled from a group of one hundred-and-nine men at the beginning to that of twenty now.[18] This was the gang with which I must go on. They completed so far only about 20 percent of the assignment, which meant there was easily one month's work ahead. I believed that I could not afford to lose any more men if we were to go on. I realized that some stabilizing influence must be exerted upon the men, as it was too easy and too free to come and go; I must make them realize that they were the members of a recognized project. I must make them feel the sense of duty and of obligation to the work. My "talks" were not showing much result; I knew the "education" was a slow process. I thought that the best idea might be to issue work cards to them through the Employment Office. I believed that it would give the crew an official status. Also, each man with a card would feel that this was his regular job. Therefore, I wrote a memorandum addressed to Evans and accompanied with a time sheet of the men for the past seven days. The note set forth the following recommendations. To advise the Recreation Department and the Fire Department to assist in burning the trash on the field. To issue work cards to the members of the crew. To forward the time sheet to the accounting department.

The following points were agreed upon between Evans and Rupkey, who were called into the consultation. The Recreation Department was composed mostly of boys of teen age, who were being accused as irresponsible "smart alecks." However, Evans promised that he would induce Dr. Powell[19] strongly for the cause. Meantime, I was to see the chief of the Fire Department. The Employment Office would also be requested to supply the work cards.

On the way back, I consulted the Japanese Fire Chief, with a letter of introduction from Evans and stressed the importance of assistance from his department. His refusal to my request was disturbing, yet his reasons were amusing. The reasons were as follows: his duty [was] to "put fire out," not to "set fire." If he had done something besides what his duty called for, he would soon be asked to pick up garbage. [Third, he argued that] the department was undermanned.

I was certain that there was no hope of getting his aid and no use of urging further. I thought I would wait until further instruction from the Engineering Department, to which we were officially assigned in the conference.

On July 6, I informed my crew of twenty-five men the details of the conference. I told them that they were henceforth officially known as the members of the "Firebreak Cleaning" crew. I demanded that if any one had any objection, he should leave right then. Among them a lengthy discussion followed, which might be summarized as follows. [One point was that] their physical condition would not allow them to work full eight hours continuously. Yet, they did not wish to work *a la* "W.P.A." They would expend their best efforts, but they should be provided with rest periods, as before.

Questions were asked if some "white guy" were to supervise their work on the field. It was obvious that they were afraid that some Caucasian would come along and would do "slave-driving." This fear and dread were apparent in later developments, treated elsewhere in this report.[20] All the men consented to continue with my assurance that I had the full responsibility and that it was I who would set any policy concerning them.

With the crew and the equipment, I moved to the area near block 53 and block 60.[21] Having learned that many persons would not object to working for a short duration and for some purpose which they could believe obviously that it was for their own benefit, I sent my assistants to the Block Managers of Quad 9[22] to solicit temporary workers. I instructed them to convey the idea that the work would require only three days and that we would move to another field unless they would assist us, which would mean no irrigation water for them. This strategy of duress had a desired effect only in Block 59, which went 7 men on the first day, 14 on the second and 10 on the third. These volunteers intermingled with the regular men, working at the same comfortable speed and with the frequent rest periods—radically different from the situation when I undertook the job on the fist day. Upon my suggestion, they built a hut, very much like that of the unloading crew, where they could rest. Although thermometer read as high as 125 degrees F., about 10 degrees higher now,[23] the men showed neither dismay nor dread of the work, except minor, occasional comments about the weather or food, of which I had no control. They were more restful and more satisfied men than the ones who had quit on me in the early days. In fact, after they were excused after three days of work, they came back one by one asking for permanent status. They said that they wanted to work for me, because they liked the way I handled the men and because they liked the way the work was arranged. At the end I had six men from Block 59 working with me on their own accord.

In the afternoon of July 7, a new Caucasian came to see me. He said his name was Meecham, just detailed from San Carlos. He told me that he was to act as a supervisor over us and that he would spend the most of time with us as this was the only assignment he had. This was contrary to what I had promised to the men. Up to this time, there was no Caucasian on the field, except that I talked to Barbour twice and to Frasier three times. I was resentful in my mind, for all this time when I was having troubles, there was no one to help me and now when I have better control over the men and the situation, this man was here to boss me.

Meecham had in his hand the time sheet, which I had handed to Evans. He informed me that it was returned by the time keeper and was not to be honored. He advised me to see Palmer immediately.

When I went to the accounting office and inquired Palmer of the reasons for his decision, he said, "Well, these Japs worked as volunteers, didn't they? That means they didn't have work cards. We can't pay wages to guys who worked without the cards. That's the rule here and I can't do anything about it."

I was angry. I thought, "My men were tricked into working by a false promise of financial return. Now this guy is refusing to pay the due compensation. That's treachery! They just wanted my men to work for nothing. They just wanted to exploit them without any intention of paying wages."

I said to myself, "God damn it! So we are Japs, are we? Ignorant bastard!"

It was difficult to keep my composure, when I said to him, "Mr. Evans promised us that we are going to be paid for what we were doing, although we don't have work cards."

He replied excitedly, "Mr. Evans doesn't set the policy of this department. He can't make promises like that without our knowledge."

I thought there was no use in arguing any further.

I left the building and looked around for Evans, but he was not in his office.

"Something must be done quickly. I must get the work cards right away. Otherwise, they would be working for nothing," I thought.

I walked to the Employment Office. There was no one but an errand boy in the office. He told me that since Miss Mahn[24] was absent I should see the Japanese head, T., who was in conference and could not be disturbed. I waited. I waited for 45 minutes. Meanwhile, my anger was aggravated by every minute of waiting, by reflecting the things that had taken place in the afternoon. When I met T. and explained my predicament, he informed me in much aloof and detached manner that he could issue the cards, but it was necessary to bring the men in for interviews; that he had no authority to honor their time previous to the issuance. I argued with him for sometime. I was losing patience at the same time. Finally he decided to take me to Miss Findley, who had been presiding over the conference just concluded. When I explained the whole thing all over again, she was silent and meditated. Then she turned to T. and said, "It is not courteous to order these men to come in the office (for the interview)." Then looking at my time sheet, "Look at the ages of these men! 59! 66! 62! If it is necessary for you to interview them, you must go to them instead. I know that is against the rule[s] here. But, Mr. T. rules are made to be broken."

Then she turned to me and said in a deliberate tone, "You are doing wonderful work. Do you know, Mr. Nishimoto, we are all judged by our deeds, not by our words?" She went on, "Don't be afraid to do anything which you are certain you are right. Keep on with your good work. Don't worry about the time sheet. I'll take care of it for you."

"What encouraging words!" I thought, "What a grand lady! She's got lots of common sense."

Although this was the only occasion to meet her and she may not remember me now, I think dearly of her as a grand lady who gave me kind words when I needed them most. I always talked reverently of her to my men, although I never mentioned this incident, which would have created more distrust toward the administration.

It was the next morning—the morning of July 8. There was a little excitement, while I was with the unloading crew on the other side of the creek. According to one middle-aged Issei, Meecham came to the field and began instructing the men how to use rakes, how to make small piles of trash, etc. The men resented these elementary instructions and one of them shouted to him, "For Christ sake! What do you think we are? Bunch of kids? You getta hell out of here!"

To this the younger men chimed in and Meecham left.

One Hawaiian Nisei came to me and supplied me with another version.

He said, "That son of bitch tried to tell us how to hold a rake. So we told him, 'You want us to clean this field, or don't you? You better shut up and getta hell out of here.'"

That was all I learned about the matter; but, since then, Meecham did not stay on the field any longer than necessary to exchange a few words with me in the morning.

On July 9, an order came from the Engineering Department that we must burn the trash in the areas—(A) and (B) on the map—without any aid from other departments. I assembled the crew together and explained the order and the situation. I knew that the task was quite dangerous and must be done early in the morning before the wind came out. Yet, I did not wish to give any definite order to them; instead, I wanted them to say from their own initiative that they would come out early in the morning and would undertake the task. So I emphasized the danger involved and lack of outside assistance and told them that it was not necessary for them to do it, if they thought it was beyond their capacity. Without hesitation after my discourse, some of them offered their service and promised me that they would report to work at 4 o'clock in the morning. I was elated that they started "the ball rolling." The rest all agreed willingly to the suggestion and they accomplished the assignment the next morning, firmly believing that they were doing something of their own accord.

The fire was so extensive, so fierce, and so tense that some soldiers rushed down from Camp II. Some residents of Block 36 came out in pajamas and nightgowns and complained that they were being "roasted." I remember a worried look on Evans' face, who had been awakened by the crimson sky and the crackling sounds and ran down to the field. He stood with me for a long time, murmuring anxiously to the fire, "Woa! Take it easy! Take it easy, will you?"

While I was conversing with him, I said unintentionally, "The code of conduct at Poston—No. 1—the path of the least resistance is to do nothing yourself and to expect nobody to do anything for you."

He was, no doubt, irritated by this statement, as he reminded me of it on two subsequent occasions. However, it represented my sentiment at the time, because every person I came in contact officially lacked the spirit of cooperation and was doing the least that his duty called for and no more.

When we were getting off duty at noon that day, Frasier came and asked me if I could take care of a little field near Block 22 next morning, as it would require only a day and lumber piles were in the way of Caterpillars leveling nearby. It so happened that this was another occasion to learn another lesson regarding the administrative set-up at Poston. It was the first time that I discovered an evidence of friction and jealousy existing among the Caucasian staff.

In the morning of July 11, when we began working on the field—the area (C)—Meecham came to see me. I could observe that he was cross and angry. I failed to ascertain why. "Who told you to work out here?" he said in an unfriendly, ugly tone.

"Frasier asked me yesterday to come over here," I replied.

"You can't do that. I am your boss; Frasier's got nothing to do with you," he retorted.

I was offended by his statement and his tone. I replied, "Hell, no one is my boss. If anyone were my boss, that's Evans."

Soon afterward, Meecham drove away in flurry; and entered on the scene Frasier, to whom I explained what had happened. While we were still talking, Meecham reappeared from nowhere and began addressing Frasier. Meecham was indignant and raging with anger; Frasier was anticipating what to come. "Well, there's no use of both of us taking charge of this crew, is there?" he opened with biting, sarcastic vein.

I walked away in a hurry, but it was apparent that heated arguments followed. I shall not go into the details of their conversation or of their previous relationship. I merely wish to add that I am informed on a good authority that this was not an isolated case of the kind.

There was another occasion on which Miss Mahn and I disagreed sharply as to the authority of my hiring and discharging of men. However, it is another repetitious example of bureaucratic incompetency and it is, therefore, omitted here.

As days passed, the crew began to show a sign of unity and cohesion. Seven men from Block 59 were added to the regular staff and were assimilated. Meanwhile, I continued with my "lecture" which was not a formal speech but common gossip tinted with a theme or themes of some ultimate purpose. I was always careful to avoid the form of "sermon." I was always anxious and cautious to attain the highest degree of casualness, so that the men would not suspect me of my ulterior motive, because I was certain that they would be resistant to lectures and sermons in their pure and naked form. Hence, my favorite medium was recounting of my personal experiences, true or fictitious. In addition to the theme on the cooperative spirit, described previously, I had another topic among my repertoire. This was, "There is so much talk going on in the camp about our status under the international law. After all, we are subjects of an enemy nation. However, much we agitate and complain under the code, we would not find ourselves back in California right now. Let's try to be happy here. And that happiness is attained by keeping ourselves busy in some gainful work and by doing the work well."

This theme was most effective when the men were talking about a certain Hayashi in Block 3, who was known as an avowed "agitator" and a "soap-box" orator of the first magnitude. This was the time when they were arguing pro and con on the question of the attempted eviction of Hayashi from the block and of the petition circulated and signed by his co-residents for the purpose.

Another topic was like that: "The American government is spending an enormous amount of money for the project. But they are doing it for our protection and for our benefit. Suppose they said, 'Get out of California. Do as you please in other states. We can't look after you!' Then, where would we have been?"

Toward the end of July, it was getting noticeable that the men developed some sense of obligation to this community and willingness to serve for its welfare and benefit, due either to the changing trend of the general sentiment or to my effort. It was about this time that we were called upon to collect rubbish in order to relieve then existing alarming condition. Subsequently, after the regular hour as an emergency duty, we were called three times in rubbish service and once for collecting 3–5 days old garbage. Even on these occasions, I had the least difficulty in soliciting volunteers among ourselves. They were not only anxious to serve, but also eager to do the work well. It was a remarkable change in their mental attitude in contrast to that of the days gone by.

The Men

At this point, it may be well to discuss some characteristics of the men who comprised the "firebreak gang."

Two days after my meeting with Miss Findley at the Employment Office, T. brought the work cards to the field and with much dignified and histrionic air, he distributed them. He emphasized that he was taking this "very unusual and irregular" procedure in recognition and in appreciation of their "meritorious" spirit and service. There was no doubt that the men were greatly impressed by his words and felt flattered. And I was appreciative of his theatrical gestures, too.

With said addition of men from Block 59, the crew expanded to that of 33 men. It is this group of 33 men, of which the following statistical studies were made. It is also mentioned, in passing, that the identical characteristics and proportionate distributions would have been discovered and prevailed if the original group of 109 men were subjected to the same studies. There was, of course, a minor fluctuation in the enrollment, later which, however, was of an inconsequential nature.

As shown in Table II, two-thirds of the crew were Isseis—those who had spent their younger days in Japan, and since then migrated to this country. The age distribution of the Isseis was 37–66, which represents about 90 percent of the age group 30–66. That is to say, all men older than thirty were Isseis,

Table I. Distribution by Residence

Block	No.
2	2
12	7
37	2
43	12
45	3
54	1
59	6
TOTAL	33

Table II. Distribution by Intra[group] Classification

Classification	No.	Percentage
Issei	22	67%
Kibei	3	9%
Hawaiian Nisei	3	9%
Continental Nisei	5	15%
TOTAL	33	

Table III. Distribution by Former Residence

District	No.	Percentage
Urban	9	27%
Rural	24	73%
TOTAL	33	

except three. They comprised the groups 40–49, 50–59, and over 60. The educational background of the Isseis, however, was much lower than those of the other groups—two university graduates, one "Chugaku"[25] educated, and the rest only with the elementary school diplomas. Thus, in Table V, all of nineteen men listed as "Elementary School Graduates" were Isseis. In Table VI, all,

Table IV. Distribution by Age

Age Group	No.	Percentage
19 or younger	2	6%
20–29	6	18%
30–39	6	18%
40–49	4	12%
50–59	9	28%
Over 60	6	18%
TOTAL	33	

Table V. Distribution by Education

School	No.	Percentage
College Graduate or Education	4	12%
High School (or Jpn. Equiv.) Grad	10	30%
Elementary School (or Jpn. Equiv.) Grad	19	58%
TOTAL	33	

Table VI. Distribution by Former Occupation

Occupation	No.	Percentage
Merchant	4	12%
Commercial Employee	4	12%
Farmer	12	37%
Farm Migratory Laborer	8	24%
Gardener	2	6%
Resident Farm Laborer	3	9%
TOTAL	33	

Table VII. Period of Inactivity

No. of days elapsed from the time of arrival at Poston to the time of obtaining their first employment

No. of Days	No.	Percentage
1–9 days	4	2%
10–19 days	2	6%
20–29 days	1	3%
30–39 days	1	3%
40–49 days	25	76%
TOTAL	33	

except one, listed under "Farmer," "Farm Migratory Laborer," and "Gardener" were Isseis. One could say, therefore, that they lived among themselves in the rural district and had had very little contact with the white Americans and the American culture. Only four of all the Isseis showed any ability to carry daily conversation in English to some degree. The rest of them were unable to either understand or make themselves understood in English. In other words, they were illiterate with respect to English—although they had fair command of Japanese in reading and writing. In their speech in Japanese, the majority used their respective dialect with their provincial enunciation and intonation—the standard form of Japanese being entirely absent except in two.

Three men listed under "Kibei" column, in Table II, were those who spent 5–10 years of their adolescent age in Japan. They had been subjected to the Japanese culture and had been trained in the Japanese habits and customs. Their records invariably revealed that, although they did not attend school in the United States, they had 1–3 years of "Chugaku" education. Therefore, their knowledge of English was limited and their vocabulary was of daily conversational variety. They had strong accent in them and were hesitant to speak English. Previous to the evacuation, they were employed by the Japanese and lived among the Japanese. That is to say, they had little contact with Americans and American ways of life. Their reading matters were in Japanese and their thinking was done in Japanese; e.g. when they do a mental calculation, they do it in terms of "*ichi, ni, san*" instead of "one, two, three." It is interesting to note that they spoke better Japanese than the farmers or the farm migratory laborers—better in form and freer from dialect or provincial intonation. They had inclination to respect and to be considerate of the older people. They addressed them in the polite, reverential form of the language[26] irrespective of the appearance, the cultural background, or the station of life.[27]

Three American-Japanese, born in the Hawaiian Islands, were reared in the vicinity of Hilo, T.H. [Territory of Hawaii], where the Japanese culture is prevalent. In the early twenties, they had migrated to the continental United States and found themselves again among the Japanese. Their ages were thirty-four, thirty-eight, and thirty-nine, respectively. Their characteristics were similar to those of the Kibeis, but milder and less accentuated. Their education varied from two years in high school to one year in a university. They spoke more fluent English with wider vocabulary, although with the accent typical of the people. They have had more contacts with the white Americans and were more appreciative of the American civilization. They spoke Japanese well without any trace of accent, although their form was crude and rough and their vocabulary was limited.

The Niseis, five in number, were high school graduates, without exception—one with one year of Junior College training. The age distribution was seventeen to twenty-three. They were all evacuees from the rural district, where they had been helping on the farms, which their family owned. They had lived outside of the school hours, entirely with their family or with the older Japanese. Although the exact data are not available, it was evident that they had some systematic Japanese training, through a Japanese language school or otherwise. They were able to converse freely with the older Isseis and to intermingle with them, although at the early stage of our work, they formed a clique with themselves. They gathered apart from the others and conversed entirely in English, as their duty was distinct from that of the Isseis. Later, however, as they handled axes and shovels in a group with the Isseis, they developed comradeship with them and the trace of clique disappeared. It is interesting to note that this comradeship was imbued in some degree with the Japanese patriarchal concept. The young boys were considerate of the older men; always willing to go out of their way to assist them. They were often the target of "joshings" and "kiddings"—some of them, I thought were crude and sarcastic, but they took them in good humor and responded in friendly retorts. Even in a friendly argument on such a timely topic as the cooperative store, they were willing to argue to a certain limit and no more, beyond which they did not stick to their point doggedly and stubbornly. Their friendship with the other groups developed to such an extent that they were together on numerous weekend fishing trips. It is my observation that the characteristics found in the

Niseis were more similar to those of the Isseis and their background was under greater Japanese influence than that of the urban Niseis whom I knew. This simplified the matter of breaking down the barrier between the two generations.

It is not difficult, therefore, to understand that the crew developed into a solid, homogeneous, and congenial group. Their ties were strong, irrespective of whether they were from urban or rural district and whether young or old. During eighty days together, there was not even a trace of friction nor any occasion for quarrel among themselves. As far as I could ascertain from different members, there was no ill feeling between any two of them. Even the men[28] who joined the crew after they had had quarrels or disputes elsewhere, were easily assimilated and stuck to the end. They worked hard and enthusiastically. They did not create any problem that I was [not] forewarned [of].

The satisfactory relationship was general. They were so well satisfied with each other that they were greatly disappointed, when the disbanding of the crew was announced in September. I believe that the high attendance record[29] and the commendable accomplishment attained by the crew, despite the extreme heat, was largely attributable to this congenial friendship.

Due to the dominance of the Issei elements, the crew as a whole displayed "Japanesey" characteristics collectively. They worked hard, intermingled with short rest periods at frequent intervals. They wanted to relax completely during the rest periods. They resumed the work after the period without any external coercion or persuasion, which they detested. They wanted to be told only what was to be done and what purpose was to be served therefrom. They wanted to use their own initiatives and experiences to determine what method or procedure was to be taken in order to accomplish the assignment. They were obedient, yet they resented to be told how to work in minute details. This was the aspect of which Meecham was ignorant and which resulted in the abusive remarks to him. In other words, they were hateful of any "nosey, meddlesome, overbearing boss." They were sensitive about their belief that their intelligence, ability, and experience were as good as those of any other race. They were proud in the belief that they were the most industrious and diligent people as a race, or as a generation.

Once when were discussing the shortage of green vegetables in our kitchens, many of the men remarked, "With the Japanese gone, that is to be expected. That's what happens when they have kicked the Japanese farmers out."

On another occasion, when I mentioned that the Mexican labor was to be imported into California, they expressed, "Those guys can't take our place.

They don't work as hard as we do. They don't know how to raise vegetables."

At another time, when we were discussing the shortage of farm labor everywhere, some said, "War or not war, we'll be back in California next year. They need us there."

It is true that I took the advantage of these "weaknesses" and exploited them to the full extent to obtain the result.

It was apparent, as the reader would have foreseen, that the group was backward in understanding and appreciation of the American government and the principles, yet they were neither defiant nor antagonistic. They were simply ignorant. Only two of the Isseis had any faint idea of what the Bill of Rights is. Even though there was neither restraint nor restriction as to the topic of their conversation, there was not even one utterance which might be deemed detrimental or disloyal to the American government. It was a consensus of their opinions that this was the best country to live in and that they were thankful for comfortable life and living which they had been provided with in America. They were, in other words, appreciative of their material gains in America. They did not possess the capacity to appreciate the abstract phase of Americanism.

On the other hand, they were critical and suspicious toward the administration and the staff at Poston. They placed credence without any examination in the story of alleged graft by Mr. Best. They did not doubt that the hospital was killing the Japanese. They thought that they were discriminated by them in favor of the Niseis in the Administrative Buildings. They thought that the white men were "slave drivers."[30] This was the problem which I endeavored to combat most vigorously. I expended every effort and every mean to alleviate the skepticism and the suspicion. I believed that I was successful in my attempt until . . . When my crew failed to receive their wages which were due to them, they were again outspokenly suspicious and resentful (discussed in the succeeding section). They suspected that somebody in the accounting department was manipulating the books and was embezzling the wage payments due to them. I felt as if I lost all the ground which I had gained, and I was disillusioned that my efforts were all in vain due to the counteractive and destructive effect of the administrative carelessness and inefficiency.

The Isseis were inherently gentle people—mature in their thought and conservative in their reaction. These qualities were manifested collectively, too, as a crew. Yet they have shown tendency to be provoked by such an inconsequential pretext as by some person showing overbearing authority. This defect was more remarkable among the urban evacuees, especially ones with higher education. Yet, this excitement was of short duration; they cooled off and became gentle quickly. It is also interesting to add that it was the Isseis of the migratory farm group with the least education who exerted a soothing and counterbalancing effect upon these men.

It was the morning of July 20, when we set fire on the field adjoining Block 43 (area D). The Japanese Fire Chief, N., came running down and questioned me if I had a permit to burn. Knowing that this was a part of our regular routine, I did not feel necessary to go through the "red tape" and told him so. N. began to scold and chide me, which I felt was obnoxiously arrogant. Meantime, Frank M., a Block Manager, appeared on the field hanging on to a dump truck with heaping load of papers and trash, which was driven by a boy of small, frail stature, who appeared to be about 15. I understood that at the time the rubbish collection service was suspended and the accumulated trash created a serious problem to the Blocks. In order to relieve the problem, M., had borrowed the truck and loaded the trash with his block residents' aid. He intended to burn them where we were working.

Just as soon as the chief noticed M. with his load, he stormed down to him. "You can't dump 'em here!" the chief shouted.

"What'ya mean I can't dump 'em here?" M. returned angrily. The rage and excitedness between the two gained momentum.

The chief's argument was . . . there was a place provided in camp for burning trash. Any burning was prohibited without a permit. All the rules must be strictly observed.

The manager's point was . . . the rubbish situation was dangerously menacing the sanitary welfare. It was safe, as thirty odd men were working in the field. M. shouted to the little driver, "Dump it! Go ahead! Dump it!" M. yelled with rage, "Go on! Drive on!"

These contrary orders were screamed to the boy continuously. Poor kid! The little boy did not know what to do and sat in the cab "dumb-struck" and "punch-drunk."

Simultaneously, my crew was gathering around and was getting nervous and excited themselves. They began to involve themselves in the heated argument on the manager's side. Someone shrieked in Japanese, "God damn it! The young punk's cocky. He's arrogant! Let's beat him up. That's the only way to teach him. Come on, let's beat him up."

Others took up the chant, "Let's beat him up!"

I was convinced that a mob violence would have resulted if the chief had not sensed the tenseness and had not driven away with the boy in the dump truck. I knew that I would not have done anything to prevent it in view of my previous experiences with the chief. It was unfortunate that he could sense the ugly atmosphere, as I was informed later that he could not understand Japanese beyond "*nagure*! [let's beat him up!]" Subsequently, I inquired my men if they understood what the chief said, as he spoke in English so fast and so nervously. They informed that they did not understand much more than "drive on." They resented his arrogant and overbearing manner. Soon afterward, some Isseis—migratory farm laborers—began to imitate comically the perplexity and bewilderment of the little driver in the dilemma; and others joined in laughter. Thus the crew regained calmness and composure.

Events must have taken place fast later in the day. A new order was announced by the administration in the same day to the effect that it would be permissible henceforth to burn trash before 10 A.M. and 150 feet clear of any object.

The men were steady and persistent, once they had started. They showed unusual stamina and perseverance in the heat of 120 to 125 degrees F. (An unofficial temperature reading was as high as 145 degrees in the open.) Even though they were benefited with frequent rests, the work required tenacious determination mentally and exhaustive effort physically. Yet all the members, except five, once they had joined the crew, remained to the end. One left to take charge of the sanitary detail. Two men were transferred, by the request of their managers, to the farming in their respective Block. Two young Niseis went to operate Caterpillars after the tractors for our use had been reduced to two and their service was no longer needed.

The record of attendance was excellent, as a study of the graph, attached elsewhere, would indicate. On the same chart, it is reported that on any one day there were no more than three absentees, the lowest point of the percentage curve being 90 degrees. For 30 days out of 59, the record was perfect; that is, without an absentee. It is also noted therein that the frequency of the curve increases after August 11. This is explained by the fact that cases of illness or of illness in their family were reported. Another interesting fact is that the low points on the percentage curve occur on Thursdays at the earlier period and on Mondays later. I failed to discover any explanation beyond a statement by some: "That's about the time you got a little tired and feel like taking a day off." The latter feature, especially for the last two weeks is accounted by the fact that the cooler weather was conducive to more vigorous outdoor activities on the week-ends.

It is my belief that the rate or the amount of compensation, that is, $12.00

per month, did not have any effect upon them. They thought they were compensated for the wage differential by my special treatments such as providing the rest periods, supplying sandwiches, etc. The people, of course, commented on the low wages, but in good humor and jokingly. The following expressions were common among them:

"Say, you are working at one-dollar-an-hour speed." Or at the end of a day, "Well, I've earned fifty cents today."

The only time a monetary matter might have had some effect upon the men was an incident when the majority of the crew failed to receive the correct wage payments for the month of July and expressed their disgust and dissatisfaction on the field. One extremist said, "What's the use of working steady? Even if you work a full month, they won't pay a full wage anyway."

One could say, therefore, that the fluctuations of the curve for August 27 to September 3 are probably accounted by the resultant reactions from this administrative incompetency, although I am inclined to minimize such effort, judging from my own sentiment and experience under a similar circumstance.[31]

The people in my charge spoke of the Niseis hatefully, belittlingly, and abusively, whenever some young men were passing in shiny sedans. Some expressed their displeasure, "The young punk is acting important."

One well-educated Issei was more emphatic, "They are getting cocky, just because they are being patronized by the *Ketos*."[32]

The vexation was more widespread, pungent, and serious, when a car was kicking up dust so badly as to envelope the workers with its smoke. It found expressions in more pugnacious form: "Let's drag him out! Let's beat him up!" Yet the tone was of reproachfulness and condemnation, rather than of criminal premeditation.[33]

A few found a source of irritation in the trousers some Niseis were wearing—they were odious of any other kind of trousers but "blue jeans."

These hateful feelings were general, in more or less degree, among the Isseis, Kibeis and the Hawaiian Japanese. They were stronger, however, among the age group 35–55 and more outspoken among the men of higher educational background and of urban extraction. Even my Niseis occasionally shared the sentiment and were critical of their contemporaries. It is interesting to add that even the Isseis—fathers of Niseis of the late teen age and of the early twenties—were contemptuous of the Niseis other than their own.

However, upon a more detailed individual check, it was found that their reasons for the irritation and resentment were superficial and not deep-rooted.

They gave their reasons such as, "They are cocky." "They want to show authority and want to act important, just because they are patronized and are in the favor of the administration." "They are discourteous." "They don't know how to talk."[34] "They sold their fathers 'down the river.'"

It is my contention that although the reasons being superficial as they are at present, the breach shall develop into a serious problem in the future unless corrective and preventive measures are applied soon.

Before closing this section, I shall add the following datum without detailed interpretations.[35] It attracted my attention as the differences existed between the generations were sharp and remarkable.

That is to say, three-fourths of the men were idle for 40 days or more since they arrived in the camp. Four men listed in the group 1–9 days were three Niseis and myself.

A further check with the men listed under the 40–9 days group, 76 percent of the entire crew, revealed that only two made any attempt to seek a position by inquiring at the Employment Office during the inactive period. In other words, 23 men were idle without making any attempt or indicating any intention to obtain an employment.

To make a contrasting study, I interviewed 20 young Niseis at random in the camp and obtained the following result:

1–9 days	17	85%
10–19 days	1	5%
20–29 days	2	10%
TOTAL	20	

That is to say, the Niseis obtained their positions as soon as they had arrived in camp. It is another evidence to prove my contention further that the Niseis are more aggressive and "go getters."

As a supplementary study of my men in relation to the general sentiment of the camp, the following observation is presented herewith. The observation was made when the War Relocation Authority announced the following regulation: " . . . each person who is offered employment and who refuses to work will be charged at the rate of $20 per month for himself and each dependent. Such charges if not paid immediately will accrue against the enlistee and a deduction will be made from his salary when he does work, to cover the amount due the United States."[36] The notice was posted at the Block Manager's office on or about July 11 and created widespread discussions pro and con.

I was curious at the time how much effect the regulations had on my men and inquired of them on the subject. The following question was asked of them individually on or about July 20: "Do you believe that the administration shall charge $20 a month to a person who does not work?"

The result compiled from 25 men of the crew was as follows:

"Yes"	8	32%
"No"	17	68%

Some comments to their "no" answers were amusing. They varied from, "Try and get it," to, "That's a Nisei big shot's scheme to get the men out to work."

On the other hand, the records in the Employment Office for the period indicate that there was some increase in the interest on the part of the residents to obtain employments, due to this announcement or otherwise.[37]

The Progress of Work

The work was progressing well and the crew was working together smoothly. By July 20, we moved into the field near the warehouses (area E). By then I was getting free from the departmental interference; and I had the complete responsibility for and authority over the crew, which they sensed and were convinced. Meecham disappeared from the picture entirely. Frasier came to see me for a short chat now and then—about twice a week—and the conversation was limited to gossiping.

It was on July 21, when we were working in that field. It was extremely hot humid day. About 2 p. m. a man came to me and complained of dizziness. I carried him to the hut, which we had built in the middle, and instructed him to lie down and relax. I was alarmed and began to inquire around. Two reported that they had a nauseating feeling. One said that he did not feel "just right." I myself did not feel "just right," although I never picked up even a piece of scrap lumber. I immediately suspended the operations and loaded them on a trailer to join the unloading crew in their larger hut on the other side of the creek, where it was much cooler. There I ordered them to lie down and to go to sleep. I lay down myself, too, among them, so that they would feel that I was one of them.

Around 3 P.M. when I heard a car approaching, I acted as if I were dozing.

Soon there was a little commotion among the men. I could hear one say in a low tone, "There's that white guy."

"Hey, better wake 'boss' up," another said.[38]

Then someone shook me and said, "'Boss,' get up! The white guy is here."

I got up sleepily and with a deliberate slow pace, walked to the car, which was parked some 50 feet away. Frasier was there and wanted to know what was the meaning of all this. After my explanation, he agreed that my procedure was proper, half skeptically, and drove away.

As I re-entered the hut many of them began to speak all at once. They said, "What did he say?" "Was he sore?" "Did he scold you?"

I answered them calmly, "No, he just wanted to know where he could find a certain tractor."

They were very much concerned as to what the white "slave driver" would have said. After this incident, they erased the last doubt from their mind that I was a white-man's "stooge" and they felt stronger than ever that I was their friend and anxious to protect them. If I had reported to them that he was "sore," they would have flared up.

On or about July 31, I sent in the morning a gang of eight men to clean up some brush and trash scattered around near the Post Office and along Block 34, in charge of the Nisei assistant. I expected them to finish the work in one hour or one hour and a half. When I went there about 10 A.M., they were all sitting around the small canteen. When I asked the assistant what had happened, he told me that they did not like to work there and that he did not coerce them, as "no coercion" was my standing order to him.

One Kibei said on my questioning, "Oh, these Nisei punks make me sick."

Another reply from a farmer evacuee was milder, "It's too dusty and noisy."

To all I said, "Come on! Come on! There is only a little more work left. Let's get it over quick and join the rest of the gang."

They went back to the work without any trace of defiance. I stayed with them another half-hour and returned to the rest together.

This abhorrence of working around the Administration Buildings had an important bearing on two decisions we had to make later on.

One of the occasions was like this. On August 4, Frasier brought two propositions between which we were to pick one, as we were completing the firebreak cleaning work. To construct raised walks, ditches for electric cooler drains, and do other dust control work around the Administration Buildings. [Also,] to subjugate high school and farm grounds.[39]

Without hesitation, I knew which work we would be doing next. However, as a matter of procedure, I assembled the men and consulted them. Before I could finish with the presentation of the former proposal, I was overwhelmed with objections. Comments started to fly thick and fast from all directions: "Not around there." "I hate the sight of Niseis and '*Ketos*' around the Administration Buildings." "Too many cars go by." "It's too noisy and too dusty around there."

Some had [a] more sincere tone and said, "It doesn't look nice to be sitting down and resting out there. And I can't work without a rest now and then."

One extremist said, "We fixed our Blocks ourselves. Hell! I don't see why those guys—meaning the employees in the administration—can't do the same. It's good for them to do a little outdoor work. Besides, the place doesn't look any worse than our own." And I knew there were two others who shared the same view.

Thus, the proposal was snowed under. However, I noticed particularly that the migratory laborers did not offer any comment. I was curious. When I questioned them later on the subject individually, they invariably replied, "I didn't mind working there, but I just wanted to 'string along' with the rest."

So the second proposal was adopted although it meant also two days of working around the Post Office and the canteen area at the start. They said laughingly, "Well, that's all right. We will just walk through, out there."

And they did walk through. The neatness and thoroughness of their work in that area were much below their standard.

With the start of this work I discarded the idea of giving 15 minutes rest every hour on the hour. Instead, I gave them fifteen to twenty minutes once in the morning and thirty to forty-five minutes once in the afternoon. They always rested in a single group, which fact made it easy for me to talk with all the men.

The length of the rest varied as there was no one to coerce them to resume the work. They must get up from their own volition. On two occasions, I made them lie down and sleep—the majority dozed and some snored. The result was, however, disappointing to me, as the men failed to get up for 45 minutes and worked without "pep" or enthusiasm afterward. Henceforth, the relaxation of this form was avoided unless it was necessary.

Once someone started a conversation on the "Battle of Midway" [June 3–6, 1942], which was currently all over the newspapers. From this, a discussion of the duration of the war ensued. Their estimates, as I remember, varied from four months to three years. Many of them could not agree and it resulted in an argument; especially, between two men—one a Kibei, and the other a younger Issei. They exchanged words heatedly. I interceded and brought the discussion to a close in time with, "After all we are in America. However long and the war may last, we are protected and safe here."

The two men kept on arguing while they worked with an axe and a shovel. Contrary to my fear that this would result in some ill-feeling, they were working happily together in a group the next morning. Since then I avoided talks on the war, and so did the men.

It was about this time the lectures on the "co-op" principles were held in various Quads. Some man mentioned that he attended one of these meetings and repeated what he had learned. Few showed any interest. However, as soon as one Issei began attacking the present community store, the interest of the men greatly increased. The sentiments were expressed in such statements as: "They are robbing the people." "Some white 'go-betweens' are pocketing a big profit." "Ogawa is making side-money." "The employees are dividing among themselves the $20.00 per week rebate from a ice cream company."

On other occasions, the "co-op" was mentioned, but it always ended happily and joyfully in scathing harsh accusations of the present store.

Once in a while we spent the time gossiping about women in the camp. Beauty of this or that person and shape and figure of this or that girl drew many laughs and light air prevailed among them even after they had resumed the work.

As the weather became cooler, after the middle of August, the crew was working with better speed and steadier constancy in swinging axes and digging with shovels. I was satisfied with and thankful of the manner they worked and the acreage they covered (five to seven acres per day). I was certain that their efficiency during the last few weeks of the assignment, would have compared favorably, if not better, with that of any group of men employed elsewhere in the country at higher wartime wages.

It was announced by the paymaster that August 27 was the pay day for Block 12. It was a great event for all of them, as all except a few had never received wages in the camp. This was to be the occasion to receive cash for the first time since the evacuation. I informed seven men from Block 12 the night before that they would be excused for the morning and kidded them, "What are you going to do with all the dough?" And, "Let's see what the government money looks like when you get it."

They beamed. Yet when they returned the next afternoon, they were furious and disappointed men. Two men reported that they received only $7.83 for 196 hours of work in the month of July. Another said that he was paid $10.81 for 180 hours. Two complained that their names were not listed on the payroll.

"Of all the people! The one who needed the cash most failed to get his pay," I said to myself, thinking of one of the men who did not receive the payment. As he was indigent and destitute, I had asked Evans for a personal loan.[40]

"That means another begging trip to Evans for a few more dollars," I thought.

Others gathered around and began commenting, "They are a bunch of imbeciles," they said, meaning the people in the accounting department. "They should all be fired."

Another one suspected and said knowingly, "I bet they are manipulating their books. I bet some guys there are putting the money in their pocket. That's easily done, you know."

"There they go again," I thought. I was afraid that these mistakes caused a disturbing effect upon the state of mind of my crew. I felt as if all my effort to create more confidence and trust in the administrative people was destroyed by a single stroke of carelessness and inefficiency of its department. I did not want to argue with the men, because I thought that they were rightfully indignant after they had worked so hard in the scorching sun.

A few days later, I received $9.28 for about 220 hours of work. And similar mistakes were reported one after another, as the Paymaster moved on. They were hurt; they were more indignant. One Nisei tractor driver came up to me and complained, "I only got $12.00 whereas I should be getting $16.00."

I replied to him, "You know, I am your foreman, yet I was paid at $12.00 per month rate."

"Yeah, but that doesn't do me any good. We ought to go and fight," he said.

"Fight? Why not?" I said with determination.

I went to see Palmer and presented the fact to him. He did not repent his mistakes beyond saying nonchalantly and mockingly, "We should be doing a little better than that, shouldn't we?"

As to my request that the foreman, the assistant foreman, and the tractor operators should be paid at the rate of $16.00 per month, he said that after all they were "just common laborers pulling stumps out." I was refused and I was angry.

I walked out of the office with rage, saying to myself, "Bastard! So we are common laborers, eh? I'll get him yet."

Afterwards, upon Evans' advice, I wrote a report on the situation, with which I attached the composite time sheets of the entire crew for the months of June, July, and August.[41] I worked on the report many hours, setting forth arguments and accusations. When I finished it, I was relieved and satisfied with the feeling that I "got even" with Palmer. Yet my thought was, "This is the last straw. I've had enough of it. Hell with the administration people for all I care."

The End of the Road

We were in the sight of the end of our assignment. I wondered what sort of work should be assigned to us next. The men were curious and inquisitive too. Among themselves, they discussed what they wanted to do. Some expressed the desire to take up the subjugation and construction of the Poston Memorial Park, which had been abandoned.[42] The rest agreed that they were willing to "go along." It was evident that their primary desire was to be together; their utmost concern was [not] to be separated from each other.

On September 10, Thursday, Frasier came to see me for the first time in the week. He informed me that we were to be transferred to the Agricultural Department and that for further detail I must see Sharp.[43] When I met Sharp, he was busy conversing with other officials and said,

"You just report to me Monday morning. I will tell you then what you are going to do."

When I returned to the field, the men were more inquisitive. As I could not answer most of their questions, I promised them that I would make further inquiries. Meanwhile, Sharp was gone for the week and the staff of the Agricultural Department could offer little information except: "Hell! We just want the two tractors you got," K., the Farm Manager, said.

"So that's it!"

I wondered what could become of the crew when the work was completed Saturday per schedule and we did not know what to do next. A few more queries on Saturday afternoon brought out that we were to be merged with "Yakura's gang"—the crew engaged in the landscaping work around the Administration Buildings. "What? Again?" I was bewildered.

I knew that if they reported Monday morning and were told to work around here, the men would balk and revolt. That would mean "showing up" Sharp and would be injurious to the reputation of the "gang" or to the dignity of the administration. I decided, hence, to call a holiday on Monday and passed the word around to the effect among the men.

That Monday morning, I consulted with Evans and Sharp and reached a compromise: that we were to take up a municipal park project, but no tractors.

Subsequently, all the members of the "firebreak gang" met in a recreation hall and to them I reported what had taken place and presented the park proposal, which was duly accepted. I added, then, the two following points. That no transportation is provided to and from work. [Also,] that I [was] relinquishing the foremanship.

A young Nisei driver got up and commented, "Last night K. said, 'I just want the tractors and hell with you guys.'"

I elaborated on the situation that the Agricultural Department had only two tractors for their farm use and was in great need of more. And no trucks were available for us on account of the tire conservation restrictions. They were not satisfied with these explanations and expressed their resentful reactions, "Hell, I see lots of guys riding," one Nisei said. "If that's the case why don't they take the cars away from the Nisei 'big shots'?" one Hawaiian-born Japanese inquired irritably.

"I don't think they appreciate what we have been doing. We worked so hard, yet they don't give a damn about us," an Issei farmer commented.

As the arguments were not leading to a conclusion, I proposed to send a delegation to see Evans and Sharp on the transportation question.

With a sigh, I said to myself, "I knew they would be sore."

Then, they demanded an explanation for my action of retiring from the crew. I told them I had no complaints against the men. My feelings toward them were all in appreciation and admiration. I was tired, [though], of "red-tape" and departmental inefficiency. I was [also] afraid that I must fight through the "bureaucracy" again to regain a "free hand" in a new department. I had exhausted courage and patience to go on. [Finally, I told them,] "I am getting to like this dump. That means I am deteriorating mentally. I must find some job in which I can do a clear and constructive thinking."

One Hawaiian-born Japanese stood up and said, "I was working just because you are the foreman."

"I don't want to work for anybody else," a Kibei followed.

"We are appreciative of what you have been doing. You know that we are getting along fine. Why can't you reconsider your decision and stay with us?" an elderly farmer said.

It was difficult for me to turn down these kind sentiments, so I offered as a compromise. "All right. If you can get transportation for yourselves, I will stay on." But I was absolutely certain that they would not get it.

The delegation was chosen and was instructed without any alternative that the crew would disband, if they failed to get either an automobile or a tractor to transport them to and from the work.

Thus, the "firebreak gang" breathed the last knell, as their request was refused.

—~—

The War Relocation Project is an extremely novel and extraordinary enterprise, on which the American government embarked as an emergency measure. By the necessity and the circumstance, it was conceived and was put into operation in the shortest possible time. It is so novel that the government lacked the concrete data and precedents to base their plannings in advance. The authority at Poston, therefore, was unable to formulate definite theories or principles in regard to the problem of the Japanese evacuees. Their orders and regulations varied from time to time as a situation demanded. It was inevitable that the chaos and confusion existed at the early stage.

They lacked the complete understanding of the Japanese and the Japanese ways, which resulted in many misunderstandings between them. The fact that its staff was manned on a short notice and the departments were set up hurriedly resulted in lack of coordination and cooperation between the departments. It was unfortunate that, as the consequence, incompetency and inefficiency were noticeable. They, in turn, created necessarily distrust and skepticism on the part of the evacuees toward the staff.

With better planning and understanding, I, too, could have done a better job. I would not have lost those 109 men assigned to me at the outset. With better cooperation from other departments, I would have carried out my duties with more contentedness and happiness.

However, I am happy to note that at this writing these defects are corrected one by one by the courageous and tireless officials. I am grateful to note that the whole picture at Poston is improving in every aspect.

The men of the "firebreak gang" were diligent and obedient people of good stock. Although they worked under abnormal strain and extraordinary circumstance, they were friendly and cooperative people; their association resulted in warm lasting friendship among themselves. They were industrious people, who would be of great value to the American agriculture and industry after the duration. These men, especially the Isseis, would have enjoyed the American ways of life, if they had had closer association and contact with the Caucasian Americans. It is, indeed, unfortunate that the financial and environmental requirements had made it impossible or impractical for them to appreciate the American civilization. It is regrettable that they had kept themselves in a circle of their own people where the old Japanese habits and customs predominated. They retained the Japanese ways of reacting, with which they had been imbued in their adolescent days. This is the aspect which gives the Caucasian people the impression that the Japanese are difficult to understand and hard to associate with. It is my belief, however, that with thorough understanding and better appreciation of their ways, the Caucasians would find the Japanese easy to intermingle [with].

In managing the Isseis and others, I believe as a labor policy at Poston that it is impractical to enforce the continual labor for eight hours a day for the summer months. It is absolutely necessary to provide them with rests at frequent intervals. It is my observation that they were accustomed to the faster pace of working than that one would find in a non-Japanese labor group; and they are ignorant of how to conserve their energy.

In closing, I wish to add that Evans was always anxious to give me valuable advice and encouragement. I am thankful and proud that I have found a great friend in John G. Evans. With utmost sincerity, I say to my men, "Thank you, fellows," and to him, "Thank you, Mr. Evans."

Notes

1. I had greater difficulty in translating Japanese slang. I used the same technique and I believe that better results were obtained. The following examples may be of value to a reader: "[Nandabakayaro,]" in the direct translation means, "What? This foolish servant," which fails to indicate what the speaker intended. There are two common inflections in enunciating the words. One denotes a highly excited emotional pitch or a fighting mood; this, depending on its context, I translated as, "God damn it!" and "You, bastard!" The other inflection denotes a mood mingled with ridicule. I translated this into "Hell with you!" or "You sap!"

The phrase, "[shima nagashi ni suru,]" is translated directly as "to let one drift to an island," meaning "to send one to a distant prison" or "to send one to a distant place." As the phrase contains a little of the punitive intent and betrayal, I thought it appropriate to translate into "to sell one down the river."

I translated "[hakujin ni peko-peko suru]" mildly into "to apple polish," although it has a vulgar tone.

2. There were 357 Japanese engaged in the outdoor projects, as of June 30, 1942. The Colorado River War Relocation Project: "Employment Report, June 30, 1942"; p. 3.

3. During the months of July and August, 1942, the following incidents were reported and were widely discussed: (1) the crews in the kitchens and mess-halls left their work in bodies at different times; (2) complaints against the Japanese foreman in the Adobe Manufacturing plant in Camp I; (3) complaints against the Japanese foreman and the timekeeper in the Guayule Division; (4) the Fish Culture crew called their meeting and demanded the change of their foreman; (5) the strike of the Dust Control crew in Camp I; (6) the strike of the Dust Control crew in Camp II; (7) the Sanitary Details had their difficulty with the personnel; and, (8) the strike of the Adobe workers in Camp II.

4. The following question was put individually on September 16 to September 19, a few days after the disbandment: "Were you satisfied while you were working with us? Was there any dissatisfaction against the foreman or any member of the crew?" Without an exception, they expressed their satisfaction and their great disappointment in the disbandment. They strongly urged me to reorganize a crew with the same personnel.

5. Evans, Rupkey, and Frasier[4] expressed the views.

6. Frank and candid opinions of each other were exchanged from time to time between myself and a male, Japanese, Ph.D. in History, Stanford University: Professor of History, UCLA; a male, Japanese, M.A. in Psychology, University of Southern California, the Principal of a Japanese Language School; a male, Japanese, A.B. in Political Science, University of Southern California.

7. See the map showing the location of wood piles.

8. The chronological progress is indicated by the lines with arrows on the map in the Appendix, "The Progress of the Subjugation Work" [not included in the available copy].

9. John G. Evans: Assistant Director, the Colorado River War Relocation Project.

10. Number of the men working: 109. Of these, about 25 were Niseis. Number of Fordson tractors with trailers: 7. Number of trucks: 3.

11. At the time, the conception that they were the prisoners of war was prevalent all over the camp among the Isseis. The provisions in the international law and of the Covenants of 1928 at Geneva pertaining to the status and the treatment of such prisoners of war were the most popular and widely discussed subject among them. In every meeting I attended the Isseis always brought out discussions upon the subject. They

4. John Evans, the assistant director of Poston and the administrator of Unit I; R. H. Rupkey, project engineer in charge of engineering at Poston; and L. B. Frasier, foreman of the engineering department.

strongly expressed openly that neither the American government nor the administration here could compel them to work in this project. Some of them either frowned upon or criticized the men who were employed. Idle Isseis were conspicuous everywhere then. (They, however, looked upon the people employed in the kitchens and the messhalls in a more friendly and favorable light as their benefactors.)

12. The following question was asked of twenty-three men remaining out of this original group on July 28: "What made you come out and work with us?"

All but two answered in substance like this: "My block manager told me to get out and work. I didn't want to refuse him, because I was afraid that the people in the block might think me lazy. Besides, I was getting tired of being cooped up in the small apartment."

The other two men answered that they were interested in the financial return therefrom, that is, $12.00 per month.

The fine difference between this sentiment and the one set forth in Note No. 11 must be appreciated. Their resistance to the idea of working was milder when they were approached individually than when they were in a group.

13. Francis Sill Wichware, "The Japanese Language," *Life* magazine, September 7, 1942; pp. 58–67, especially, the pictorial graph, ibid. p. 58.

It is the most concise and accurate sketch that I have seen in the recent months. The effect of use of improper or mistaken form upon a person addressed is so great that it is beyond the imagination of the western mind. It is my belief that a great part of the friction between the Isseis and the Niseis at Poston is resultant of the improper usage of Japanese by the Niseis. For instance, if a young Nisei should say to me, "*Te o arae*" for "Wash your hands" or "*Do ka*?" for "How are you?" I would be provoked. Proper forms for him to use are, "*Te o aratte kudasai*" and "*Ikaga desuka*?" respectively.

14. See "Map 1."

15. Officially, 108 degrees F. in the shade at noon.

16. About two weeks later, many of them told me that when they were leaving for lunch at noon they discussed and decided to quit at the end of the day. They said that they were as sour as the others. But for the break in the routine and in realizing that I was doing everything possible to make the work bearable, they changed their mind and stayed on.

17. L. B. Frasier, Foreman, Engineering Department, The Colorado River War Relocation Project.

18. On July 4 there were thirty-eight men working, of which thirteen were temporary workers just for one day.

19. Director of the Recreation Department, The Colorado River War Relocation Project.

20. On July 28 the following question was asked of the twenty-seven members of

the crew: "Do you object to working under a Caucasian Foreman?" The result was as follows:

Group I ....Yes 8
Group II.....................No 7
Group III
"It depends on the foreman"
[and]
"If he is good, I don't mind" .. 12

The cleavage of the men with respect to the answers was sharp.

The characteristics of each group are described as follows: Group I were men of higher educational background (University graduates, college men, high school graduates). Group II were migratory farm laborers. Group III was composed of farmers and resident farm hands.

The reasons given by them for their objections were as follows: "They are dumb and incompetent." "They want to act superior." "They don't understand the habits and customs of the Japanese workers." "They make us work too hard."

21. See "Map I."

22. Block 53, Block 54, Block 59, and Block 60.

23. See "Record of Attendance" in the Appendix [not included here].

24. The Director, The Employment Office, The Colorado River War Relocation Project.

25. *Shogaku-ko* [is the Japanese equivalent of] Elementary School; *Chugaku* of Intermediate School or High School; *Koto Gakuko* of Junior College, and *Daigaku* of a University.

26. See Note No. 13.

27. Piety for the parents and respect for the elders are the ideas pounded into one since one's first school year in Japan.

28. Two men quarreled and disagreed with their respective foreman, while they were working elsewhere. Three men—an Issei, a Kibei, and a Hawaii born Japanese—quarreled and left their kitchens. One of them was described to me as a "trouble maker" and an "agitator for a strike."

29. See "Record of Attendance" in the Appendix [not included in the available copy].

30. See footnote #20.

31. For the month of July I work approximately 220 hours and expected to be paid at the wage rate of $16.00 per month. When I walked up to the Paymaster and received only $9.28, I felt I was insulted and was furious. I thought irrationally at the time that they did not appreciate my work in which I had put all the best in me. Yet, I had no thought of staying off the work.

32. "*Keto*" is a derogatory and derisive term for Caucasians.

33. In Chugaku and Koto Gakuko, it was common for a mob of three to ten upper-class men [upperclassmen] to subject younger boys to some form of physical violence, the use of fists most prevalent. Their motives were simple and superficial, never involving any intention of serious bodily harm. It was their way of reproaching and chiding.

While I was in Chugaku in Japan, I was a victim of such violence, at least on three separate occasions, by such self-styled "vigilantes." Once, I was "beaten up," because I failed to kowtow and offer words of greeting when I met an upper-classman on a street earlier in the day. At another time, they did the mob act, because they thought I was cocky. Thinking retrospectively now, I believe that it was beneficial in teaching me to be more considerate of others' feelings.

34. Again, see footnote #13.

35. Between September 16 and September 19, I attempted to determine the reasons for such long period of inactivity. The answers given were all attributable to the excessive heat and lack of acclimatization, for example, "It was too hot and I wasn't used to the weather." Knowing these men for the past three months, I could not believe that that was the only reason for their inactivity. Hence, I attempted further to determine their opinions as to the evacuation at that time. They invariably answered in this form: "We, being enemy aliens, felt that we must accept such destiny and must be reconciled to the idea of the evacuation. We were thankful that we were to be protected and provided for by the government."

I could not believe the veracity of the men, except of two or three. The answer showed too much of influence of my idea and my conversation. I was certain that it was not a true indicative of their sentiment at that time. Therefore, I abandoned my inquiries along this line.

36. The Colorado River War Relocation Project: "Circular No. 5, Amendment No. 1," Lines 31–36.

37. In order to determine the intensity of the interest or the desire, for the period June 29–July 25, on the part of the residents in Camp I to seek employment in this project, I experimented with the following tabulations: for determination of the interest in the camp, I calculated the number of the inquiries made at the Employment Office per person; that is,

$$\frac{\text{Inquiries}}{\text{Population}}$$

For determination of the interest for a unit job available in the camp, I obtained the quotients

$$\frac{\text{Inquiries}}{\text{Positions Open for the Day}}$$

Then, these figures were plotted on a coordinate paper and the graph, attached in the Appendix, was obtained [not included in the available copy].

It is noted therein that for June 29–July 2, the period of the arrival of the evacuees from the Salinas Assembly Center, the activities were very lively in the office, due partly to the opening of the new Block Manager's offices, new kitchens, etc. Then the curves indicate a lull period for July 3–July 11. For the subsequent period, July 13–July 21, the curves fluctuate at the higher level, that is, more activities in the Employment Office for inquiries and placements of jobs and more interest to obtain employments on the part of the residents.

38. About this time, the farmers and the farm migratory laborers began to call me in this term reverently.

39. See "Map II"—"The Progress of the Subjugation Work" in the Appendix [missing from the available copy].

40. The Social Welfare Department was without a fund and could not take care of the needy people.

41. At this writing, no wage payments for the months of June and August have been made to the "firebreak gang."

42. I was interested to find why they wanted to work on the cemetery project and inquired of them. The answer was generally in this form—the sentiment a little stronger with the men who had been to funeral services there: "The cemetery looks too dilapidated. We must pay more respect and reverence to the deceased."

I wondered if this reply had any connection with their religious concept or belief. As soon as I attempted to inquire along this line, I noticed that they were reluctant and hesitant to answer. Therefore, I abandoned the inquiries, as I did not wish to antagonize them unnecessarily.

43. Acting Director, The Department of Agriculture and Industry, The Colorado River War Relocation Project.

LEISURE

Nishimoto's Report on Gambling at Poston

Introduction

"Gambling at Poston" is easily one of Nishimoto's most fascinating research projects. Here, as in the previous selection, Nishimoto documents a dimension of the Japanese American experience that is occasionally noted in the literature but which has received hardly any systematic coverage.[1]

Taking a decidedly historical approach, Nishimoto frames the specific topic of gambling in Poston vis-à-vis an extended portrait of gambling as an important leisure activity among Issei and Nisei in California before World War II. He begins, for example, by discussing informal gambling practices before the war, covering everything from casual games played among friends to more serious betting on the ordinary Japanese games that the Issei played, like *hana*,[2] to bets placed on the lotteries, which were popular among the Issei, and the pinball machine games that became the rage among young working-class Nisei men in urban settings like Los Angeles during the 1930s.[3] Moreover, in his discussion Nishimoto also situates gambling in the larger context of ordinary pastimes of the Japanese American community, including Japanese games such as *go* and *shogi*,[4] American sports such as baseball, and popular forms of entertainment like the movies.

Most important, Nishimoto traces the evolution of the infamous Tokyo Club gambling syndicate in detail. The gambling clubs that the Issei pioneers frequented were often run by Chinese entrepreneurs who had established such operations prior to the arrival of the Japanese in the late nineteenth century. Nishimoto's uncanny understanding of the forces that led to organized gambling, which eventually took the form of the Tokyo Club and organizations up and down the West Coast, allows the reader to see how and why the club became an integral, if semiclandestine, part of the Japanese American community.[5] As Isami Arifuku Waugh has so brilliantly argued in an historical interpretation based on Nishimoto's research, the Tokyo Club itself represents a critically important chapter of Japanese American history that has long been buried, perhaps because it goes against the grain of the "model minority" image of a law-abiding people.[6]

However horrible "enforcement" techniques and the internecine struggles for control of the Tokyo Club were—and both clearly involved murders—Nishimoto's commentary prefigures the conclusion developed later by others that gambling was wildly popular because it appeared to offer a quick and easy means to wealth, and this appealed to the Issei, who were a generation influenced by the *dekasegi* ideal. Basically, the dekasegi orientation involved a sojourner mentality common during the initial period of arrival of many European and Asian immigrant men to America. The immigrants saw labor in the United States as a temporary pursuit undertaken to earn an income that it would not have been possible to earn back home. The men assumed, at least in the beginning, that they would eventually return home. For the Issei, the ideal was to strike it rich and return to Japan to live a life of leisure.[7] Gambling must have seemed like an easy way to achieve the dream to those who worked so hard, often for little return. What is more, for the Issei and the older Nisei, whose upward social and occupational mobility was typically blocked by racial prejudice and discrimination, especially before World War II, gambling was not only a form of entertainment and a social activity, it was also a form of resistance to constraint.[8]

When and if it became too noticeable, however, "responsible" elements within the Japanese American population opposed gambling, especially in light of its serious consequences. At various times in the late nineteenth century, Japanese consular officials tried to discourage gamblers and gambling. Interestingly enough, they were concerned that the Issei might be too easily confused with the Chinese if they gambled in Chinese establishments and might thus suffer a fate similar to that entailed in the passage of the Chinese Exclusion Act of 1882 and subsequent legislation. Community leaders also noted that vast amounts of money were being lost by Japanese laborers in Chinese gambling houses. In 1907 in the California city of Fresno alone, Japanese laborers were reported to have lost on the order of $200,000 immediately following the end of the harvesting season in the nineteen gambling houses in operation there.[9]

By the early twentieth century, some of the Christian congregations were keeping tabs on the situation and were trying to discourage gaming. Kazuo Ito notes that "[c]hurch leaders were most worried about it. . . . [T]roops of Salvation Army workers came to San Francisco, Los Angeles, Stockton, Seattle and other cities, and gave speeches on the streets, arguing for moral reform of the Japanese."[10] Ministers and their churches also initiated antigambling campaigns on behalf of families who were suffering the consequences, as well as on behalf of the Japanese American community at large, whose reputation and image were partly at stake. This could be dangerous, however, and Ito notes that in Stockton in 1920 one Teikichi Takeha, "secretary of an association for the abolition of gambling, was assassinated" apparently because he was too effectively threatening entrenched economic interests.[11] Despite such efforts, gambling was a very popular pastime and was impossible to curtail. By the 1920s the Tokyo Club, albeit illegal, had become a community-based institution that addressed the dreams and needs of a population that did not have full access to mainstream occupations or leisure activities, let alone full opportunities for marrying and raising a family.[12]

The historical framework thus offers us a context for understanding the importance that gambling assumed among the incarcerated population at Poston. For its part, the War Relocation Authority realized the importance of cooperating to provide as many forms of less objectionable activities in camp as possible. Just as they had before the war, sports teams of all kinds proliferated, and Japanese and American board games provided many hours of friendly competition. Encouraged by the WRA staff, Japanese Americans established newspapers, offered adult education classes, and organized classes and schools for various crafts like sewing and dressmaking. They also showed movies, organized music and dance performances (which were extremely popular), and set up branches of mainstream society groups such as the Scouts, the Red Cross, the YMCA, and the YWCA. Various arts flourished in the camps, including painting and drawing, carving, various kinds of writing, including poetry, and even horticulture, gardening, and landscaping.[13]

Still, the old motives—the need to kill time, the hope of making a fortune, and the excitement both of gambling and of thumbing one's nose at the authorities—were still there. Further, the Japanese Americans may have been more susceptible than usual to gambling because of their frustration and anger

Residents of Poston's Unit I built this outdoor stage in Block 4. Patterned after the traditional Shibai (Japanese drama) theater, it was also used as a venue for pageants, variety shows, and community meetings. (Courtesy of Roberta Shiroma)

Under the direction of their chief, policemen from Unit I carve wooden billy clubs from mesquite wood. By early 1943 the War Relocation Authority had established a policy of maintaining a Japanese American police force to handle internal security at each camp. In Unit I the police were under the supervision of the assistant project director, John Evans. (Courtesy of the Bancroft Library)

about an unjust and overly regimented and institutionalized confinement. In particular, as Nishimoto's study details, the camp environment seemed to exacerbate many of the negative reasons that caused people to gamble, so much so that gambling turned into a decidedly destructive activity in Poston after 1943, especially among men in their teens and twenties. To make matters worse, from time to time rumors had it that the Japanese American members of the Poston police force, as well as certain community leaders, knew what was going on but, because of bribery and nepotism, did little to change it.

In the final analysis, it is noteworthy that, when the situation grew increasingly troublesome, the residents banded together with the block managers, ministers, and emboldened community leaders who had not been compromised to try to put an end to open gambling and the associated climate of corruption and lawlessness once and for all.[14] As Nishimoto's historical ethnography of gambling reveals, however, this was an old pattern within the Japanese American community. He was therefore reluctant to conclude that the efforts to curtail gambling in Poston would be likely to succeed. After all, they never had before.

Notes

1. Brief accounts of gambling as a leisure activity in the WRA camps are available in Spicer et al., *Impounded People: Japanese-Americans in the Relocation Centers* (Tucson: University of Arizona Press, 1969), 219, and in specific studies of camps, such as Sandra C. Taylor, *Jewel of the Desert: Japanese American Internment at Topaz* (Berkeley: University of California Press, 1993), 163, 183.

2. *Hana* is a popular Japanese card game.

3. Nishimoto's observations are fully consistent with available primary and secondary materials. Kazuo Ito's compilation *Issei: A History of Japanese Immigrants in North America* (Seattle: Executive Committee for the Publication of *Issei*, 1973) has a whole chapter of firsthand accounts of gambling based primarily on written reminiscences of numerous first-generation men. Yuji Ichioka presents a brief overview of the subject in *The Issei: The World of the First Generation Immigrants, 1885–1924* (New York: Free Press, 1988). He indicates that gambling was a frequent pastime among Japanese laborers from the mining camps of the central mountain states to the fishing and canning camps of Alaska and the Pacific Northwest. Tsurutani Hisashi observes that gambling and other crimes were an especially serious problem during the initial frontier period of the late nineteenth and early twentieth centuries, following the early immigration of single Japanese men to the United States; see *America Bound: The Japanese and the Opening of the American West* (Tokyo: Japan Times, 1977). Interested readers can also trace the impact of gambling on an Issei family in two books by Akemi Kikumura, *Through Harsh Winters* (Novato, Calif.: Chandler and Sharp, 1981), and *Promises Kept: The Life of an Issei Man* (Novato, Calif.: Chandler and Sharp, 1991). Isami Arifuku Waugh notes in her study "Hidden Crime and Deviance in the Japanese American Community, 1920–1946" (Ph.D. diss., University of California, Berkeley, 1978) that a rich source of insight on the impact of gambling on Issei family life is available in short stories by Nisei women writers, some of which appear to be semifictionalized accounts often presented from a woman's point of view. See, for example, Hisaye Yamamoto's short stories

"The Brown House" and "Las Vegas Charley" in her book *Seventeen Syllables and Other Stories* (Latham, N.Y.: Kitchen Table: Women of Color Press, 1988), and Wakako Yamauchi, "The Sensei," in *Yardbird Reader* 3 (1974): 245–54. Waugh pioneered the use of fiction as both an index of and an instrument for the study of crime and deviance in Japanese American families and communities; see "Hidden Crime and Deviance."

4. These games are Japanese equivalents of chess and checkers.

5. See the section "Gambling Chain on the Pacific Coast" in Ito, *Issei*, 754–58. A friend of Nishimoto once told me that Nishimoto enjoyed gambling himself and after the war particularly liked to bet on horses. In his autobiographical letter, above, Nishimoto indicates that, while he did not know how to play cards when he arrived in the United States, he was an enthusiastic player by the time he was at Stanford. Although he doesn't mention his personal interest or experiences apart from this, one of the reasons that his report on gambling is so convincing, both in detail and interpretation, is that it may reflect the fact that he was in a position to combine information drawn from interviews and other documentary sources with his own firsthand participant observation.

6. See Waugh, "Hidden Crime and Deviance," 1–20, 86–90.

7. Yuji Ichioka discusses the *dekasegi* ideal and how it relates to Issei's interest in gambling in his book *The Issei*, 3–4, 87, and passim.

8. An examination of gambling as a form of both popular resistance and community self-determination has been advanced by Raymond Lou in a scholarly study of the role of gambling in the Chinese American community; see "Community Resistance of Los Angeles Chinese Americans, 1870–1900: A Case Study of Gaming," in *The Chinese American Experience: Papers from the Second National Conference on Chinese American Studies (1980)*, ed. Genny Lim et al. (San Francisco: Chinese Historical Society of America, and the Chinese Culture Foundation of America, 1984), 160–69.

9. Ichioka, *The Issei*, 86.

10. Ito, *Issei*, 754.

11. Ibid.

12. Limits on Japanese Americans' opportunities included the fact that Issei were ineligible for naturalization and as a result were restricted on many economic fronts. For example, as early as 1913 an alien land law was passed in California stipulating that no person ineligible for U.S. citizenship would be allowed to purchase and own land. Further, the Issei were legally barred from intermarrying with Euro-Americans in California and in practice were barred from visiting many public venues of leisure and entertainment.

13. A number of books illustrate the various forms of artistic production carried out in camp, including Allen H. Eaton's classic study *Beauty behind Barbed Wire: The Arts of the Japanese in Our War Relocation Camps* (New York: Harper, 1952), which presents a variety of art forms and styles; *The View from Within: Japanese American Art from the*

Internment Camps, 1942–1945, ed. Karin M. Higa, (Los Angeles: Wright Gallery, the Japanese American National Museum, and the Asian American Studies Center, 1992), most of the illustrations for which are paintings, water colors, and sketches; and Kazue Matsuda de Cristoforo, *Poetic Reflections of the Tule Lake Concentration Camp, 1944* (Santa Clara, Calif.: Privately printed, 1988).

14. Waugh emphasizes that the camps were a breeding ground for various kinds of social problems, not just gambling. Waugh's discussion covers the illegal distilling and consumption of liquor, extramarital relations, family breakdown, delinquency, youth gangs, and even, apparently, prostitution. See Waugh, "Hidden Crime and Deviance."

GAMBLING AT POSTON

"How can we control and eliminate gambling effectively and speedily here?" is the most paramount current[1] question discussed seriously among the evacuees at the Colorado River Relocation Center.[[1]] The public sentiment against gambling was fostered gradually by the church groups and by the evacuee officials, especially since the November incident,[[2]] and was intensified greatly recently because of several cases of flagrant disregard by the gamblers for other residents. An analysis of the gambling history at Poston presents repetition of many familiar patterns and attitudes of the pre–Pearl-Harbor Japanese communities in California. The Poston situation may be divided into the following stages.

1. Coordination of "hana" game and poker for small stakes.
2. Organization by a small group of men of commercial gambling houses.
3. Increase in the amount of stakes.
4. Use of intimidation and bribery by the promoters to further their interest.
5. Fear and anxiety of the community residents for a syndicate to gain

---

1. Japanese American Evacuation and Resettlement Study Collection, Bancroft Library, University of California, Berkeley, J 6.09.
2. Nishimoto is referring to the Poston strike of November 1942, which he describes later in this document.

stronghold. Their increasing resentment against the evil and the abuses.

6. Intensified and increased gambling activity by young people. Alarm by their parents.
7. Public meetings to stamp it out.

These Poston aspects were not uncommon among the Japanese communities in California. The Japanese were usually slow to act until juvenile delinquent cases became alarmingly serious before they could successfully campaign against the professional gamblers. Some of the crusades were successful in stamping out vice groups, while others failed completely. Such campaigns were more successful in the smaller rural communities, whereas in the larger cities such as Los Angeles, San Francisco, Sacramento, etc., a syndicate was so well organized because of the corruption of the public officials that the conscientious residents were powerless in crusading. Especially in Los Angeles, the vice syndicate, the Tokyo Club, enjoyed a monopoly, its annual intake aggregating in excess of one million dollars, and wielded a great political influence over the Japanese. Inasmuch as Poston is comprised of the evacuees mostly from Southern California, a brief account of the recent history of gambling in Los Angeles and the surrounding communities shall aid the reader in gaining insight into the gambling condition by the Japanese at this relocation camp.

Private Games

The District Attorney for the county of Los Angeles remarked a few years ago, "The Japanese are the best law-abiding people. There are no major crimes among you. Only cases come up for our attention are those of gambling, which, I am sorry to say, are numerous."

As he said, arrests for gambling were frequent in the Japanese community, indicating widespread participation by the Japanese people. It was not uncommon to overhear people talking this or that residence had been raided by the police. Yet despite the arrests the gambling flourished unabated. Let us first present private games, those enjoyed among friends in homes. The common games played in private residences are hana, poker, dice throwing, and mah jong. Among these hana was the most popular game. It is a game the Japanese immigrants brought over with them. Whenever three or four or five Issei were seen together around a table, they were invariably playing hana. In fact, it was not an exaggeration if one had said that the Issei did not know any other device of game but hana. They did not take on American games, but they stuck to the Japanese game as though it were the only game existing. Especially in the districts where Japanese of the lower class were concentrated one did not encounter any difficulty in locating the game and joining in it. In "boarding houses"[2] for gardeners in the "Tenth Street District"[3] or "*Seinan-ku*"[4] or in the fisherman's barracks of Terminal Island,[5] men and women were found absorbed in playing the hana game in tobacco-smoke-filled rooms nightly or whenever they could not work due to the inclement weather condition. Their stake varied anywhere from five cents to one dollar a game; that is to say, five cents to one dollar changed hand within five to ten minutes. The victor's spoil for an evening in such games averaged about one dollar for the five-cent game and about twenty or thirty dollars for the one-dollar game. However, it was more common among the gardeners and the fishermen to set the stake at twenty-five cents a game—an evening's haul for the victor being about ten dollars.

As it has been noted, hana was more widely played among the older Japanese of the lower class or of the lower income group. Gardeners, fishermen, older produce men, farmers, migratory farm laborers had especial liking for the game. But who else were there among the Issei in California? Very, very few others. As the census would reveal almost all the Issei in California were engaged either in farming, gardening, fishing, or domestic service. Therefore, it was often correctly expressed that the game had an universal appeal for the older Japanese. Of them, it was more frequently played among the fishermen, the gardeners, and the migratory laborers, because they either lived closely together or had more opportunities to assemble in one place in addition to having frequent idle or unemployed periods. As a corollary, the farmers and the domestics indulged in it only occasionally, since they lived scattered and had less opportunity to assemble together.

In passing, it is interesting to note that in the upper and the middle classes of Japan abstention from the game is strictly self-enforced not only for fear of the police and social criticism, but also, for pride in adhering to the moral standards of the classes. It is only among the lower class people and the people of special groups such as theatrical people and professional entertainers that the game is condoned. And it is from this lower class of Japan that the California Japanese population extracted its largest, if not almost entire, portion.

Then, why is hana so popular among the California Issei? No doubt, there may be many reasons; each student having his own deduction why it is prevalent among the people. The writer, however, believes that the reasons for the popularity can be summarized in the following aspects.

Hana is a simple game. It is somewhat like rummy. Its rules are easy to grasp. Only a few players are needed for the game. Two men can play it. It also can be played by as many as seven persons, although it is most usual and best to have four or five contestants. The paraphernalia are inexpensive. It requires a set of cards, which is sold for about twenty-five cents. The set is durable and can be used for days and days, unlike the playing cards which are changed for a new set every hour or so during one poker session. There is an equal chance for every participant. No special skill is necessary after one becomes familiar with the simple technique. Unlike poker, the skill of betting or of bluffing is not needed. [Further,] the game is comparatively free from cheating. It is an exceptional person who can cheat with hana. It takes years and years of practice before one can cheat with the hana cards, besides laymen regularly avoid to play with these "professionals", whose reputation spreads rapidly in the community. The Issei, since coming over to this country, congregated among themselves and had little social contact with the Caucasians of the community. They failed to absorb the American ways of life, although most of them had been here more than thirty years. Hana playing, *go*, *shogi*, picture shows in Japanese, etc. are the only means of their recreating. They did not develop appreciation in participation of sports or watching of sports. Baseball was the only game which the Issei took on as spectators with enthusiasm, especially in the twenties. Even this was limited only to the small portion of the population. The Issei could not enjoy American movies due to their inability to understand English, of which one could hear them say defensively, "There is nothing in movies. Kisses and kisses. That's all. A man and a woman get together and they go through all kinds of erotic gestures on the screen. I don't enjoy things like that." Thus the variety of recreation they can enjoy were very limited, indicating that their history of immigration was that of hard struggles and they had very little leisure to themselves.

In contrast with the popularity of hana among the Issei, the game failed completely to permeate among the Nisei. Occasionally young people are seen playing the game, but they are almost always Kibei. With the Nisei, poker was most popular. The young men were meeting together in their friends' homes regularly and were holding "sessions". With the young business and professional men of Little Tokyo, the "market boys"[6] and the fruit stand employees, the "sessions" were more frequent and more regular, since they toiled only for the short union hours daily and had their evenings free, besides they had steady income and were comfortably set economically. With many of them the poker "session" was the basis of a clique and the common ground of their friendship. Some of these cliques held their "meetings" as often as three times a week, each one taking turn and inviting the others to his home. One young man would say to another, say on a street in Little Tokyo or in the Wholesale Produce Market, "Hey, Joe! At Jimmie's tonight. Eight o'clock."

The size of stake of their game varied from penny-ante/two-bits limits to nickel-ante/table-limit. The former was common among high school boys, who also liked the game and played it behind the backs of their parents. The latter was most prevalent in the older Nisei circle; it meant that the minimum of ante is five cents and the chips in his possession are the limit of one betting. The player bought the original chips[,] varying in the amount from ten to twenty dollars, at the beginning of the "session" from the "bank", usually the host for the evening. As the evening progressed, the unlucky ones had to buy more chips with cash again and again from the "bank" and the chips in circulation increased as the game went on. It increased to such an extent that it was not rare among them to see in one single pot chips worth more than seventy-five dollars or more. However, since such large winnings received publicity out of proper proportion among the clique acquaintances and were talked about more widely than others, it is safer to report that it was more usual in an ordinary "session" to find cash in the amount of twenty to thirty dollars changing hands in one evening.

The poker "session" also served as a social meeting for the middle class Nisei. During the evening many gossips concerning their friends and their community were exchanged among them. The host or his wife served refreshments; for the cost of food and the decks of cards the host was generally privileged to take out ten cents or twenty-five cents from the larger pots from time to time. To be called a "charming" or "nice" lady and to avoid being called a "joy-killer" or an "old battle axe" the host's wife had to wait on the guests gracefully with smile, even though she might have condemnation and contempt for her husband for gambling. It was her duty as a "perfect" hostess to keep her even disposition even if the "meeting" lasted into the early morning hours.

The common kinds of poker played by these people were five-card stud poker, seven-card poker, and draw poker. Of these the young Nisei liked seven-card poker, as they would say, "the pot gets bigger", while the high school boys enjoyed small five-card stud or draw poker, satisfying themselves with a spoil of one dollar or one dollar-and-a-half for a day.

Along with poker games, "twenty-one" was played sometimes among them, especially among the adolescents; it did not, however, gain popularity and limited only to the extent of "killing time" for one hour or so with a twenty-five cent or fifty cent capital.

In the somewhat same degree of popularity for "twenty-one" in the Japanese community the dice-throwing could also be classed. It was played for the similar purpose of "killing time"; it never gained the widespread favor of hana or poker and was played only occasionally among a small portion of the Nisei. Sometimes the Nisei were seen throwing the dice after the peak business hours in the dark corner of wholesale produce houses or in the wash-room of fruit stands; and it was very rare to see the older Issei indulging in the dice-throwing.

Other games of chance such as Mah Jong and Pin Ball machines had their ups and downs in the scale of popularity. The height of fad for Mah Jong in Los Angeles and its vicinities was in 1925–1930. During this period the Chinese game struck fancy of the middle class Japanese like a wildfire and they all began to learn it. Its rules, however, were so complicated and its paraphernalia were so expensive—a set costing about fifteen to thirty dollars depending upon its quality—that many of the beginners dropped out before they could master it. At the end it was mostly the shop owners and the artisans of Little Tokyo and the produce market owners who kept on with the game. They invited their friends in the evening and played a game or two, as a game would last about one hour-and-a-half to two hours-and-a-half. At this stage of the Mah Jong fad they were intent upon improving their skill and enjoyed it as a form of amusement without having a cash stake. Rivalry of skill and luck was sufficient to satisfy them, although the rivalry within the closed circle of family friends failed eventually to satiate the increasing egotism of their own skill and consequently outside competitions were sought out whenever possible. Such a desire to have competition with unfamiliar players culminated in holding a Mah Jong tournament. The first of the tournaments was held in 1928, and thereafter such a meeting was held monthly or bi-monthly, usually on Sunday. They rented a large reception hall of a Japanese restaurant in Little Tokyo for the occasion, beginning the game early in the afternoon and lasting until nine or ten o'clock at night. Its sponsors customarily charged each player one dollar or one dollar-and-a-half as entry fee, for which they served good dinners in the evening in addition to many prizes offered to the winners. The tournament was given ample publicity well in advance of the date in the Japanese newspapers and always drew a good mixed crowd, often numbering more than one hundred contestants. It always turned out to be a jolly, happy Sunday for the players, enjoying the merry, friendly atmosphere. If one was a winner, he received not only a prize such as a trophy or a fountain pen set but also a mention in the Japanese newspaper articles reporting the tournament.

In spite of the avid indulgence by the business men and the artisans and their wives, Mah Jong playing failed to penetrate either deeply or extensively into the Japanese society. To the farmers or the fishermen, for instance, it was something mysterious; and to the Nisei it was something tedious and foreign. The farmers or the fishermen were too busy with their chores or too impatient to learn the complicated rules. The Nisei desired "snappier" games. Therefore, it was not surprising at all that support by the select group was not enough and the fad for the Chinese game gradually died down after the peak of 1928–1929.

It was about 1932 when the popularity of Mah Jong playing revived and caught on with new addicts. This time, however, it was not as a form of amusement; but it deteriorated into a device of gambling. In private homes, where it was played formerly only for fun of playing it, the people were betting one-tenth-of-a-cent a point. It meant that the original investment for a game for each player was one dollar, as he was given two thousand points to start with. It also meant that his average winning or loss for a game was about fifty cents to one dollar. As it is always the case, they could not be satisfied long with such a small amount of money at stake. The stake gradually increased to one-fifth-of-a-cent a point and eventually to one-cent a point; that is to say, the original capital increased to two dollars and finally to twenty dollars, and the player's average turn over for a game was anywhere from one dollar or one dollar-and-a-half to ten or fifteen dollars. With the increase of stake the game attracted "bums" and "Nisei undesirables", who were not equipped with either the paraphernalia or place to play. In order to accommodate the need of these men "with too much time and don't know what to do with it", Mah Jong clubs sprang up in Little Tokyo. The purpose of the clubs was to arrange for a foursome and supply the set and a table and to charge a nominal fee, generally fifteen cents per game per player. Some of these clubs were quite respectable and catered [to] the Mah Jong playing middle class Japanese men, as it was convenient to walk in and find the partners for a game anytime they desired, although the Japanese women frowned upon such places. The stake of one-fifth-a-cent a point was most common and larger stakes were not encouraged at these places; as one proprietor remarked, "if they play for too big money, there are always big losers. The big losers can't come back and play some more. I don't want to lose my customers."

At the height, in 1933, there were as many as six Mah Jong clubs prospering in the downtown Japanese section. And it was a rule rather than an exception then that the players were going full blast with the Chinese bamboo blocks as late as two or three o'clock in the morning. But the prosperity for these establishments was of a short duration, as it again failed to draw new converts in a great number and the support by the "hoodlums" and a few respectable men alone was not enough to sustain the intensity of the fad for long. By 1935 all but one of these clubs closed their doors and the game returned to the homes of the middle class Japanese, although they retained the habit of gambling for small stakes. To indicate that the Mah Jong craze in the Japanese community waned rapidly and could not regain its old glory one could say that during 1935–1941 there were only two or three tournaments, which did not possess the gayness or merriment of the bygone days and that there was only one Mah Jong club existing in the city at the time of the evacuation meagerly as a side-business for a pool hall. One could also add that dust and dirt had piled thick on the Mah Jong sets in attics and basements when the Japanese were packing for the Assembly centers.

Like the fate of Mah Jong was the rise and fall of Pin Ball games. The first time that the machines were used as devices for gambling was soon after their appearance in the town in 1932. At the early stage of this gambling, a few men were clustered around a machine and were shooting the balls in the machine one by one, manipulating the handle spring carefully and aiming at the preselected pin expertly. Each player bet ten cents and the highest scorer took possession of the dimes in the pot. Soon the stake was hiked up to twenty-five cents and then to fifty cents. Later on, since the manipulating and aiming took time and were tedious, they banged away at once all the ten balls in the machine with one violent stroke. That is, if five boys were playing together and betting fifty cents each, a game was decided within ten minutes and the winner took two dollars-and-fifty cents in the pot. A variation of this form—at a faster pace to minimize the time spent for a game—was for a player to take a turn at the machine as before but to put up a certain arbitrary amount of cash, say two dollars, challenging the non-players that he would score a certain total point previously agreed upon between them. The spectators then would "cover" the bet individually or collectively that the player would not score the total. The game was decided within two minutes and money changed hands more rapidly. This form was especially popular with some Nisei business and professional men and "market boys". In extreme cases, when the Pin Ball game was at its peak in 1934, men were betting anywhere from fifty dollars to one hundred and fifty dollars for one game. The writer witnessed these "big games" quite often in the drug store at the corner of San Pedro and East First Streets, right in the heart of Little Tokyo. In one of these "contests", there were about fifteen prominent young business men gathered around a machine. The player was putting up twenty-five dollars and the bet was covered by two men. In addition to this pool, the spectators were betting separately among themselves, some betting fifteen dollars that the player would make the total point and finding a taker in the crowd, another pair betting ten dollars between them, and still another staking twenty dollars. With a single violent bang at the machine by the player, twenty-five dollars changed hands between the player and the two men who had covered the bet, while ten dollars, fifteen dollars, twenty dollars, and so on passed in many separate sets of betters severally. In this single game which lasted less than one minute, cash in excess of one hundred and fifty dollars in aggregate exchanged the owners. At this drugstore it was interesting to observe then that the policeman detailed to the traffic at the street intersection was a busy participant in this crowd.

The "big time" Pin Ball gambling at the drugstore went on ostentatiously everyday for a few months from the early hours in the afternoon to the closing time of the store[,] attracting a good sized, enthusiastic crowd until it suddenly disappeared and small betting games of the former days returned. The story about what had taken place meanwhile was this: the Japanese organized gambling syndicate was alarmed over thousands of dollars "transacted" in the store in a day and evidently its business volume, especially the sale of lottery tickets, dropped. The organization feared the increasing popularity of the competition from the Pin Ball machines in the community that it sent one day a gang of "huskies" to the owner of the store and "warned" him to stop the big stake gambling at his place. There was another place, it was reported, in the wholesale produce district which had been operating a similar gambling [operation] and returned to smaller stakes about the same time.

In spite of the fact that the gambling syndicate was alarmed over the machine playing, the fad did not penetrate the Japanese population extensively. It was only confined among the young "downtown crowd" and the "market boys," that is, among the Nisei in their twenties. It utterly failed to catch on with the Issei or with the rural Japanese. It was because of the intense craze among those Nisei who were their profitable clients and loss of prestige to have their monopoly of the gambling business violated that created concern among the syndicate.

Thus the gambling with the Pin Ball machines for the bigger amount of cash was eliminated by the external pressure for the selfish motive, but the machines playing for nominal stakes was flourishing unabated among the young men. With the advent of more complicated, electrically operated machines about 1936 even this practice of competing for the small sums at stake practically disappeared. The boys were satisfied with playing the new electric gadgets without betting and were more intent upon winning the prizes offered by the house. The owner of the machines were also careful to stimulate and sustain the interest of these boys in them by exchanging the old ones with newer and more and more intricate models from time to time.

Then what was the profit from these machines for the owner of a restaurant or a drugstore, who had the gadget installed in his premises and made it available for players? It was reported that there were two ways of obtaining the use of such machines, which were exclusively owned by two or three syndicates exclusively in Los Angeles most of the syndicate members with whom the writer was acquainted were invariably Jewish. One of the two ways of renting was on a percentage basis and the other was on straight set rental basis. The machine was never sold outright. With the percentage basis, the owner and the operator generally split the intake fifty-fifty, although this ratio varied slightly in some cases. With the latter form the monthly rentals varied from twenty to thirty-five dollars. It was said by many operators that it was much more profitable to rent them on the cash basis, as the following figures would reveal. In 1932, a very early, crude model rented for twenty or twenty-five dollars per month. One restaurant owner in Little Tokyo who had such a machine in his place, reported that the average daily gross income was approximately five dollars-and-fifty cents. That is to say, his net earning from the gadget for one month was one hundred and forty dollars after deducting the rental of twenty-five dollars. The owner of the infamous drugstore at the intersection of San Pedro and East First Streets, who also operated one machine confided once that he averaged about nine dollars daily. It meant that he was earning about three hundred dollars monthly by just letting the boys play the Pin Ball games.

With the introduction of more intricate models and overabundance of machines available for the community, it was true that the operators' intake decreased considerably. Even then the earning was lucrative enough. In 1938 the same drugstore owner reported that he was taking in about ten dollars daily from three machines of different patterns. His net income, it showed, was still in excess of two hundred dollars a month. One restaurant owner in the city Wholesale Produce Market district, who operated two machines, reported about the same time that his monthly net income from them averaged about one hundred-fifty dollars. It might be true that the cases cited here are those of extremely profitable establishments. Even if a concession is made to regard these cases to be those of special prosperous ones, it is still quite evident that a monthly profit of thirty or forty dollars from a machine was not at all difficult. It was no wonder that every drugstore owner or restaurant owner was fighting to get new and novel machines and was anxious to attract the pleasure-seeking boys for they took up little floor space and required little attention of shopkeepers.

The Pin Ball machines in Los Angeles went out of existence completely in 1940 when the Bowron administration decided to clean up vice in the city. With a single stroke of the police vice squad, gone were the glamorous days for the gadgets. The operators raised their hands in horror and lamented the passing of never-miss profit-making instrument. Of course, they protested vigorously but their protestation fell on deaf ears and was in vain. The prohibition of operation put an end to the source of lucrative extra income and endangered the existence of some of the stores which depended heavily on such earnings. The writer remembers two cases of store closing soon after the incident. Both of these were restaurants in the wholesale produce market district. The owner of one of these said, "I was making the store rent from the machines. Now with those machines gone there ain't enough profit to stay in the business." The other owner complained, "I have been going in the hole ever since those machines were taken out by the police. Why don't those politicians go after big guys? They shouldn't have bothered with those machines. They are alright; they are for clean fun."

Of less importance was contract bridge playing. It was only among a handful of the middle class or college bred Nisei that the popular American game found favor. Although they were enthusiastic adherents and held parties among themselves often, gambling with money was unknown to them generally. They took on bridge playing, it seemed, as a substitute for poker or hana, which was frowned upon by them as cheap. They had been playing the game many years, some known to be playing since as early as 1925, but outside of their circle it failed to spread far. Many Japanese sneered at their bridge playing as trying to be "uppish" or "fashionable."

Therefore, one could say in broad perspective that there were only two means of gambling for money as the privately played games in the Japanese community which held any significance because of its intensiveness, extensiveness, and permanency—namely, hana for the older Japanese and poker for the Nisei. Should the reader comprehend the extravagant grip of these two games over the Japanese people, he has an excellent insight into the unorganized, unsyndicated gambling of the Japanese community in California. Hana and poker were interwoven with the daily life of most of the Japanese to such an extent that they could not feel the moral restraint of violating a penal code and they were playing the games ostentatiously and openly in the sanctum of private homes. When some fellow countrymen happened to visit such a home, the players without any sign of shame kept on with the game and did not make any attempt to conceal it from the intruders. It was not necessary at all to hide the game from other Japanese because the Japanese community as a whole accepted and condoned the hana playing in the greater degree and the poker playing in somewhat less degree as the inevitable and "legitimate" sources of recreation.

The Organized Gambling

Every discussion of the organized or syndicated gambling in the Japanese community of California must necessarily be centered around the activities of the powerful Japanese organization, the Tokyo Club. And every discussion of the Tokyo Club, in turn, must be focused upon the activities of the Los Angeles Tokyo Club, which was the main office and the holding company of other Tokyo Clubs in the vast network extending not only throughout the state of California but also into Oregon, Washington, and Utah.

First, let us survey the early history of the organization briefly. One old Issei, who immigrated into America in 1900 as a young boy, reminisced recently about his younger days. He said that he always liked gambling. He said that as soon as he set foot in California he began to migrate seasonally from farm to farm as a harvest helper in company of several Japanese men. He reflected, "of course, we played hana almost every night among ourselves. But that was not enough. You keep on playing one kind of game in the same company and soon you crave for some diversion. One Saturday night some of the boys took me to a chop suey restaurant in a nearby town. We ate a nice dinner and then they took me to the back of the restaurant. There, there were some Chinamen and Japanese playing 'sheeko'[7] and lottery tickets. They taught me how to play 'sheeko.' It wasn't difficult to learn. All you have to do is to place your money on a certain number. The dealer counts the beans and you know within a short time whether you win or lose. I remember I won some money that night. And that was the beginning. I got the habit of going to these joints as soon as I got the pay. Oh yes, I moved from a farm to another, but there was always at least one Chinese gambling joint in a town nearby."

"Remember," he continued, "that was back in 1900's. There was no Tokyo Club then. All our gambling except hana games was done in these Chinese joints. I gave all my pay money to these Chinese; I was young then and never thought of saving. I worked from a payday to next payday and then took the pay-money there and splurged it away. Don't think I was a special case; all the other Japanese I knew were doing the same. We sure were swell customers for those Chinese; they took away all the wages from all of us Japanese. I don't know how many tens of thousands dollars the California Japanese were pouring into the caches of the Chinese. We sure were suckers. Then a few years after the Earthquake of San Francisco some bright Japanese saw a gold mine in the business and opened a place in the Japanese town of San Francisco. I don't remember if they called it Tokyo Club then or not; but anyway, this was the beginning of the Tokyo Club. It was patterned after those Chinese places; there you could play *sooko*, dice games, blackjack, poker, *gaham*,[8] or lottery tickets. Yes, I patronized the place whenever I was in San Francisco; and so did other Japanese. They began to do a swell business. Soon the club sent its boys out to other towns in California where Japanese were congregated densely and set up similar joints. We went to these Japanese places now instead of the Chinese gambling houses. You know, it is always nicer to patronize your own people rather than other races. There were lots of Tokyo Clubs all over California one time, but some died out, because of poor business or the opposition from respectable Japanese of the communities, while others survived till today."

"Yeah, the gambling got into my bone," he lamented, "because of gambling I was never able to get married, although I worked hard and earned lots of money. If I had saved those money, I would be sitting pretty now with a nice wife and family. I wouldn't be going around from farm to farm from season to another like this. And I bet there are many, many other Japanese who are in the same shoe."

"By the way, how about women?" he was asked. "Women? I am too old and no good any more. Sure, when I was younger, I wouldn't say I didn't visit prostitutes. But there were very few Japanese 'women' then. It had to be with either Chinese or white prostitutes. No, the Tokyo Club had nothing to do with 'women'. Those guys themselves had to visit those whites or Chinese. As I remember there were only two red light joints with Japanese women in California, and they were in San Francisco. These places were privately operated and the Tokyo Club had no interest in them. They are all gone now, though."

As the old man narrated, it is most probably true that the first Tokyo Club was established sometime around 1910 as an imitation and a rival of Chinese gambling places. Their games were the same as those found in the Chinese places and their intention was to draw away the Japanese customers from the Chinese. However, it is unfortunate that no account of the history of the activities of the Tokyo Club syndicate could be authenticated, since it was an ultra secret organization and its members and employees were extremely tight-lipped.

It was also true that all Tokyo Clubs set up in the smaller California cities were operated by the men who had been sent out by the San Francisco house. These branches, so to speak, were controlled by the main office in San Francisco until the control was transferred to Los Angeles later. A branch house was evidently sending in at regular intervals the net earnings to the main house after deducting its own operating expense. However, it was not until sometime in the early twenties when the main office moved to Los Angeles that the syndicate was firmly entrenched in the Japanese community and began to wield a great influence over the Japanese, its annual earning exceeding a million dollar mark. Its existence was still shaky about the time of the World War, as the old reminiscing Issei inferred. Many of the houses opened by the syndicate met opposition from the Japanese residents and some of them closed their doors after a short unprofitable operation. Even in their golden days of the twenties all the attempts of the Tokyo Club syndicate to "muscle" into new and unexploited territories were not successful, especially in the smaller towns, where the united front of public condemnation and vigorous crusading by the leading Japanese was too much for the organized gambling to survive. The writer witnessed in one of these smaller towns a crusade by the residents against the encroachment of such an organized gambling into their community life when the syndicate had opened a branch and began to draw crowds.

It was in Vacaville, California, in 1924. Vacaville, as you know, is situated on the outer rim of the fertile Sacramento Valley. It was a thriving town, being the center of prosperous fruit orchards, which were noted for producing and shipping to the Eastern markets many varieties of fruit at least one month ahead of the orchards in other sections of California. The early appearance of their produce in the markets for the public hunger for novel and different fruits commanded enviable price. And almost all of these favorably endowed ranches were operated by the Japanese, who had settled down in their respective places for many years; their tenancy with one contract usually lasted for four or five years and was generally renewed as long as they wished to stay. These Japanese farmers had made money through the past profitable years and saved. They were, therefore, steady, economically secure people who seldom toiled themselves but merely directed others in their chores on the farms.

Besides these middle class Japanese there were permanent farm helpers who resided on the ranches with the operators all year around, usually drawing set monthly wages; these, too, were steady and stable because of permanency of employment and regularity of income.

As the harvest season approached, which would begin in April and last until October, migratory Japanese laborers flocked into the town from other sections of the state. The season here provided them with abundant opportunities and attractive wages. As the season reached its peak in the summer, the Japanese population in and around the town increased to about one thousand. And as it is always the case wherever Japanese people congregate, there was a sizable prosperous colony of their own in one section of the town, which was composed of Japanese shops, restaurants, pool halls, employment offices, and cheap inns, which were supported by and catered more or less exclusively to them.

One day in the spring of 1924 in this colony a gambling house was found, where all the sundry paraphernalia of various devices of gambling had been pretentiously installed. It was whispered among the townfolk that the place was financed by the big Tokyo Club capital. Within a month Japanese, young and old, were passing through its door in droves. Soon some ranchers began to grumble about the house of gambling. They complained because their hired helpers failed to return to the ranches for days and sometimes for a week, should they hit the town on Saturday night when they had been paid for the week. These laborers stayed in town to gamble in the house as long as their money lasted. When they had lost every penny they had, they came back to work; and again they were gone for days after they earned some money. Other ranchers complained more loudly because the harvest work was impaired and was running short of help due to the uncalled for absence of laborers.

Now, the "leading" citizens, *yushi*, of the colony took up the chant, joined enthusiastically by the Christian pastor and the Buddhist priest. "Something must be done, and done quickly," they said. "Let's do something," others said. This chorus of "Something must be done" and "let's do something" resulted in an emergency meeting of the Japanese Association, a town meeting for the ranchers and the townfolk in the town hall. There the leading citizens got up on the floor and made impassioned speeches in the crowded hall. (For some reason meetings of this sort always draw a big crowd among the Japanese.) One *yushi* said, "The invasion of organized gambling into our community perils our prosperous industry. The peace-disturbers are keeping our workers away from the orchards. We had depended upon these men for our harvesting; but now with inroad of the vice what is going to become of our crops? Not only these innocent workers are easy prey of the professionals and their future is being destroyed, but our whole existence, life or death of all of us, is challenged and threatened. This situation is of a great concern to us. The house of ill fame must go and go right away."

"Look at those young men who are frequenting the place of vice," shouted another, "They were the exemplary models and the flower of our young manhood. They were once diligent and industrious. They were working hard and saving for the happy day when he would take a wonderful girl as his proud bride to make a blissful home with her. (How often has one heard the plea of model young manhood? This was certainly one of the most popular themes or logic of the Issei in the past.) Now, their future is destroyed; our happy dream and anticipation of their bright future have been completely shattered. The gambling is contaminating the innocent and delicate minds of the young Japanese. It is a deplorable condition. I am fearful of the future of our race. Organized gambling must go. We must put a stop to it not only to save those who had been addicted but also those who are yet to come under the diabolic influence. If our race in America is to survive and to perpetuate our good name which we had established, we must close the house."

After many speeches of similar themes were made by others passionately and excitedly, someone asked, "What can we do to stop it?"

Many suggestions were offered. One was to contact the men who were known to be gambling in the place and advise them to stay away—it carried a tone of "or else", meaning that those who refused to abide by the advice would be socially ostracized and made unpleasant to stay in the town. A rancher offered another suggestion; he wanted every orchard operator to make a pledge with him to refuse to hire those who were frequenting the infamous establishment. All present, however, agreed that it was impractical and impossible to close the house forcibly; so these two methods of combating the evil—social ostracism and boycotting of the gamblers—were adopted officially by the town hall meeting.

At the close of the meeting, which lasted more than three hours, a resolution of condemning the organized gambling and those who gamble was passed by the wild-eyed throng in excitement and uproar.

What actually took place during the ensuing days was not revealed to the writer, but men passing through the door of the house gradually decreased and ceased to be noticed eventually. Those who had to gamble habitually did go into the place under the cover of darkness, endeavoring not to be seen by anyone; and even those became negligible in number as the time went on. Soon afterward, the gambling house closed its door inconspicuously and the Japanese people returned to the old routine of playing hana games for small stakes in the backrooms of the shops, restaurants, and inns or in the workers' barracks.

A similar incident of frustrating an attempt by the Tokyo Club interest to establish its branch was reported by the secretary of a Japanese Association. Let us have his story now.

"It was about six months after I got out of the University of Southern California," he commenced, "I got an offer from the *yushi* in the Gardena Valley[9] for the job as the secretary of the Japanese Association in that section. It sounds good when I say the executive secretary, but that was the only employee they had. Their office was located in an old, shabby two-by-four house. But I took the job because I couldn't find anything else to do and it paid pretty well—one hundred dollars a month with rooms and utilities—that wasn't bad at all—I was engaged to a girl and had to save as much and as quickly as possible. I moved with my bag and all into my residence, which was composed of two rooms, bath and kitchen in the back of the office. It was back in February of 1928.

"As soon as I had settled in my swivel chair, I had many members of the Association coming into the office with sundry business every day. After all, the Association had the membership of about three hundred Japanese families; that meant about two thousand Japanese, male and female, young and old. It was next to the largest of its kind in Southern California, the largest being the one in Los Angeles. These members were mostly truck gardeners and "haul men."[10] Anyway, this is where I began to work.

"Very soon afterward," he continued, "these Issei farmers were coming to see me about a gambling joint down the street. They complained that lots of

Japanese were gambling there every night. Some of them stayed there so late that they couldn't work in the fields the next day. "And mind you, these men are the fathers of many children," they said. It seemed that the wives of these frequenters of the gambling house were worried about their play-loving husbands, yet they were powerless before them to do anything about their indulgence. Instead, these women went to their neighbors and sought sympathy for their grievance. Well, as you know, Japanese farmers are altruistic and helpful whenever others are in trouble, often to the point of being 'busy-bodies.' They would say, 'I will tell the Japanese Association to do something about it. What are they doing anyway? Are they asleep?'"

"Other complainants had more selfish motives. They said that some of the 'haul men' with whom their garden products were entrusted for consignment marketing were parking their loaded trucks and were gambling in there beyond the opening hour of the wholesale market, thereby missing the early market hours during which produce would usually sell for higher price. They would also say that it is very easy to cheat the sale price and the weight of the consigned goods, because no one could check up on their transactions. Well, their arguments is that when there is greater temptation to cheat, especially if they had lost in games, they are most likely to cheat. My argument to that would be that if that is the case why don't they tell those 'haul men' face to face themselves; or why can't they change the 'haul man' and consign their produce to someone else. They either haven't got 'guts' or don't want to say anything unpleasant or offensive themselves and want someone else to say it for them. I know they are sly and shoving the buck, but being the new secretary I couldn't tell them so.

"I remember a couple of old men who came to my office and said that their sons were gambling there habitually but they could not do anything to stop it. Should they chide their sons they would revolt and big family squabbles would follow. So these old men wanted me to do something about it. Their primary worry was that these grown up sons were stealing the income from their produce, for which every member of their families had toiled and were squandering it away. But they would say, 'the presence of gambling place in the community is unhealthy for the young mind.'

"You know how they get excited quickly," the secretary continued on, "and how they get heated over such a moral issue. They were clamoring for action, but they all wanted me to do something about it and none of them wanted to take the leadership. I was new in the job and was anxious to satisfy the members; I didn't want them to criticize behind my back, 'the new secretary we got is incompetent and lazy.' So I called an officers' meeting one evening and consulted the big shots of the Association about what procedure was to be taken. Yes, they readily agreed that the joint must be driven out of the town 'for the sake of the younger generation.' To them their hana playing in the presence of their sons and daughters are all right but not the place with permanent gambling facilities. I was ordered to call a mass meeting of all the members, which meant just about calling all the heads of the Japanese families in the alley. When these people assembled in our Japanese language school hall, we presented the résumé of the situation, which they had already been aware—stories travel mouths to mouths awfully quick among the Japanese in a hush-hush manner. There were many speeches made in that meeting; you know how they do it—speeches of flowery words, of the importance of maintaining the moral standard, on the virtuous mission of the older people to guide the young generation, and so on. To you and me these speeches would sound spurious and superficial or make an impression as if they were talking just for oratory's sake. When it reached to the point of determining the definite steps to be taken to curb out the organized gambling, they were stuck. They couldn't suggest any concrete suggestion. Finally, after a long indecisive discussion they selected a committee and asked them to take action."

"The committee met the next day in my office and again couldn't decide what to do and told me to figure out a solution. Yes, they too passed the buck. Well, I had to make good. I contacted a few husky Judo men of the valley and obtained their support for the crusade. With these physical marvels I called on the boss of the gambling house and argued with him why his place should be closed. He half-heartedly consented that he would not do anything to encourage people to come into his place, although he would not restrain them from doing so. He had been living in the town for some time, although he had some connection with the Tokyo Club syndicate. He said that he liked the community and wanted to live there. He did not want to 'defy the strong public opinion' nor did he wish his family to be [']looked upon by other Japanese askance.' Our work was half done; something we had been thinking almost impossible was accomplished. So from that night our gang stood vigilantly about fifty feet away from the entrance of the place and stopped every one coming toward it. We told him that we were there to curb gambling and advised him to stay away; some heeded while others went around the house and sneaked in from the back door. We kept on with this for several nights. Meanwhile the news of the vigilantes spread around the community and the people began to rally around. We were encouraged by the public support because we had been afraid how the syndicate men would take our action and fearful of their reprisal; now we were confident that we were safe.

"Well, we were successful in stamping out the organized gambling from our town," he boasted. "The boss of the house confined his activities thereafter to promoting of shows and running of a restaurant. He is still living in the town, but I don't think he will try to run a gambling place anymore, knowing that [he] will meet a stern opposition from the community. Anyway, I certainly had guts to buck against the racketeers, but those were my younger days and I was new in this job. I wouldn't dare to do a thing like that now."

These cases which have been cited are two of a few instances in which the Tokyo Club syndicate failed in their attempt to extend their control over a new territory because of public opposition. It was, however, more usual for them to succeed rather than fail wherever they had wished to extend their interest; and once they had established it, it was practically impossible to curb them out.

In the golden days of the twenties they held the monopoly of gambling among the Japanese and their far flung network was entrenched firmly in many cities and towns. The main office was located in Los Angeles and the branches were found in San Francisco, San Jose, Sacramento, Stockton, Lodi, Fresno, Watsonville, Salinas, Martinez, and Walnut Grove in the northern part of California, and in San Diego, El Centro, and Bakersfield in the southern part. Those in Portland, Seattle, and Salt Lake City enjoyed more autonomous privileges and [were] more loosely connected with the California chain.

The Tokyo Club of Los Angeles was situated on Jackson Street at the foot of Central Avenue in Little Tokyo, occupying a three-story building. The place of business was located on the third floor of the building, three flights of narrow steps leading up directly from the street to the entrance. At this entrance, there was a heavy, thick, impressive door, on which a small opening with its own small door was found. Through this peep hole, a man looked searchingly from the other side as a customer came up the stairs. If the oncoming man was a Japanese, the watcher opened the heavy door without a moment's hesitation. Through this door, one went through another door and then into a large smoke-filled, electric-lit hall, where Japanese of every walk of life were found busily absorbed in many kinds of game—faro, sheeko, blackjack, dice throwing, poker, gaham, and lottery, each of these games occupying a neatly arranged area in the hall respectively. It was known that the place opened for its daily business at two in the afternoon and closed sometimes around one, and that about eight o'clock or thereafter every night this hall with about seventy-five feet by one hundred feet floor space was filled with game participants and spectators, numbering at least one hundred or so, not including about thirty employees. At one corner of the hall there was a wire cage like the one seen in a bank, behind which a few men stood. One of these men was a chief cashier, an important man placed high up in the hierarchy of the syndicate, and he took charge of the huge, massive safe behind the counter, which was reputed to contain cash of at least seventy-five thousand dollars constantly. On one side of the hall there was a dining room and an adjoining kitchen, and there *shaoko-tai*,[11] or bums, were regularly fed together with the employees and bona-fide customers free of charge. Amid the crowd several tall men of muscular physique were moving about; they were the 'bouncers' of the house, entrusted with the duty of maintaining peace and order or of bouncing obnoxious or disturbing clients out. Once in awhile these men, too, relieved the dealers and the bankers and took charge of the tables. Although the exact figure was not revealed, it was said by the people in the know that five thousand dollars' worth of "business" was transacted there daily. From this information it was easily conceivable that their profit was enormous and lucrative.

The second floor of the concrete building owned by Tokyo Club was fitted as an auditorium, with a stage and a hall with a seating capacity of about eight hundred. This was called Yamato Hall, which was operated by *Beikoku Kogyo Kaisha*, or the American Entertainment Company, a subsidiary of the chain. Stage shows were imported by them from Japan and were staged there, or shows of local talents were put on. The auditorium was also often used for *minshu taikai*, or mass meeting, for the Japanese people of Los Angeles in order to fan public agitation for this or that purpose. Frequently, especially in the late thirties, hundreds of Japanese not only from the city proper but also from the towns all over the Southern California assembled for *koen-kai*, or lecture meeting, given by a *meishi*, or a noted personage, who was passing through the city from or to Japan. The lecturers included the front-page names—statesmen, members of the diet, newspapermen, and army and navy officers of Japan. As the cloud of crisis between America and Japan darkened, the interest of Japanese was intensified in what these men in the know would have to say. Some of the big names attracted such a tremendous crowd overflowing into the street, for whom a public address system had to be installed from the stage. It was in these speeches that the Issei were told that war was certain to come and they should be reconciled to the eventuality. One of the speakers said once, "If war comes, which is only a question of time, don't expect the Japanese government to do anything for you. It is going to come very suddenly.

You are not *imin*, or immigrants, but *kimin*, or forsaken subjects." A naval officer assured the throng on another occasion "Japan is invincible. We have prepared. We are ready." Another commander boasted, "We have been balked and humiliated by America for many years. When the time comes, we will crush America. We will attack them; we will bomb them." One army captain was reported to have said that Japan would attack Hawaii: "She would capture the Philippines and Singapore."

The contests of the speeches were discussed and re-discussed in whispers in the Japanese shops and farms; they reverberated days and weeks from the platform of Yamato Hall into the Japanese community. The warnings and assurances pointed the way for the Issei in the event of war. The student of the Japanese, especially for the period after the outbreak of the war, cannot minimize the important role played by the lectures in Yamato Hall, the second floor of the Tokyo Club building. Many beliefs, convictions, and rumors of the Issei after Pearl Harbor had their origin in these "fight talks."

The tenant of the second floor, *Kogyo Kaisha*, aside from operating Yamato Hall, was the owner of *Fuji Kan*, the only Japanese theater in the United States which was showing Japan-made films daily. The theater was located in the heart of Little Tokyo on East First Street and a bright spot of the Japanese "Great Whiteway." Although the excessive admission of seventy-five cents was charged, old Issei men and women flocked to the theater as they craved for amusement and entertainment of their own culture, which was very limited, if not denied, to them. On Saturdays and Sundays the movie house drew crowds from far and wide and it was not unusual for it to hang "Standing Room Only," or *oiri Manin*, signs.

Kogyo Kaisha, in addition to the successful and exclusive operation of the theater, imported the films made in Japan. Some of those films were directly brought from Japan, but more likely most of them were obtained from the Japanese theater chain in Hawaii after they were shown to the island Japanese, as some critical Japanese used to remark, "Those are discarded obsolete films which were picked up in Hawaii almost for nothing." Although these pictures might have been obsolete and cheap intrinsically, they were just the same novel and entertaining to the Japanese in California. After the first showing at Fuji Kan, they were taken around for a one "night stand" throughout smaller towns in California, the local Tokyo Clubs promoting and sponsoring these shows. And these shows were invariably profitable both to the promoters and the film owners.

The street floor was leased by the Japanese language newspaper, *Rafu Nichi-*

bei, or the *Los Angeles Japanese American Daily News*, until it failed in 1931 when the publishers incurred the wrath of the public and their paper was boycotted due to the mishandling of a labor dispute with the employees. Even during their heydays, the newspaper had difficulty in operating itself profitably, as true with any other vernacular paper,[12] because the fixed expense is enormously high in comparison with the limited possibility in volume for subscribers. It was common knowledge that the Japanese newspaper game was not for money making, but for "social prestige," that is to say, the newspapermen were looked upon with respect and could wield a great deal of influence over the community. The *Rafu Nichibei*, too, had more than its share of financial difficulty and was known that their rent was in arrears for many months. This, in turn, created a special obligatory relation between the tenant and the lessor making the paper constantly considerate of the whim of the gambling interest. It was careful not to offend them, although they might not publicly endorse their activities. However, whenever the syndicate or its subsidiary was promoting some "legitimate" undertaking, the paper gave ample space for its publicity.

After the failure of this paper, in about 1935, another Japanese newspaper, *San Gyo Nippon*, commenced its publication on the ground floor of the building and met the same fate of its predecessor.

Speaking of vernacular newspapers it is important to add that one of the two others in Los Angeles was published by a popular "pro-Axis" man, Sei Fujii, who for many years had been the legal counselor for the chain, while the other of the two was operated by a man who had intimate social and business connections with the officials of the gambling hierarchy. One could say, therefore, that the papers did not dare to provoke their wrath and tacitly condoned the existence of the organized gambling for expediency.

"Wasn't there any other group which might impede and oppose the work of the syndicate?" one would ask. The answer to this question is "no." The Japanese religious groups were careful not to mention the name of this organization whenever they preached the evil of gambling. They were willing to condemn the gambling in general as a principle, but were afraid to cite the specific instances of abuses of powerful Tokyo Club. There were good reasons: first of all, it must be stated that the leaders of the hierarchy were more than willing to donate a considerable sum of money for charities and good causes freely and lavishly. It would not be an exaggeration to say that every church or temple of Los Angeles at one time or another received financial aid from these underground men, although neither side of the transactions was anxious to divulge the names of donors and the amounts. Some churches and temples had to rely on the shady donations in order to complete their new building projects; and the erection of a new church or temple building was undertaken one after another in the twenties as if it were the only right thing for them to do. To them the "bosses" were the ace in hole in pinches, because they could get money easily without any resultant unfavorable publicity.

Secondly, it was very difficult to create public sentiment against the Tokyo Club by any group, religious or political, on account of, first, the geographical distribution of the population. The residences of the Japanese were scattered all over the unrestricted zones of Los Angeles, the Boyle Heights, "Virgil Street," "Hollywood," "Central Avenue," "Tenth Street," the Lincoln Height, *Seinan-ku*, Sawtelle, etc. Without the aid of newspapers it was impossible to create and unite public opinion. Second, [there was] the new steady influx of Japanese into the city. There was a great inflow of Japanese from other parts of the United States since 1920, especially from Seattle and San Francisco, attracted by the purportedly abundant economic opportunities. The community as a whole assumed the metropolitan attitude of laissez faire and "mind my own business" and did not have the meddlesome "we must do something for our neighbor" attitude of small towns, where everyone knew what everyone else was doing. People [came] to the Tokyo Club to gamble from a wide area from Bakersfield and Santa Barbara in the north to San Diego in the south. Thirdly, the leading business men of Little Tokyo had some business connections either directly or indirectly with the club itself or the club members. And these men were the political leaders of the Japanese colony, occupying the official positions of the Japanese Association of Los Angeles. For instance, Sei Fujii, the legal counselor and newspaper publisher, was at one time the president of the Association for some years. A recent president also was closely connected with the chain and took over its subsidiary, the amusement company, when it was in a legal difficulty in 1939. It was no wonder that the political organization was inactive in gambling crusading.

Lastly, instances of intimidation and physical violence by the "strong men" of the Tokyo Club were whispered among the Japanese. These were enough to frighten away the Japanese from risking their own selves in a crusade, which might bring on reprisals. These will be discussed more in detail later.

Because of these factors, the Tokyo Club in Los Angeles had a clear field to prosperity without meeting any serious opposition for their existence from the community.

From the police, too, the Tokyo Club was free of interference, due to the corruption of public officials. They were buying the "protection" from the police through a well worked-out bribery system. It was more likely to be correct, although variously rumored, to conjecture the amount of bribery to be around two thousand dollars a month. With such an unauthorized permission from the vice squad, the gambling place was free from raids. During the successive administrations of Mayor Porter and Mayor Shaw, the police and the underworld were partners in the intricate understanding so that the Japanese gambling organization had no fear whatsoever of arrests and penal punishments. It was true that during those years a few raids on the establishment were made, but they were of a make believe nature. The vice squad, it was said, tipped off the house in advance of such a raid, and when they did actually break into the place, only a score of men were present in the hall, the gambling paraphernalia having been hidden away. Even though these men were brought before the court after their nominal arrest, they were charged with some minor offense and were freed on small fines. Aside from police "protection," they were doubly cautious in posting a lookout station in the guise of a cigar stand at the street corner several doors away from the building. Its purpose was to signal emergencies such as a raid by some police squad other than that of policemen in the ring.

Thus the force of legal and social sanctions failed with the Tokyo Club in Los Angeles; there was nothing in their way to obstruct them from reaping an enormous profit. Then the question is: how did they make money? What difference was there compared with a gambling place in a Caucasian community?

As it was mentioned in this report previously, various games were operated on the third floor of the Tokyo Club building. Of these blackjack, dice throwing, poker, and faro were the same as those found at Caucasian establishments, while sheeko, gaham, and lottery were seen in Chinese places. The characteristic difference with the Japanese organization, however, was the extensiveness of lottery ticket sale outside of the premise[s]. A man who was taking charge of the lottery department reported that more than four-fifths of the total ticket sale were brought in from streets by their "salesmen." There were usually about five of them, all being Issei beyond fifty years of age, each having his own territory. Three of them were assigned to the Little Tokyo district. They started their rounds every morning about ten o'clock, calling on regular customers in the business town. They also had their "agencies" established in the backrooms of restaurants and soda fountains and called on them at regular intervals on a prearranged time table; the prospective customers had a choice of either waiting for the "salesman" or of leaving their marked tickets [on] the premise[s]. Two other salesmen took care of the wholesale produce districts and the wholesale flower market earlier in the morning while these markets were open for business. All these men reported back to the Tokyo Club at half past one in the afternoon and deposited the tickets with the lottery manager and the cash to the cashier.

At two o'clock sharp the drawing was made and the result was known half an hour later. The "salesman" again walked into the streets with the result sheets and the prizes, if any, and went over the same route which he had visited earlier in the day, giving out the result sheet to each customer and each "agency." In this manner, the interested parties could find out how they lost (more likely than winning) their money. The post mortem discussions were lively among these habitues; their typical expression was, "I could have guessed that the marks would come out this way. Shucks, I missed a chance of making three hundred dollars."

The "salesmen" again early in the evening resumed the same routing for the eight o'clock drawing, and returned to the streets by nine o'clock.

What, then, was the compensation for these lottery ticket sellers? They charged five cents on each dollar from the purchaser and a five percent commission from the house. For an ace salesman in the golden era it was not difficult to sell three hundred dollars' worth of lottery tickets in a day, which meant that his profit was at least thirty-dollars for the day. In addition to these sources of income, they received a bonus from the winners; it was a gambler's ethic to express his appreciation for selling him the lucky ticket by giving the seller a cut of five to ten percent of the winning. The lottery man, then, split this gift fifty-fifty with his "agent" if the ticket happened to be sold at the "agency." This custom might have some connection with their oft expressed statement, "I am lucky if I buy the ticket from so-and-so," or with a superstition that to be generous after a winning is to preserve that good luck. At any rate, the one who failed to show "appreciation" was looked with askance and regarded as a "cheap bum." On the other side of the ledger for the "salesman," there were only those expenses paid for gifts such as sacks of rice, kegs of soy sauce, boxes of noodles, etc., which were sent at frequent intervals to the "agents." Therefore, one could conceive that lottery ticket selling among the Los Angeles Japanese was a very lucrative business, netting the seller several hundred dollars a month. Consequently it resulted in a keen competition to obtain the franchise from the gambling organization, although posting of cash bond was required and the right commanded a high value of royalty. The writer knew two such lottery men who returned to Japan with sizable sums of money after a few years in the business—one of them, according to rumors, with fifty thousand dollars.

"How does a lottery ticket look?" and "What do you do with it?" are the next questions to be taken up. A lottery ticket was about five inches by six inches in size and was made of cheap pulp paper, on the top of which the name of the "company," or brand, appeared. The Tokyo Club of Los Angeles operated four brands, namely, Tokyo, Yokohama, Kobe, and Kyoto. In other words, they had four separate lottery drawings successively according to the brand at each drawing time. The purposes of having the four different brands were to give a wider choice to the buyer in selecting his ticket and to get more varied results of drawings in order to increase one's greedy appetite for gambling. It was a well conceived idea on the part of the gambling syndicate, because it could not only increase the business volume but also could give unfortunate lottery players an outlet of consolation and self-pity that it was not his choice of ideographs to be marked which were at fault but his selection of brand of "company." One could often hear "God damn it! I should have bought Tokyo instead of Kobe. Look! I missed a chance for fifty-five dollars." As the result it was common for many to buy simultaneously tickets of two or more different brands to "safeguard their hunches," especially when they had "lucky dreams." In this case tickets of different brands were marked exactly alike.

Under the name of brand, eighty Chinese ideographs were printed as shown in the following diagram,[3] each brand printed with ink of different colors; specifically, Tokyo in black, Yokohama in red, Kyoto in purple, and Kobe in green. Each ticket also carried a statement, "Ten thousand dollars limit."

A player received a sheet of this lottery ticket from the "salesman" and with a calligraphic brush and ink he blotted black any nine of these ideographs. The habitual players had definite patterns or conceptions as to which nine characters should be marked. For example, some marked the ticket exactly the same every time he bought it; others held the superstition that if one had dreamed of serpents, of fire, or of running river he should mark it in a certain definite pattern, conventional for each dream, to be lucky. The Japanese held a dream of snakes specially as a lucky omen and were willing to wager more money in

3. The diagram mentioned here is missing from the version in the archives.

such a case. The lottery man, then, copied over the markings on another sheet in his presence and handed the copy to the buyer, while retaining the original. The price wagered on each ticket was any multiple sums of thirty-five cents, the minimum being set at one dollar-and-five cents; then, one dollar-and-forty cents, one dollar-and-seventy-five cents, and so on without any limit. To the Japanese a wagering of three dollars-and-a-half was not at all surprising, although one-dollar-and-five-cent tickets were sold most commonly. As the player bet more money, he could win more; the rate of return was calculated so much for each thirty-five cents.

The result was determined by drawings twice a day, as already mentioned. At each drawing time, four separate drawings were made, one for each brand. This was the way the drawing was done: there were eighty square sheets of paper, on each of which one character of the eighty appearing on the lottery ticket was printed, and were placed in a container after they were carefully folded. Out of this container a man picked out twenty pieces, that is, he picked twenty different ideographs. These drawn ideographs were, then, transcribed on lottery sheets by perforating; in other words, the Chinese characters which represented those drawn out of the container were punched out of the sheets. These were called *do gami* or result sheets.

In order to explain how the wagers were rewarded, let us assume that you hold a ticket and paid one dollar-and-five-cents for it. You take out the copy of your marking and compare it with the result sheet. In case you find any four of your nine marks correspond with four of those twenty characters punched out of the result sheet, you are paid forty-five cents, if five, six dollars-and-fifteen cents; if six, fifty-five dollars and some odd cents; if seven, three hundred-and-forty-five dollars; if eight, one thousand and some dollars; if nine, the limit of ten thousand dollars. (The last two figures never need to be verified). However, you need not worry about how to get your winning money if you have hit better than "six marks," because the lottery ticket man will most probably be looking around the town for you so that he will be given a "cut" and will try to make you buy more tickets.

What were the chances of winning? One or two examples will suffice to explain that the chances were slim and the lottery ticket was a one-sided business all in favor of the house. One Issei said, "I have been buying a one-dollar ticket every day for the last two years, but so far I got back fifty-five dollars twice and six dollars not more than ten times. You would ask why I buy them then, if I knew I would lose the money. Well, it's a habit. Every time I see a lottery man, I feel positive that I will hit it this time. I get an urge from inside of me that I have a good hunch. This is more so when I dream. I follow up the dream for many days thinking 'perhaps.' Yeah, when I gave up and changed the marking, the marks came out. You often hear people say, 'So and so got one thousand dollars' or 'He's gotten six spots.' Yeah, but, you should ask those guys how much they have lost so far. Now, you would ask why I don't quit. It got into my blood and it's no use to tell me to quit."

Another man said, "I quit the lottery. I don't know how much money I have spent, I bet it's more than five hundred dollars. And only thing I got out of it was one fifty-five-dollar win and several six-dollar ones. You bet, it was hard to quit. Now I buy them only when I had good dreams." It is interesting to note that although he claimed that he had gotten rid of the habit, he was still buying tickets occasionally when he had hunches from his dreams. The tie-up of dreams and the lottery among the Japanese. A great many Japanese held the belief that dreams are never-to-be-missed guidance in the lottery ticket marking. Common were those expressions such as "I must buy a lottery ticket today, because I dreamt of snakes last night," and "I had a dream last night, I am going to Los Angeles to buy a ticket." To these men, it was no hindrance to travel, say twenty miles from Terminal Island to Los Angeles.

About 1933, the Tokyo Club instituted another game, on the same order of lottery, to appeal to the greed of the general public. This was called *Tomikuji*, or "Lucky Lot," working on the same principle of "Bank Night." They sold an artistically designed card, each bearing a number, for one dollar. The card buyer was registered and his name was recorded with the syndicate. On this card the rules were printed together with the date of drawing—twice a year, one in the spring and the other in the fall. The highest prize was cash of ten thousand dollars; the second was two thousand dollars, and so forth down to five-dollar prizes. There were approximately two hundred prizes in all.

As usual agencies were established and salesmen were sent out all over Southern California. And the success of the "sales" campaign was phenomenal due to the novelty of the game and the then economic unrest among the Japanese. The people reported and believed that, for the first Tomikuji, the syndicate sold at least fifty thousand tickets before the lot drawing time and their net earning was calculated to be around fifteen to twenty thousand dollars.

One day in November of that year the drawing of the first Tomikuji was held pretentiously in Yamato Hall before the general public which filled the hall to capacity. On the stage there was a huge glass container which held small number-containing capsules. After the container had been spun and rotated, a kimono clad girl took out the capsules one by one and handed them over to the judges, who were the representatives from the local vernacular newspapers. The judges then opened the capsules and announced the numbers contained in them amid cheers and groans of the crowd. Within a few hours after the final number had been drawn from the container, the prize-winning numbers were printed and dispatched throughout the territory. The Japanese newspapers of that evening also carried large advertisements by the syndicate informing the readers that the lot had been drawn and the reports announcing the winning numbers were being distributed; in this connection it should be noted that they carefully avoided to announce the numbers in the advertisements, since it was a flagrant violation of the postal regulation, although they dared to print that the lot drawing had been made.

The second Tomikuji cards were sold again in the next spring for the drawing in May of 1934. And there were a few more drawings in subsequent seasons. As the Tomikuji sale was repeated, the interest of the public gradually waned; the decreased public interest resulted toward the end in failure to pay the advertised prize of ten thousand dollars. The first prize at one time was a little over eight thousand dollars and that at later time was something like six thousand dollars. Meanwhile, there were several instances that the Tomikuji salesmen were arrested, mostly in the outlying towns, while selling the cards. There was one arrest which the writer witnessed in Long Beach in 1935—a man who had come all the way from Los Angeles was selling the tickets to the Japanese operators of the stalls in the Municipal Market. He was apprehended by a detective in the act of selling and was taken to the city jail. Afterwards, it was said that the man was fined heavily in court and the fine was paid by the Tokyo Club interest.

Although the exact reason has never been revealed, the sale of Tomikuji was suspended entirely in 1936 never to be revived. There were many conjectures by the public as to the discontinuance of the lot drawing. Although there were "tall" stories circulated in the community, any one of the following explanations or a combination of them was more plausible and nearer to the truth: (1) decline of public interest in Tomikuji; hence, decrease in the sales volume; (2) although they were considerably free from police interference in the city of Los Angeles, they experienced a great deal of difficulty with the law enforcement agencies of other towns. This was understandable because there were no "agreements" between the syndicate and the law officers of other towns. As the sales dropped in the city proper, they had to depend more and more upon the "clients" in the outlying districts, which eventually extended as far north as Fresno and Sacramento; (3) fear of complication with postal regulations; (4) the enormous overhead—the prize cashes, the commissions to the salesmen, etc.—was too great in proportion to the net return to the house. They were operating more profitable games.

Indeed, the Tokyo Club of Los Angeles built a tremendous business in a score of years; in retrospect, however, its history reveals more than its share of struggles to sustain the gigantic business in full swing and to preserve the monopoly of gambling and entertainments in the Japanese community. About 1920, the chain was still in a disorganized stage; its headquarters had just moved from San Francisco to Los Angeles, whence the center of the Japanese population was shifting and where the business was increasing at a surprising rate. With this move one Itani was chosen as the president of the Tokyo Club of Los Angeles and with it carried the title of the president of the entire Tokyo Club syndicate, all inclusive of Beikoku Kogyo Kaisha and the Tokyo Clubs scattered all over the west coast. Befitting the great responsibility and the broad scope of the activity the duty required, this man was of an exceptional executive ability with forcefulness and resourcefulness. As soon as he assumed the office he began the work of consolidating and unifying in one central organization in Los Angeles as the cog and the absolute authority all its holdings and subsidiaries, which had been independently operated and loosely coordinated. He instituted the system of sending out from headquarters a supervisor and an auditor periodically to examine the business activities and records of each branch. He exercised the appointive power vested in him to the full extent, recalling inefficient or corrupt branch employees and substituting them with men of better ability who had been trained at the head office. In cases of insubordination and disobedience he was severe in meeting out the penalty; he sent out his gang of powerful burly men to take care of these rebels in the Chicago gangland manner. In most cases the disciplinary measure stopped at just beating, although some of them were so severely beaten to require hospitalization. In two or three extreme cases, so the grapevine reported, men were actually murdered and their bodies were disposed of so well that even the police detection failed.

In attempts to establish competition to the Tokyo Club activities the men who dared to defy the powerful organization were treated in the same manner. They met the same fate as the balking employees at the hands of gangsters. These drastic actions, in turn, had self-accentuating effect in curbing or stamping out any future attempt at revolt or of competition, since the tales of the use of force and violence agreed with the taste and satisfied the appetite of sensation-loving Japanese. Many stories of punishments were told and retold, and magnified and exaggerated, and again told and retold.

The gangland technique was successful in establishing and maintaining order within the ranks and files of the organization; the attendant publicity, if not actual application, was effective in maintaining and preserving the monopolistic control in the Japanese gambling and amusement fields. It was so effective that the policy was inherited by the succeeding presidents of the syndicate after Itani retired with a reputed bonus of a quarter of a million dollars and returned to Japan to live the rest of his life luxuriously.[13] The despotic, ruthless policy, however, at the end worked as a boomerang on the organization bring[ing] about its own downfall. Inasmuch as the application of violence in perpetuating its own business was instrumental in creating fear and dread toward the Tokyo Club syndicate and their members among the Japanese in California, a few of such instances as told by the men of the street are recorded in the following paragraphs.

In the early years there were minor beating cases, which were in general confined to disobedient employees and disorderly customers; the club was more concerned and occupied with keeping order within the house itself. One heard that a man was thrown out of the hall of the third floor of the Tokyo Club building in a battered condition, or that the boss of the Lodi branch was deposed of his office after his life had been threatened, or that an employee in the Sacramento house was severely banged up. There was a story of a little more severe case told in the Los Angeles community. It was in 1927—one employee was chided by a gang of henchmen for an insubordinate act, but he was arrogant and talked back. Incensed by his sullen attitude, the gang beat him, but due to concussion of the brain or heart failure the victim who had been felled on the floor could not be revived. Perturbed as to the disposal of the body, the assailants finally decided to carry it in an automobile and sped through the darkness of night. They chose a cliff on the Palos Verdes Hill[14] as the most desirable of all places for the purpose in the vicinity, whence the body was thrown into the Pacific Ocean with a heavy weight attached. It was ironical in that they had chosen the place, albeit unintentional, because within miles of the cliff there were no other residents but Japanese families raising vegetables. This tale fanned out from these farmers and through the grapevines was known to the Japanese community within a short time; in effect, it increased the fear held by the Japanese toward the Club people, having been convinced more than ever that they "meant business" and their order was accompanied with "or else."

After the collapse of the Hoover prosperity, it was more evident that many "big time" games incompatible with the Tokyo Club activities were on the increase and required more attention by the Tokyo Club "goon squad." The case of pin-ball games at the corner drugstore, which has been reported, is a typical example. Several poker games for big stakes which were going on in the backrooms of restaurants were intimidated and busted up. The writer observed one such case one day after midnight in front of a Japanese restaurant in Little Tokyo. As the players came into the street from the place, where it was known that a big stake poker session was operated frequently, three burly men appeared from nowhere in the darkness. It was obvious that they were waylaying them. They approached one of the players and gripped his coat lapels in jujitsu style. One of the waylayers said, "You know what's good for you. Quit the game." The victim was not freed until he had said apologetically, "I am awfully sorry. I won't do it again."

The same procedure was repeated with the next group of men coming out of the house within a few minutes. Within a few days afterward it was heard that the games at the place ceased to exist and even when it was resumed at a much later date it was for small stakes.

A similar case occurred in 1934 involving a man by the name of Kensaku Nadaoka,[15] who attempted to sell sweepstakes tickets competing with Tomikuji. This man Nadaoka was the manager of a jobbing house, which held the exclusive agency right for the Japanese territory of the Lucky Lager beer and the sole agency contract for the continental United States of certain brands of sake manufactured in Hawaii. Some years previously he had been a newspaper man for the *Rafu Nichibei*, then a seller of some patented therapeutical gadget. He was a sly, shrewd business man, who tried to manipulate capital belonging to some one else and made profits for himself. He was keen and ambitious in seizing any money-making opportunity, although shiftless and impatient. He always dreamed of a get-rich-quick scheme, since he spent more money than he earned. No doubt he had observed the phenomenal sales of Tomikuji and was envious. He searched for a similar scheme and perchance hit upon the sweepstakes tickets sold by a New York underworld organization. He immediately obtained the exclusive concession for the sale in the Japanese community from the Eastern firm and undertook a sales campaign with extensive newspaper advertisements, giving it a Japanese name *Takara Sagashi* or "Treasure

Hunt." Within a month, however, he was visited by the *Teppo Gumi*[16] of the Tokyo Club. When he was told to suspend selling of his tickets as they were incompatible with the policy of the Tokyo Club, he argued back that inasmuch as his tickets were issued by a Caucasian organization and the Tokyo Club did not control the Caucasian underworld, he has no reason to discard his scheme. His reasoning, needless to say, could not convince the gangsters and he was severely beaten in the presence of a few employees who were standing by helplessly. The bystanders could not do anything to aid the manager who was lying on the floor unconscious until the gangsters had left the premise[s]. He was immediately taken to a hospital and the next day the capitalist and owner of the firm went to the Tokyo Club headquarters with a gift—a case of sake—to apologize for the "insolent act" of his manager and pledged that they would no longer sell the sweepstakes tickets to jeopardize the prosperity of Tomikuji.

As it has been stated, the maintenance of law and order among the rank and file of the syndicate was successfully administered by the masterful strokes of the first president, Itani. Subsequent to his retirement, the great prosperity and prestige became a source and a factor contributing toward the increase of jealousy and discontent among themselves. The succeeding presidents, who were weaker and less endowed, often had difficulty in coping with insubordination or of rivalry between the employees. The second president, one Yasuda, was being criticized in his back that he was too anxious to amass a fortune for his own personal gain. He was accused of favoritism, patronizing one faction at the expense of another. He was suspected of diverting the money belonging rightfully to the cache of the organization into his personal fund. The discontented elements aligned themselves with the man next highest in command in the hierarchy and the rivalry between the two factions was intensified. One day in 1929 it reached the breaking point; a delegation from the hostile faction demanded the resignation of the president face to face and was refused. A short time afterwards, the newspapers carried the news that Yasuda was murdered with pistol shots by unknown assailants in front of his residence. Beyond the casual reporting, the papers in unison minimized the news[,] confining themselves only to the facts directly pertaining to the murder itself; none of them mentioned the background of the victim or the probable motives behind the murder. The homicide squad made routine examinations and reported the clues were scant. There were no suspects apprehended in so far as public knowledge was concerned, and police detection utterly failed. Meanwhile, the funeral for Yasuda was the most elaborate and ornate in the history of the Los Angeles Japanese colony; every notable, dignitary, leading business man, and politicians of the colony were eager to express his condolence to the bereaved family. Within a few days after the funeral the murder news disappeared completely from the pages of newspapers as if it had been forgotten. One could accuse also that the detectives lacked zeal and enthusiasm to solve the mystery, which to this day remains as an unsolved crime in the annals of the police department. In contrast, however, stories of the murder were circulated in the community for weeks and weeks unabated with fervor. These stories in general agreed that Yasuda was murdered by the "trigger men" of the rival faction within his own organization. He had a premonition of his imminent danger and had a bodyguard with him, but this precaution was useless because the bodyguard himself belonged to the enemy camp and was instrumental in bringing his master into the prearranged trap. Another version went as far as to say that the police had been paid off heavily and it was absurd to anticipate the arrest of the assassins. Incidentally, in the ensuing years, the body guard, George Yamato, who had double-crossed his employer, was receiving compensation regularly from the house without performing any noticeable service.

In 1930 another man, Oku, the boss of the San Francisco branch, was murdered by unknown attackers, who were never detected by the police. Again the vernacular papers failed to report the murder in detail, to which the curious public had no access save through the grapevine. According to information offered by laymen, the murder was a repercussion of Yasuda's. Oku was a staunch enemy of Yasuda and was one of the behind-the-scene men who schemed and arranged his murder. After the event he was discontented and dissatisfied because one Yamawaki was elected to the presidency, for which he had held a secret ambition. Oku's subsequent uncooperative attitude made the position of the men in power precarious, since they had once been the partners in one crime. The murder was accomplished in order to seal the mouth of the insurgent and to eliminate any chance of downfall of the in-group.

Murders of members were the extreme measure of discipline the Tokyo Club resorted to. They were usually more tolerant of violation by a member of their special code of conduct and meted out much milder punishments.

In 1933, a certain Iwanami, a cashier, was charged with tampering with the account books and embezzling the Club fund. In this case, the offender was presented with a gift of a few hundred dollars and was ordered to leave for Japan.

In the same year, there was a more interesting case concerning an employee—one Isobe. He was a "bouncer," about 30 years of age. He was a son of a Shinto priest. A few years previously he had fallen in love with a Nisei prostitute and since then had been living with her without marital status. In the course of time, a child was born between them. For some reason a rift developed between the two; the man began to stay away from home and the wife was seeing a young Nisei during her husband's working hours. Once it was whispered that she was caught with her paramour and was beaten by her husband; this was followed by another story that they—the wife and the paramour—disappeared from the city leaving the child alone in the home. It was variously reported—some said that they went to Nevada, while others said that they ran away to the East. Speaking from the standard of the syndicate code, Isobe lost "face" in that he had lost his woman to another man and had disgraced the name of the organization. He was given the usual sentence—an order to leave for Japan with a gift of a few hundred dollars. Recently news was brought back from China that he was doing well in Shanghai as a member of the Japanese police force, after he had joined a nationalistic organization of the city which received orders directly from Japan.

With the advent of Fletcher Bowron into the Mayor's office, one of his platforms for election, crusading of vice and the underworld, was undertaken vigorously. With the repeated shake-ups in the police department, inefficient or shady officers were either demoted or transferred to other divisions where they would be of no value to the tie-up with the underworld. As a result, many gambling resorts were raided and closed, and even Guy McAfee[17] had to leave the city to seek a haven in Nevada. The Tokyo Club, too, met more interference from the police and it became increasingly difficult to keep the house open. One night a police squad broke in from the skylight of the hall and arrested a sizable crowd who had no time to seek cover. After this round-up[,] operation was suspended for a long time. When it opened again for business, it was only for a short duration as it was involved in a legal mess from which they could never again disentangle themselves, marking the final blow to the once glorious existence of the Tokyo Club of Los Angeles. This case is called the State of California vs. Yamatoda, et al.[18]

As one old Japanese has philosophized, "Violence brings more violence. Success in use of violence is tempting for one to use more violence again to solve a difficulty. Eventually the user of violence becomes careless and is doomed." The employees of the Tokyo Club one night in 1939 became careless in the use of force upon an obnoxious player.

There was a truck parked on a street in Little Tokyo for days without any trace of having been moved. The police, when notified by some in the neighborhood, traced its owner to one Namba, whose family revealed that he had left his home for Los Angeles with a load of vegetables about two weeks previously and was missing since then. His family was concerned about his failure to return and had been conducting a search among his acquaintances. The family asked the police now for a further search for the missing man, since the news had been known by the public.

Somehow, a story began to go around the town that Namba had been murdered on the third floor of the Tokyo Club building and his body had been disposed of. The police on the tip-off arrested the employees and their grilling finally produced a few confessions as some of them[19] had turned as state witnesses. It was true, they said, that Namba had been murdered, although accidentally, by the Club employees. The trouble started when he had lost in games several hundred dollars and demanded of the house a donation of a few dollars for traveling expense to return home. When he was refused his request, he became vehemently vociferous and pugnacious. In order to quell him and to restore order in the house, a few hired men rushed to him and "ganged up" on him, some with fists, one with an abacus, another with a stick. They had no intention of killing him, they protested.

After they were arraigned for the murder charge in the Superior Court of Los Angeles and while they were awaiting trial on bail, this difficulty bred another trouble. One faction within the chain, which was dissatisfied with and had ill feeling toward the then president, Yamatoda, staged a *coup d'etat.* They kidnapped Yamatoda and took him forcibly across the border into Mexico, although the attempt was frustrated in El Centro and the kidnappers were arrested. These two cases go to show that there no longer existed within the syndicate the unity and harmony which once prevailed; it was, indeed, in a chaotic condition. In due course of time the defendants of both cases were given jail terms, although Yamatoda was successful in "jumping the bail" and escaping to Japan on a tramp freighter.

The remnants of the Tokyo Club made a final desperate attempt in 1940 to reopen the gambling house and were entrapped by the police with whom they were "negotiating" for a term. In this delegation which visited a city hall office, which had been installed with dictaphones, there was one of the leading Nisei attorneys, Carl Iwanaga. Subsequently [he] was disbarred and served sentence for one year after a trial.

At the close of the discussion of the organized gambling activities in the Japanese community the writer wishes to point out again the significance of fear and dread held by the Japanese as a whole toward the Club and its members and resentment toward its abuses although powerless before them. In other words, the Japanese fully realized the evils of the Tokyo Club but were afraid to speak up. They dared to criticize the gambling chain only when they were certain of ample support from the public at large. They were awed and overpowered until the syndicate crumbled from within.

The Post Pearl Harbor Period

December 7, 1941! The Japanese Attack Pearl Harbor!

The world was stunned. The Japanese in California were stupefied. True, these Japanese had had the premonition and wished that it would not happen. It did happen: the Japanese become "enemies" overnight. No longer could they remain aloof of the fast changing world events. Every turn of the events had vital effects on them. Their very existence was threatened; they did not know what was to become of them tomorrow. The foundation of their life—the source of income—was periled. Americans stayed away from the places of business operated by Japanese; Americans terminated the employment of Japanese. Governmental restrictions were promulgated to curtail the personal liberty of the Japanese in several aspects, for the violations of which many arrests were made. The FBI agents combed every corner of the Japanese community for "saboteurs" and "contrabands" which were reported on the front pages of newspapers in bold type with malicious falsification and paranoiac imagination. Public sentiment toward the Japanese in California became worse every day. Rumors flew far and wide among the Japanese. Wild stories went around thick and fast. A Japanese baby was burnt to death in burning oil by incensed whites, one story said. A young woman was assaulted by a gang of hoodlums, another reported. A young Nisei was stabbed in the back by an unknown assailant, still another rumor had it. The Japanese were frightened in full realization that their physical safety, too, was not secure. Their primary concern was what was to become of themselves and their families. Their paramount worry was what was to become of their business and properties.

The war necessitated revolutionary changes in the mode of living for the

Japanese. The anxiety persisted and worry occupied the minds of Japanese every minute of their waking hours. They were concerned only with one thought—their security in the future. In this revolutionalized way of life gambling found no place to exist. The Japanese suddenly dropped the perennial habit of gambling. Gone were the hana games from the boarding houses; gone were the poker games from the backrooms of restaurants. People met in the homes of their friends, not to play hana or poker, but instead to talk about the war, about FBI arrests, about the California Japanese, and about their own future.

It was not until the first contingent of volunteer evacuees left for Manzanar that the Japanese people began to gamble among themselves again. They had realized that the evacuation was something of actuality and resigned to the idea that the foundation which the Japanese immigrants had built in scores of years was to be destroyed completely. They were reconciled to the idea that they were to leave for the "concentration camps." It was also true that the people were out of gainful occupation—some had closed their places of business long ago and others had lost their jobs—since the vernacular newspapers had been advising the people everyday that the mass evacuation might be ordered tomorrow. "Get ready," the papers said, "the army will not wait for you." They had gotten ready, after selling their properties for any price in panic, and waited for the army order. But the evacuation was a slow process to the Japanese and the army order they were awaiting did not come. They all had too much time and did not know what to do with it. Sources of recreation and amusement were denied to them and the curfew restriction compelled them to remain at home. The only things they could think of doing was to gamble—hana and poker games were thus resumed in private homes, although for small stakes. (They had no source of income and were afraid to gamble for bigger stakes.) In effect, the revival of gambling was an escape on one hand and a means of "killing time" on the other hand.

As the evacuation orders began to be announced one after another more rapidly, the Japanese reflected, "How am I to spend time in the camp? I must do something to kill time. I am going to make it a 'vacation.'" Thus the stores in Little Tokyo had a big sudden pick-up in the sale of playing cards, hana cards, sets of go, and of shogi. For instance, a box of hana cards which contained two packs of cards, was originally selling for seventy-five cents, but within about two weeks due to profiteering it was sold for as high as two dollars-and-fifty cents. Even at the exorbitant price the people bought them uncomplainingly. They added laughingly, "It's too high if it's ordinary time. But I can't buy these hana cards after I leave Los Angeles for the assembly center. Maybe I will get the money back in the camp." On the eve of the departure with the army escort the Japanese packed the paraphernalia of go, of shogi, of Mah Jong, of poker, and of hana. They knew then what they were going to do when they arrived at these assembly or relocation centers.

By the end of April, 1942, information was coming out from the Santa Anita Assembly Center that gambling among the camp residents was going on at a furious pace and that most of the Tokyo Club remnants had moved there *en masse.* It was this clique, it revealed, that operated "big time" gambling, involving hundreds and thousands of dollars, and that the Caucasians and Japanese police officers were receiving "hush money." Of this the men who were still awaiting the evacuation order to come commented, "It's the same old story."

At the end of May as the last contingent of evacuees from the county of Los Angeles arrived at the Colorado River War Relocation Center, the situation of gambling that existed there was surprisingly different from what they had heard previously in connection with other assembly centers. Unlike other places there was no regular establishment for the purpose of gambling by the residents of Poston. Whatever gambling was done was confined to only groups of friends and acquaintances; it was done only as a source of recreation. No doubt, many games were going on in different living quarters, but these were played for nominal sums and the games played were limited to hana and poker. It was merely an extension of what they were doing in private homes just prior to the migration. The Poston police, however, had another conception of law enforcement. The police force, then comprised mostly of young men who had reached the majority not long ago, were seen all over the camp carrying crudely made clubs of mesquite tree and proudly showing the arm bands bearing the letter "P." Indeed, they made arrests too, but they were limited to gambling cases. They made raids into the apartments where it was known to have gamblers gathered. In groups of sevens and eights they sneaked up to these quarters and broke in through the unlocked doors. The participants, having been taken by surprise, had no time to hide their money or cards and were caught flat-footed. They were then led into the police truck and were taken to the city jail, a twenty feet by twenty-five feet apartment in back of the police station, whose address was Block 28, Barrack 1, Apartment A. These raids were not confined to evenings or nights; they were conducted even during the daylight hours. The men who were taken to the jail stayed there overnight and were freed the next day without trial, as there was no machinery to conduct such a trial. It is significant to add that these men were almost always old Issei, who were charged with playing hana games, and Nisei were seldom detained.

The Nisei were known to be playing poker here and there in the camp just as much and as frequently as Issei's hana, but they were clever to play the games unnoticeably in the evenings. Even though these places were raided, the police were satisfied with merely breaking the party up without making the arrests. The writer observed one of these raids one night, sometime in June of 1942. A group of young Nisei bachelors made it a habit to get together in the evenings in their apartment in Block 45. It was going on for about two weeks until that night. About eleven o'clock six policemen came through the door, which was unlocked, with clubs swinging in their hands. The boys were caught playing. One of the policemen said authoritatively, "Break it up, boys! Break it up!"; the rest of them stood behind this spokesman watching for any emergency. The players collected the chips and cards scattered on the table in silence. As soon as the table had been cleared of the paraphernalia, the spokesman again commanded, "Don't let us catch you again. The next time it means the can," and with the rest left the apartment. For days afterward the boys argued how "the police got wise" to their game. "I bet some Issei joy killers tipped the police," some said, while others contradicted, "No, the police just got the wind of it." Whatever the source of information might have been, it was successful in discontinuing their games for the next two or three months until sometime before the November disturbance.

This was the typical method by which poker games of Nisei were curbed by the police, who refused to take Nisei offenders to the jail. However, in extreme cases in which young men failed to heed and kept on with their playing defiantly, more stringent measures were taken. In one case on the second raid to the same apartment within a week, the raiding squad was headed by Chief of Police Shimada [a pseudonym], a burly six feet two, two hundred pounder. The chief walked into the apartment and found the same gang of young boys playing poker as usual. The chief chided the boys for not heeding the police order and told them to quit for good. It seems that some of the boys talked back arrogantly and insolently as most Poston boys would do. The quick-tempered Shimada, it was told by one of the police later, did not wait another moment and swung his fist into the face of this boy and knocked him on the floor. He then hit two other boys and repeated the routine. "He sure beat the hell out of them," the reporter said, "Chief then said to them, 'You know what's good for you. If I were you, I would remember this.' And we had no trouble from these boys since then."

About this time, the religious workers were alarmed over the gambling condition which was on the upward trend. In order to combat the evil they met several times to discuss feasible countermeasures. The Christian workers and the Buddhist priests met together and decided to endeavor for the cause hand in hand. They made it the subject of their sermons. They issued circulars and distributed them to the residents, which in substance said that gambling was observed all over Poston. "It is increasing everyday; it has become alarmingly grave. Should it remain unchecked, we fear its evil influence upon our young people. No right thinking men can remain aloof any longer. We, therefore, solicit your full hearted cooperation in our earnest effort to curb this evil."

The paper was delivered to every block and then to each apartment, but the reaction of readers was lukewarm in contrast to the serious tone of the statement. Some commented, "Those are small games. They aren't so bad. Let them enjoy themselves; after all we are vacationing here." "They are harmless," others said. Still others said, "We don't want to be involved. Let those church people fight it. It's their business." Another comment was, "It's too hot even to be thinking of such a thing." Many were non-committant and sitting back quietly, and it was only a handful of people who rallied to the cause. To the appeal of the religious groups the Poston people were passive and undisturbed, if not contrary minded.

Meanwhile, reflecting such contrary sentiment of the people, the police department received a protest from some block managers that the police should notify them of intended raids, reasoning that the full authority of the managers over the block residents must be respected. The argument was that the managers would lose "face" if the raids were carried out without their knowledge. True, the reason of the block managers was far fetched, but it only goes to prove that they were hard pressed by the residents' complaints against the police raids of these games. To this the police department was furious and argued their own points, and the bickerings went on for some time between them without any result and to fade away eventually.

The Temporary Community Council of Poston, too, was cognizant of the gambling situation. Soon after the legislative body was elected by the residents of Poston, it created the Judicial Committee within itself, headed by Seiichi Sumida.[20] The first task of the committee was drafting of the penal code for Poston in order to organize a trial court, the Municipal Court, and to define offenses and their punishments. "Those criminals shouldn't be turned loose after staying in the jail overnight without trial. You have to put teeth in the arrests," Sumida said about that time. There were many crimes committed in Poston everyday which required attention by a judicial body, let alone those gambling offenses. The drafting of the penal code was immediately undertaken by the committee in consultation with the Project Attorney, Ted Haas, and the Legal Department. According to Sumida, they copied the sections which they believed were vital in preserving law and order in the community from the Penal Code of the State of California, "taking out what we want" and modifying the word[s] and the penalties to be adaptable to the existing conditions at Poston. Upon examination of the final draft of the Poston code, a casual observer would receive an impression that the committee had a preconceived conception as to what offenses were to be included in the code book, because, after all, the California code book of several hundred pages was condensed and abridged into sixteen typewritten pages. The Poston code confined itself only to the cases of gambling, of assault and battery, of theft and embezzlement, of forgery and extortion, of intoxication, and of prostitution and other sex crimes. It is very significant that the final draft begins with the sections on gambling on its very first page, indicating where the utmost concern of the committee had been and how much they were worried about gambling in the future. The grave concern on the part of the committee about the gambling offenses is conceivable and understandable as Sumida, the chairman, had been the legal counselor and one of the officers of the Tokyo Club chain for more than ten years and was well versed in their evils and abuses. The sections pertaining to gambling in the code of offenses for Poston in its final draft read as follows:

> Section 1. *Gambling.* Every person who shall deal, carry on, or open, or cause to be opened, or who shall conduct, either as owner, proprietor or employee, whether for hire or not, any game of faro, monte, roulette, lasquenet, rouge et noir, rondo, vingtun, or twenty-one, poker, stud-poker, draw poker, bluff, fan tan, thaw, seven and one-half, chuck-a-luck, blackjack, "panginki," mah jong, or any similar game whatsoever, played with cards, dice, or any other device, and every slot machine, punch-board, or machine of like character, whether the same be played for money, checks, credits or any other representative of value within the state of Arizona; and every person who shall participate in any of the above enumerated games dealt, carried on or opened or caused to be opened by any other person in the state of Arizona; shall be guilty of misdemeanor, and upon conviction thereof, is punishable by a fine of not less than one hundred dollars

($100) not more than three hundred dollars ($300), or by imprisonment for not more than six (6) months or both such fine and imprisonment.

Section 1a. *Permitting Gambling in House.* Every person who knowingly permits any of the games mentioned in Section 1 of this code to be played, conducted, or dealt in any house occupied by such person, is punishable as provided in the preceding section.

As a sidelight, the reader may be interested in the following incident. The Judicial Committee, upon completion of the final draft, sent it to the Bureau of Sociological Research, which the Administration regarded highly then and of which Ted Haas was a staunch supporter,[21] for their advice and recommendation. In compliance with this request Dr. A. H. Leighton and Dr. E. Spicer sent a memorandum recommending the committee to delete the sections pertaining to gambling and prostitution.[22] The reason, in Dr. Leighton's own words, was, "There isn't any use in having laws which you know you can't enforce. The people will be violating them anyway; this reduces their respect toward the entire code." According to Sumida, "Dr. Leighton recommended no restriction whatsoever on gambling and advocated the French system for prostitution. If you take those sections out of the code, there's nothing left." Sumida chucked the Bureau recommendations into the waste-basket and sent it unchanged to Ted Haas, who at the time was attending a WRA regional conference in San Francisco, for final approval. "Well, Dr. Provinse[23] saw the draft there and praised that the Poston code is the best among all the codes submitted by the relocation centers," Sumida boasted in his typical Hawaiian accent. "The Code of Offenses for Poston" was duly approved by the Project Attorney, and later by the Temporary Community Council. The Chairman of the committee since then refers to Dr. Leighton and Dr. Spicer as "those broad minded an-thro-polo-gists."

When the same topic was mentioned by Sumida to a group of his friends some weeks later, one of the listeners said, "Why didn't you recommend to Dr. Leighton to hire one of the wards in the hospital to practice the French system. Well, say, station an examining doctor at the entrance and to install a ticket selling booth as it might be a land-office business. And tell him to get a few girls for nineteen bucks a month." Sumida laughingly retorted, "Yeah! The whole trouble is Dr. Leighton might do it."

In August the machinery of judicial organization was set in motion; the Judicial Committee members were appointed by the Council to become the judges of the Municipal Court of Poston. The first judges were Seiichi Sumida of Block 45, George Imamura of Block 6, and George S. Fujii of Block 28, all being Council members representing their respective blocks. The very first case that came before the court was that of traffic violation[,] then of hana gambling, and so forth. With traffic violations, the judges gave suspended sentences with a proviso to report weekly to the police department for a certain length of time. With the gambling cases the judges meted out suspended sentences also, the heaviest penalty being "three days suspended." This was indicative of the fact that the police was arresting just the small time gamblers only and not that there was no gambling of bigger scale in Poston at that time. It was not until fifty cases had been disposed of by the judge that a more serious case came up before them—and this was not of gambling, but a case of private profiteering. It is ironical to point out that the Municipal Court held its sessions in the City Jail and this practice is still continued at present, although one of the present judges abhors the practice.

Although the gambling cases brought before the court were of a minor nature, it could not be said that there was no "big time" gambling in Poston. About the time the court began to function a story was going around the camp that big gambling was going on day and night in Barrack 13 of Block 54.[24] Barrack 13 was a building where male bachelors were housed, and Block 54 was occupied by the evacuees from Imperial Valley. Upon questioning, a resident of the Block said, "Yeah, there's big gambling going on in that barrack. What they are playing is 'gaham' and they are betting one hundred and two hundred like nothing. I saw it. I wonder where they got that much money. The guys playing out there are all Issei, most of them from some other blocks. They tell me that some former Tokyo Club big shots of the Valley, who are residing in the northeastern section of the camp, are behind this game. They are playing it in the professional way, charging the house-take."

"Why don't you people do something about it?" he was asked.

"We are kind of scared. Those guys are tough. We don't want to stick our neck out, though the block people are talking resentfully about it."

In September the rumor was rife that the police chief, Shimada, was flashing five dollar bills and buying the men in his department ice cream and cigarettes. They said, "He is getting the money from the Block 54 guys."

Simultaneously with this story, the camp residents were told of beatings of boys, who had been accused of being *inu* [literally, "dogs"] and FBI informers. It was no wonder that the Block 54 residents were afraid of either informing the police of the gambling house or actually taking the leadership to curb it themselves.

The beatings did not stop just with frightening the block people from any active attempt for prevention of gambling; they also had a great effect upon the police force. Sensing the increasing political power of the Issei and the gravely threatened unrest in the camp, the police became reluctant in making arrests[,] resulting in a rapid decrease in the number of cases brought before the Municipal Court. The laxity of the police in the law enforcement resulted in the further increase of gambling all over the camp. It was at this time that the Block 45 boys, who had been warned and ceased playing, resumed their games. In almost all the mess-halls the crews were seen playing hana games much more publicly than before.

The beatings of "inu" continued and the wave of gambling remained unchecked.

Then, November 18th [1942; i.e., the date of the Poston strike]. It was a *coup-d'etat* staged by the Issei extremists and the Issei-ish Nisei. They began to demonstrate in front of the police station and the jail for the release of two attackers of the alleged FBI informers. The original crowd numbered about 1,000, but it increased rapidly as the time went on without a concession from the authority. The demonstration continued for days and nights undiminished in its fervor.

When the difficulty between the administration and the administered was settled after a few days' wrangling, it proved one thing conclusively among many others—the police were powerless, without courage, and sensitive to the dictates of extremists. In other words, they always "checked which way the wind was blowing" before they would undertake anything.

The respect of the residents toward the police waned, and in the same proportion gambling games were observable more conspicuously and the players were more brazen. Reports were coming in from the school teachers that Nisei school boys were gathering in many places and were gambling without attending classes. The Community Enterprises reported that their stores were broken in by thieves on several different occasions. They also added that some of their employees, the younger ones, were suspected of pocketing sales money while the stores were crowded with purchasers. One of the Community Enterprises officials lamented, "It's always young kids, who break into the stores or do stealing. The other night, they got into the main canteen[25] and stole a gold wrist watch worth forty dollars and cartons of cigarettes. Oh, those shop liftings are nothing unusual at all; gangs of boys come in and walk out with merchandise—you watch them next time, one or two of the gang occupy the clerk's attention and the rest swipe the goods. We can't catch them, because we are always busy and short-handed and the store itself is a make-shift affair.

Those kids need money to gamble. And they lose and need more money, so they have to steal some more."

The residents in the northeastern section were telling in January of 1943 that there was a gambling place in Block 3[26] and "their games are sure big." They said that "gaham" was the game and it was run by the same people who operated the Block 54 place. The operation at this new place was so prosperous that they were serving the customers refreshments and drinks of whiskey free of charge. Another rumor had it that similar gambling places were found in the adjoining blocks, Block 4 and Block 14.

Rumors were going around the camp thick and fast. The stories of gambling were lively subjects for the men in idle minutes. Now the tale of the bribing of the police chief had new twists. One of them said, "It's no trouble to buy Shimada. He is making a big business for himself." Another said, "Some of the police force are grumbling, because the chief won't give them enough cut." Another reported, "Shimada and those old Tokyo Club people are inseparably connected. They are both making lots of money." It was the same situation again—the tie-up between gambling interests and the police[,] and the community being reluctant to do anything to curb the evil. It was also true that no one in the camp doubted that Shimada was being bribed regularly or did he minimize the consequences should the Tokyo Club remnants once establish themselves at Poston; but none of the evacuees was willing to take the initiative. Indeed, they were more than willing to gossip about the resultant evils of gambling and the crimes directly affiliated with gambling in the camp; yet they had an attitude either of *laissez faire* or of "let George do it." In order to convey the grave condition which existed since the beginning of 1943, a few instances are cited in the following paragraphs.

Judge Sumida revealed the young Nisei were losing their government or garnishing factory checks in a single night to these professionals in Block 3. As the residents had considerable difficulty in cashing their checks and the house was too glad to do the service, many went there for cashing of their checks, but only to be attracted into gambling themselves. He commented, "Too bad. They lose one month's wages in one night. Those young kids haven't got a chance with the Club guys." This comment truly is from the man who should know.

The Block 3 organization build a new place for gambling within the block. They dug a basement below two adjoining apartments, about 8 feet deep, made of concrete walls supported by wood beams. It was also installed with electric lights. This was an ultra-luxurious palace for Poston and the building materials were obtained free of charge in the typical Poston manner—stolen government properties "leased for the duration."

At the time of the fiasco between The Central Executive Board and The Issei Advisory Board in the beginning of February, the standard bearer of one camp, M. Nagai, sought support from the gambling interests. One of the "professional gamblers" from Los Angeles, one Nakashima, was after N. Mizushima, the leader of Nagai's opposing camp, and broadcast a story himself that he and his gang would beat Mizushima should he not abandon his ill-thought scheme to *coup-d'etat* the Central Executive Board. This story was enough to intimidate the Issei Board vice-chairman and was responsible for his face-about in his ambition.

Games for stakes were prevalent in the Police Department, the Fire Department, and the warehouses.

Those houses in Block 4 and Block 14 wanted cement for their walls, too; and some connected with them went over to the Elementary School Adobe Building Project and stole twenty sacks of cement "in the presence of nightwatchmen" during one night. The next morning the building crew were without cement for their concrete mixer and had to suspend the work for the day until a new load was obtained.

One of the nightwatchmen complained, "When those people come in a gang, you can't do anything. We look the other way and let them steal. Being a Japanese myself, I don't want to arrest fellow Japanese and prosecute them." Indeed, he would not admit that he was afraid.

A rumor—"Chief Shimada is drinking whiskey a bottle a day. And you can't buy it for less than nine dollars in the camp, you know."

The situation of gambling took a sudden and more grave turn in March. Here are the stories which were most rife in Poston Unit I at the time; all those stories were verified to some extent, but the authenticity to the last detail is not vouchsafed.

This is the story of a boy from Los Angeles, who was a juvenile delinquent even before the evacuation. He is a son of the principal of the First Japanese Language School (*Dai Ichi Gakuen*) of Los Angeles, K. S., who was interned on December 7, 1941, and now detained in Camp Livingston, Louisiana. He came to Poston with his mother and is now residing in Block 26, the Orange County section. He is about nineteen years old; he quit going to school some years ago without graduating. This boy, "Junji," was the leader of a gang of teen age boys—some out of school and others still of school age. He and the gang boys were gathering in one room of the Block 26 Recreating Hall and were gambling for money every day from morning to late at night. These young people could not be satisfied completely with their own recreation among themselves and became obnoxious to the residents at large. They were getting rowdy and "corner boyish" in their behavior day-by-day. One day, in the classroom of the elementary school next to their assembly room a teacher was having a geography lesson. The teacher said to the pupils, "What city is the capital of Illinois?" Before the pupils had time to answer, the gambling boys across the thin partitioning wall shouted, "Chicago." Shameless they were, because they did not realize that they had made a mistake in geography, let alone obstructing the teacher.

The teacher, an old Caucasian woman, was evidently perturbed by the boys and came over to the wall between the rooms and banging on it shouted, "Stop it! Boys! Stop it!" To this earnest appeal the only response from the other side was wild bangings on the wall.

The teacher was incensed and reported the incident to the Department of Education, which in turn sent an urgent appeal to the manager of Block 26. Manager Morimoto realized that he was powerless to undertake anything all by himself and called an emergency meeting of the block council, composed generally of the yushi of the block. As the minds of Issei would work in such a case, the yushi did not desire to publicize the case or to publicly shame the boy "for the sake of his future." Instead, they chose delegates who went over quietly to his mother and informed her of her boy's activity. The mother's answer was again typical of an old Issei woman; she refused to accept the wrong doing of her boy as gospel truth. Perhaps she did not wish to lose "face" in front of the delegate. She said defiantly, "My boy? My son, of all persons! I can't believe it. It isn't true. It can't be true for my son." It is only she who knew whether she had spoken her real mind or had subterfuged to cover up her own embarrassment.

When the delegates reported back to the block council, they were angry, "With our utmost kindness and sincerity we spoke to her. She does not accept our unselfish motive. Now we must push the case to the limit."[27] The council members with the block manager, after a lengthy discussion, decided to pass and promulgate a block rule to the effect that no gambling within the block would be tolerated and the room in the Recreating Hall should be cleaned of delinquent boys. As often the case with those block meetings, there was an old man who strenuously and stubbornly objected to the passing of this rule. His argument was, "This is an extreme measure. I can't believe it of Mr. S.'s son. Even if it were true, it is not entirely his fault; it must be the influence of the boys with whom he associates. We don't know for sure that the boy is really involved with the boys in the room; we don't have evidence to substantiate it. If we pass this rule, it means that we are publicly accusing the boy and his mother without conclusive evidence. Besides, his father is a great educator, who has contributed toward the well-being of our offsprings. We cannot defame the great name of his father." No doubt, the advocate of the dissenting opinion was a friend of S. His stubbornness and insistence further angered the rest. The meeting finally ended with the resignation of the block manager and the members of the council *en masse.* They said indignantly, "Hell! If you must insist on contradicting our idea, alone[,] which the rest of us have agreed unitedly, we quit. You take over and handle the situation yourself then." This old man took over the duty of the block manager's office for his pride and from defiance.

In April the "corner boys" somehow moved their place of activity to the neighboring block, Block 27.

Incidentally, the S. boy was accused of living with a young unmarried girl whose parents are in the Heart Mountain Relocation Center and who was suspected of running away from her parents just prior to the evacuation deadline. Of this, his mother says, "There is nothing wrong between the two. We are just taking care of the girl." Of this Judge Sumida had an entirely different interpretation, "'Just taking care of the girl?' Hell! When a young boy lives with a girl in a same room what do you have? Why don't they get married and get it over with?" What the judge was accusing was that the boy was violating the sections of the Poston Code of Offenses pertaining to illicit cohabitation and fornication.

Speaking of the block manager, he is working now for the Community Enterprises as a cashier. Recently he remarked, "Boy! I am glad I am not the block manager anymore. There are lots of troubles in the block yet. Those Issei sure don't know what they want to do." (The source of this information—Manager Morimoto, Judge Sumida, and a resident of Block 26.)

Rumor—"Sumida is splitting the bribery money with Chief Shimada." (The writer has complete faith in Sumida's honesty and integrity, and cannot believe this story to be true.)

This is another story of the boy of an internee. The father had some property—farm equipment, tractor, and such—left in California under the name of his son, as the Issei generally entrusted their property to their children who possessed American citizenship. After the father was detained by the Federal Government and the family was evacuated, the property was sold by the family and the money was made in the form of a cashier's check in favor of the son, which amounted to something like one thousand dollars. It is quite understandable that his mother sold the property outright and the check was made in her son's name. She evidently was very much concerned over the current rumor that the property belonging to internees would be confiscated and the money belonging to them would be impounded by the government, since the American government was contemplating repatriating them to Japan. She believed the story in as much as it passed among the residents with the absolute credence.

One day she found out that the check was gone and was alarmed. She naturally cast her suspicious eyes to her son and questioned him, which brought out the fact that he had taken the check to one of the gambling houses and had lost every bit of it. It was too late and her appeal to the gambling people was of no avail. She was perplexed and indignant. Upon advice of her friends, she took the case to the Executive Board and pleadingly asked the chairman, M. Nagai, "My son has sinned. My son took our money and gambled it away. One thousand dollars for which we sold everything we had in California. That money was taken away by the professional gamblers, to whom he was an easy prey as if taking a 'sucker away from a baby.' We had depended on that money for our post relocation days. Now it's gone! I don't question that my son was at fault. But the blame cannot stop with my son alone, because I am positive that there are similar tragedies involving boys like mine. It is a fault of yours; it is the fault of the community. It is a fault of yours and theirs, because the responsibility of guiding the young and of preserving law and order here rests with you and them. How can you remain calm without doing anything? I beg you to carry out your duty."

By the ardent appeal of the mother, Nagai was moved and promised that he would take immediate action. (The source of this information—Sumida, one PTA representative, and the chief cashier of the Community Enterprises.)

Another story was told that a boy who had a cashier's check for two thousand dollars swindled it away to the professional gamblers. This tale, however, is very much similar to the one above and may be properly treated as an exaggerated version of the same incident.

The chief cashier of the Community Enterprises in a recent interview reported, "Many checks in large amounts are brought in to me for cashing, since there is no other facility in camp. You would be surprised if you knew how big the checks are. It is not unusual to have checks for one thousand dollars in exchange for cash. No, these checks don't come from the urban evacuees; they all come from the former rural residents, among them the Salinas people seem to be richer on the average. It also goes to show how poor the Los Angeles people are and how much hard pressed economically they were before the evacuation. Of course, we can't cash them on sight. At present the daily sale of the canteens for three camps are two thousand dollars, of which only five hundred dollars are in cash. So we send these checks out to Phoenix.

"About the middle of March, a Nisei boy, about nineteen years of age, came into my office with a cashier's check pretty close to one thousand dollars and requested cash for it. I said to him, 'How come you have so much money? Where did you get this money anyway? Isn't it funny that you have so much money? If you want this check cashed, you should bring your parent or some responsible person with you.'

"To this the boy answered angrily in a loud tone, 'This is a cashier's check made out to me. What's wrong with cashing my own check? Whatta hell! If you don't want to cash it, I will take it to some place else. I can cash it any darn place I please. I will take it to Parker—they will be glad to cash it for me.' And he left the office in a flurry.

"'Cash it in Parker?' Hell! Who's got one thousand dollars in cash on hand in Parker? Besides, how can they trust a young kid like that?" he went on. "A few days afterward, an Issei woman came to see me and said, 'I found out that my son came to you with a check of big sum. When he asked you to check [cash?] it for him, you refused. I don't know how to thank you for that, because that check was stolen from me, although it is in his name. You have saved me. I can't ever thank you too much for your kind deed.' Yeah, most likely this kid was hard up [for] gambling money."

A story was told in the northeastern section of the camp that a boy took out forty dollars from his mother's cache, which contained eighty dollars. He lost it in games with his friends. It was told that he thought the stealing of a part of the hidden money would not be detected by his mother.

Many thefts of personal properties were reported all over the camp. Even in the section unaffected by professional gambling[28] there were a few instances of theft by young boys. In Quad 6[29] the residents were warned to look out for two boys who are residing in Block 35, both of them about seventeen years of age. They were going into the male latrines and pick-pocketing watches and cash from the trousers of men who were taking showers in the adjoining room.

One resident of the block said, "We know those boys are stealing, and stealing for gambling money. Some of the block people approached the parents of those boys and told them of the fact, but they flatly refused to believe the wrong deeds of their sons. So what can we do with those blind parents? The best thing to do is to catch the boys and beat them up. They are afraid of physical pain to themselves, all right. There was one man in our block who could not locate his gold watch, and suspected these boys as the thieves although not certain. Anyway, this man went up to the boys and said knowingly, 'Hey, boys! Give back my watch!' One of the boys reluctantly took out the gold watch from his pocket and said without shame, 'Mister![30] Was this your watch?' Can you beat that?" The informant was shaking his head in disgust.

Poston in March of 1943 was a wide-open town. The cases reported in this paper were undoubtedly only a few representatives of abundantly numerous ones throughout the community. The residents were acutely aware of the existing condition and convinced that something should be done to remedy it. Only a few conscientious ones were willing to take [it] upon themselves to do something about it; and these men, too, did not know where to begin. The course they invariably selected was to go to the office of the Executive Board and to accuse the members of negligence and dereliction of their duty and responsibility. In other words, they were shoving the buck to the Executive Board and did not wish to "Stick their neck out."

The Executive Board, too, realized that the condition was grave and serious and getting out of control of authority. Yet they too felt not powerful enough to combat the evils alone. Nagai consulted the president of the Parent Teachers Association, that meek, good-natured Mohri of Block 31. Upon his request Mohri immediately called an emergency meeting of the organization one evening in the latter part of March and the methods of curbing gambling was the topic on the agenda. The chairman of the Executive Board was the first and main speaker, who presented to the body how serious and how grave the condition was in the camp. In his "pedantic and academic"[31] manner he argued that this was a critical problem for the young generation should the condition remain unremedied. After his speech, the representatives from each block undertook a discussion among themselves about what to be done about the request for cooperation by Nagai. As a whole, the tone of arguments from the floor was apathetic and indifferent. One speaker set forward, "This task is too great. We are not strong enough to take upon ourselves the difficult duty of the crusade."

Another man stood up to accuse Nagai, "This is your job. The Executive Board was created to handle those situations. What you are doing is to shift the responsibility to us."

To this accusation, Nagai pleaded, "We are powerless. We cannot do anything. The whole police force is corrupt and rotten. It is receiving bribery and refusing to cooperate with us."

The same man retorted, "Well, if you are powerless as you say, how can you expect us to be of any value?"

Another one suggested, "The maintenance of law and order of the camp as a whole must depend on the maintenance of law and order within each and every block. Every block must be responsible for the conduct of the block residents. Therefore, it should be called upon such a block to stamp out the gambling within that block."

The fruit of this emergency meeting did not go beyond the fact that each representative would take the problem back to his block and would assist in arousing public opinion against gambling. The constructive and positive aid sought by the Executive Board was never materialized to meet the emergency. Furthermore, many of the delegates failed to fulfill their promise of the meeting and did not report the proceedings of the meeting to "arouse public agitation."

The Executive Board at the same time approached the religious group. But the Buddhist and Christian workers were only successful in ruffling ripples in a great big pond.

Meanwhile, the attitude of the Police Department was getting to be conspicuously inattentive of the general welfare of the public; it was reported here and there that some policemen were actively soliciting bribes. Another report said that they were disdainful and contemptuous of the conscientious residents, who were endeavoring to obtain public support in the crusade. They said, "What can they do? Let them try it." Indeed, they were defiant.

Furthermore, the political opponents of Nagai were quick to take advantage of the chairman's dilemma; they accused, "The block in which Nagai resides, Block 3, is the core of the whole difficulty. If he thinks he is the leader of the camp, he should be able to close the house in his own block. How can he ask other people with a straight face to drive gambling out of other blocks when he has failed to do the same with his own?" In about the same vein, N. Mizushima, who took over the chairmanship of the Issei Advisory Board when the former chairman, Kato, had been appointed General Manager of the Community Enterprises and who was a perennial enemy of Nagai, said, "I hear that Nagai is at the back of the whole thing. People are talking that he is making money with the professional people." To the writer it sounded that Mizushima wanted the people to gossip that Nagai was receiving bribery, not that they were actually saying so. It was a projection typical of Mizushima.

In the face of growing criticism against him, Nagai could no longer be sitting in the back seat. It was in the beginning of April that Nagai went over to the underground chamber of his block and demanded that the professional gamblers close the place. He threatened them, "If you don't stop, I will see to it that you would be arrested. It will not stop with your gambling. I will see to it that you would be arrested for stealing government property and using stolen goods for personal gain. All this lumber, cement, and electric wires are stolen government property, I know. Let me tell you now that these offenses are tried in Yuma and not in Poston."

Nagai's words were enough to intimidate the operators and the house was closed in a few days.

The ice was broken; the first attempt of Nagai was successful. Now the chairman of the Executive Board went before the Temporary Community Council and received their approval to call a conference of block council members to discuss both the gambling and manpower shortage problems inasmuch as the latter was a grave problem facing Poston simultaneously with gambling. He argued that it was vitally essential to create consciousness among residents of the acute existing problems and to obtain the support of the public at large for their solution. In the past the problems discussed in the Community Council sessions were not reported to the block and the people were ignorant of the conditions; there was too much gap between the residents and their representatives, who were regarded as a separate entity as if they were Caucasian "appointees." The members of the council themselves realized that they were remote from the people and endorsed the plan full-heartedly.

As a result, on April 18, the Executive Secretary of the Executive Board, Nobuo Matsubara, sent a memorandum to each block manager. It read as follows. Our TCC is planning to sponsor a conference of Block Council members and Block Managers the first of its kind in the history of Poston in the very near future. We were requested by the TCC to submit the names of the Block Council members.

Please assist us by informing us with the following data: the names of the Block Council members; and the name of the Block Manager (or Assistant

Block Manager if the managership is vacant). Upon receipt of the names, the Executive Board sent out an invitation to the conference to each block council member in the name of the chairman of the TCC, Franklin Sugiyama. The invitations were written only in Japanese and the English version did not accompany them.

In the April 21 issue of the *Poston Chronicle*, an article appeared announcing this conference. It read:

TCC to Hold Meeting on Council's Policies

Under the auspices of the TCC I, a series of meetings to inform the Block Council of each block on Council's policies will be held starting this Wed. night, April 21, it was decided at the weekly meeting held at Rec. 5.

The Program is to educate the public of the community problems both from the Council's viewpoint and the community's outlook to achieve closer cooperation.

As there are 9 quads, 3 quads at a time will convene at Mess 32, which has been tentatively chosen as the site. The first meeting on Wednesday will be repeated the following Thursday and Friday nights, April 22 and 23, with W. Wade Head expected to speak at the first meeting.

The Japanese section of the same issue carried an article much more detailed:

United Conference of Both Legislative and Administrative Machineries To Be Held For Three Days Under the Auspices of TCC

The mode of living in this center is rapidly changing due to the changes in the WRA policies, which in turn are affected by the changes in the internal conditions of the United States. In order to solve many new problems arising out of these changes, it was believed essential to have better understanding and cooperation of the two machineries, legislative and administrative (Block Managers, Block Councils, The Executive Board, The Labor Relation Board, the Temporary Community Council, and its Issei Advisory Board). For this reason, it was decided to hold under the auspices of TCC joint conferences for three days beginning the night of this 21st (Wednesday) in the Block 32 Mess Hall. The program is as follows:

Program

Chairman: Yasutsugu Kushiyama

1. Address, TCC Chairman: Franklin Sugiyama
2. Address, LAB Chairman: Nagisa Mizushima
3. Reports:

(1) The Executive Board—Masakichi Nagai
(2) The Labor Relation Board—Nisakichi Nakachi, "The Problems We, The Poston Residents, Are Facing At Present."
(3) The Temporary Community Council—Frank Fukuda, "About the Manpower Commission"
(4) Speaker from every block representing his Block Council, "The Methods and Solution for My Block Problems and Difficulties in the Past"
(5) Questions and Answers
(6) Discussion (regarding the policies to solve the existing problems).

The issue of April 22 carried an article mentioning something about the gambling condition in camp for the first time in the history of its publication, and even this was confined only to the Japanese section. Under the headline,

Crusade of Gambling in the Center Which Is in Alarming Condition
Several Proposals Decided by TCC

it carried a short paragraph saying,

> TCC I held its regular meeting on 17th at 10 A.M. in the Block 5 Rec. Hall. Besides the plan to hold a joint conference of the legislative and administrative branches, which was reported to you yesterday, they decided as follows: 1. To take steps to curb gambling in camp, which has reached a grave and alarming stage. . . .

It was not until April 23, that the English section of the *Poston Chronicle* mentioned gambling for the first time. It was in a short article.

TCC to Curb Gambling

> Drastic steps to curb gambling, which has reached alarming proportions in the Unit, will be taken, it was decided at the last TCC I meeting at Block 5.
> Also during the meeting, a committee consisting of G. Kurata . . .

The original plan was changed and the joint conference was held in two sessions, dividing the camp into two; otherwise the proceedings were the same as announced in the newspaper. The conference was held in the south wing of the Block 32 Mess Hall[32] in which two long lines of mess tables were lined parallel to the walls. On each of these tables which are big enough to seat eight persons, cards bearing the numbers of blocks, were placed. In the center of one line of tables, the speakers were seated. When the meeting opened at quarter to nine, forty-five minutes behind the scheduled time, almost every seat was occupied by delegates. These delegates were either Issei or Kibei, although white-haired or bald headed persons were more noticeable.

One should sympathize with the predicament of the first speaker, Franklin Sugiyama, who had to speak in unfamiliar Japanese, as the meeting was conducted entirely in Japanese. He explained with difficulty that there were many problems in camp which could not be solved without the aid of the people present. The purpose of the evening was to acquaint them with the pending problems and the policies of the TCC and the administrative branch.

The second speaker, N. Mizushima, related the necessity of close cooperation between those elected officers and the residents at large; he emphasized that the gap must be eliminated.

With the next speaker the meeting went into the main topic. M. Nagai, the chairman of the Executive Board and the self-styled Mayor of Poston, commenced in his characteristic Japanese oratory, "We are facing a deplorable condition. It is a shameful thing for the flowers of the great East Asia races (*Toa Minzoku*)—the Japanese. I am speaking of our gambling habit in Poston . . .

"Just because the older people are setting bad examples, the young men are thereby influenced and affected. They are delinquent. They are gambling, neglecting the performance of their rightful duties. When I see them gambling at their tender age, I grieve for their future, since the habit of it should once get into their blood, will be an incurable malignant disease. I grieve for the future of our race in America . . . "

Then he cited the case of the boy who had wasted away one thousand dollars belonging to his family. "His mother could not stop tears coming in her eyes. I, too, cried with her. She said, 'Now you know what happened. Please do something.' To her I said, 'If we succeed in saving not only your son but other sons also, the money you have lost is a very cheap price to pay. You should be proud that with that money, you have saved our young generation. Let us now undertake the crusade to save our young manhood . . . '"

At one stage of his speech, Nagai said, "If a person wins in a gambling game, he does not work because he has made easy money. If he loses, he is angry and irritated; he stays in bed without working. In either way the person who gambles does not desire to work. Gambling makes one lazy and irresponsible . . . "

After twenty minutes of ardent appeal to the audience, he concluded, "Let us together save and guide the young generation, who has a great promise and a great mission to accomplish in the future. It is not too late yet. It is yet possible to cure the disease these young men are afflicted with at present. With your aid let us curb this gambling evil in this center. We need your unselfish and full-hearted assistance to carry out our great duty."

The remaining speeches, one by Nakachi and the other by Fukuda, were on the manpower shortage problem.

As soon as the delegates had access to the floor, a discussion of the gambling problem was resumed livelily. One delegate said, "I heard that the police is receiving bribery from the gambling interests."

Another commented, "I know a certain person who was caught gambling and was put in jail. There he saw the policeman gambling in the police station. This man told me, 'The next time we are thrown into jail, we are taking sets of hana cards and we are going to gamble in jail.' When such a condition exists with the law enforcing agency, how can you expect us to prevent gambling in the camp?"

"I want to offer this incident," a block council member said. "A friend of mine was caught in the act of gambling and was taken before the court and was duly sentenced. On the next day, after about twenty-four hours stay in jail, I saw him in our mess hall. I asked him what happened. He said, 'I came home to eat, because they told me to come here and eat. Hell, I am not returning to the jail any more.' And he refused to return to serve the rest of his sentence and yet nothing happened to him."

One man stood up and spoke indignantly and accusingly, "Isn't it your duty, Mr. Nagai, to see that the police department performs its duty rightfully? Isn't it the duty of the Executive Board to supervise the activities of the police?"

To this query Nagai spoke evasively, "When the duties and the functions of the Executive Board are interpreted broadly, it may be said that the police department is under our jurisdiction. However, in practice, we are not authorized to supervise the department. It is under a separate authority. On the other hand, the police are arguing that they cannot exercise the police authority to the full extent without public opinion supporting the enforcement. In my estimation, we have the police in camp, but in effort, it is the same as not having any police."

On this attempt of Nagai to shift the blame of inefficiency elsewhere there were comments in whispers in the audience, "What's the use of the *Tosei-bu* (the Executive Board) if they don't have jurisdiction over the police?" "What's he trying to do anyway?" Or, "Nagai is evading the blame."

Nagai was again put on the defense by another man who asked, "Mr. Nagai, we have heard from you this evening about the deplorable proportions of gambling. But I am sorry to call your attention that you have not said a word about any concrete and constructive plan to curb the evils. You should at least have some idea as to what you intend to do. Will you let us hear from you what you propose to do?"

Nagai answered this questioner hesitantly, "We do not have any definite plan except that we have asked the Parents Teachers Association and the religious groups to take the initiative. I do believe that the responsibility falls on these people. We must depend on them to take the leadership with our support." At this time the reaction that Nagai was trying to pass the buck to others was rampant among those present in the hall.

When the conference broke up about midnight the delegates went home with the feeling that nothing concrete and substantial had been gained during the evening.

However, the conference was effective in making the gamblers in the camp, especially the professional gamblers, realize that the people were disturbed and were rallying to the righteous cause and that public sanction was about to work upon the corrupt police and selfish gamblers. It was enough to intimidate them and all the gambling houses were closed within a few days after the meeting. It was also true that police warnings were instrumental in the retreat of the gamblers. The reasons for the sudden police vigilance were two fold: first, the police had received the support of public agitation against the gamblers for which they were clamoring; second, the Chief and the entire force were under fire and were accused publicly of their corruption. Nevertheless, there was one exception—the place in Block 27—which the police could not close. It was the place where the young boys of the "J" gang held their gambling establishment. Rumors had it, although without credence, that Shimada was receiving fifty dollars a day and had been threatened by them, "If we go, we take you with us." At the end, however, this group which defied the Chief's closing order, too, moved away from the block by the pressure of the block residents.

Meantime, in the morning of April 23, the Project Director, W. Wade Head, called into his office Police Chief Shimada and the members of the Judicial Commission, Seiichi Sumida, and Elmer Yamamoto, a former Los Angeles Nisei attorney. Head explained that cash in the excess of four hundred fifty thousand dollars was to be paid to the Poston evacuees within the next four weeks by the project and demanded the tightening of law enforcement, especially a curtailment of gambling in order to protect the residents.

To the request of Project Director Head, the Police Chief, who was at odds with the Commissioners and was disturbed by current stories of his corruption, pointed his accusing finger at Sumida. He argued, in general substance, that real police enforcement could not be effected without stringent penalties pronounced by the Municipal Court against arrested gamblers. So far, whenever the offenders were brought before the justice, the court was turning them loose with either suspended sentences or probations. The chief especially emphasized that the laxity of the court was responsible for the present situation; this same laxity nullified the effectiveness of the police.

Sumida, of course, could not take this accusation with hands down. He retorted that all cases which were brought before the court up to date were minor violations and he could not with a right mind and justice impose heavier penalties. He added, "Don't catch small fries. When you bring big ones, I'll give it to 'em." Shimada, no doubt, understood the hidden insinuation of the judge.

At the end of this conference Head was reported to have said, "I will guarantee all of you that I will give every bit of support for enforcement. I will invoke the authority vested in me by Administrative Instruction No. 84. Just get one witness who will testify that he has seen certain persons play games for money. That's sufficient for me. I will issue a warrant immediately."

W. Wade Head intimated in this statement that he would exercise the full authority granted him by WRA Administrative Instruction No. 84 in making those arrests. The instruction reads in part as follows:

> . . . A police officer may make an arrest without a warrant only of an evacuee who has committed, or is committing an offense in his presence.
>
> The arrest of an evacuee for an offense not committed in the presence of a police officer may be only pursuant to a warrant of arrest issued by the Project Director.
>
> The Project Director may issue a warrant of arrest—
>
> 1. On the application of a police officer who makes a signed written statement that he has reason to believe that an offense has been committed and that the person for whom the warrant is requested had committed the offense. The Project Director in his discretion, may require such additional details to be included in the statement as he may believe desirable. When it is urgent that the warrant be issued at the earliest possible moment, the Project Director shall normally not require more than such a written statement by the officer that he believes an offense has been committed and that the person for whom the warrant requested has committed it. When the issuance of a warrant is less urgent, the Project Director shall normally require the statement by the police officer to state briefly why he believes the person for whom the warrant is requested has committed

> an offense. In any case in which the Project Director finds that the belief of the police officer that an offense has been committed, is clearly unwarranted, he shall refuse to issue a warrant.
>
> 2. On the application of any evacuee, any member of the staff of the War Relocation Authority, or any other person within a relocation center, who makes a signed, written statement that he has reason to believe an offense has been committed, setting forth his reasons for such belief, and that he has reason to believe that the person for whom the warrant is requested has committed the offense, setting forth his reasons for such belief—except that the Project Director shall not issue a warrant in those cases unless he is satisfied from the statement that there are reasonable grounds to believe that an offense has been committed and that the person for whom a warrant is sought has committed it. . . .

After the conference of joint Block Councils, the circulation of wild stories about Chief Shimada was accelerated. One rumor accused the chief of having received at least fifteen thousand dollars as bribery since he came to the camp in last May. Other rumors placed the figure at a smaller amount. Judge Sumida's version was also substantiating the story, "I think fifteen thousand dollars are a little exaggerated. I think it's somewhere around nine thousand or ten thousand dollars. He is the guy who put an ad in the *Chronicle* some time ago to purchase a tractor. Shimada is from Terminal Island and didn't have any money before he came to Poston. Now he's got enough money to buy a tractor for cash. Figure that out for yourself."

The rumors about the Police Chief were somewhat at variance, but they all agreed that he was receiving "protection" money. There was, however, one person who contradicted this story. He was M[izushima], the Issei Advisory Board Chairman. He said to his acquaintances, "Shimada is a nice boy. I taught him when I was teaching the Japanese language school in Montebello. I don't think he's got any money from the gambling interests. I think it's just talk. His father told me, 'I swear to God that my boy is honest and innocent.'" The listeners immediately repudiated Mizushima, "How can you tell that he didn't take bribe? If you don't pipe down, people will start suspecting that you are with him." The chairman did not have another word, as he was aware that his political position was precarious and that he himself was being suspected by certain elements in the camp of having some connection with the FBI.

On April 26, the Temporary Community Council met with the Legal Department and discussed ways and means of revitalizing and reorganizing the Police Department. The councilmen were particularly concerned about the rampant rumors about the bribe taking police chief. As the first measure, they decided to call in the chief.

On the next day, April 27, the Council called in Chief Shimada before the body and recommended him to resign before they would act upon it. He was told, "You'd better save your face. We are going to oust you anyway." Sensing the consequence, Shimada immediately tendered his resignation to the Internal Security Officer, Miller, and to the Council.

Seiichi Sumida commented on this resignation, "He'd better get out of camp. That guy made too much promises to the professional guys. They are after him now."

With the resignation of the police chief, some of the policemen left their jobs one by one; the number remaining in the force was reduced to twelve on April 30. About this some said sneeringly, "those are the smelly guys. The ones left in the department now are honest and around this a new force should be formed."

On May 1, the *Poston Chronicle* printed an article announcing the change of the chief in its Japanese section.

Retirement of Chief Shimada
Mr. Ota Appointed as the New Chief

> Chief Shimada, who was responsible for the maintenance of law and order in Camp I since his arrival here, decided to retire and tendered his resignation to the Temporary Community Council. The council, having judged his reasons for resignation reasonable and proper, accepted it; subsequently they were searching for the right person to fill the vacancy and agreed that Assistant Chief Ota was the most logical person, as he is most popular among the police force. As Mr. Ota willingly accepted the appointment which was approved by Project Director Head, he was formally appointed as the new chief.

During the night of May 1, the following mimeographed paper was posted all over the camp—in the latrines, on the mess hall walls, and on the bulletin boards of all the blocks in Unit I.

Something Was Rotten in Denmark

> Poston was a wide-open town. Commercialized vice and syndicated gambling has flourished, winked at by an official who has been appointed for the express purpose of keeping the lid down on stinking corruption.
>
> Rumors are rife that there was a monthly pay-off for "protection." That only small-time penny-ante games and crap-shooters rolling dice for nickels and dimes were apprehended, while the big controlled games were unmolested.

> Of course, this may be just another rumor. But there's the old-time saying that "where there's smoke, there's fire."
>
> It is high time that something be done at once to clean up the corruption in organized crime.
>
> Poston must clean house! Throw out whom would line his pocket with filthy money!
>
> Resignation from a $19 job is not necessarily means atoned for his sins.
>
> We are ready to drive out this whole stinking mess. Racketeering and dishonesty must go! You know whom we are talking about!

The same mimeographed papers disappeared during the night of May 2. No one in camp could explain this mysterious appearance and disappearance. No one could say with authority who put out this paper and who took it away. The only plausible conjecture was that they were not printed in the Administration Buildings, as the Caucasian superintendent would not allow printing of papers other than those of the project. Besides these machines, the mimeographing can be done in the *Chronicle* office and the Community Enterprises. In addition, there are two privately owned mimeograph machine in the camp and to these owners—Christian workers living in the volunteer evacuee section—the credit of printing and posting of these sheets was given. And the Shimada supporters were suspected of being responsible for the disappearance.

On May 4, the *Poston Chronicle* in its Japanese section reported as follows:

> Six Commissioners Appointed
> Strengthening of the Police Department
>
> As reported, Mr. "Jumbo" Ota was appointed as the Chief when Mr. Shimada retired. Now the Temporary Community Council formally announced with the approval of Director Head the appointment of the following persons as the Police Commissioners. It is the duty of these men to act as the advisors to the chief and to be consulted on the policies of the department in maintaining law and order in the camp: William Fukuda, Masaharu Hano, Frank Kadawaki, Tsuneo Sumida, Setsuichi Masukane, George Fujii.

The first person named in the report, William Fukuda, is a Nisei who is working in the warehouses. Masaharu Hano and Setsuichi Masukane are both members of the Issei Advisory Board, while Tsuneo Sumida, also an Issei, is the Manager of Block 16. The other Nisei beside Fukuda, namely George Fujii, is a member of the Temporary Community Council.

The condition in camp was getting under control; it was an anti-climax by May 5, when the newly organized Police Commission sent a memorandum attached to a notice from the Project Director. The memorandum reads as follows:

To: Block Manager

As you know, it would be much more preferable to prevent the continuance of these evils rather than enforcing stringent penalties after the violations have occurred.

May I ask your cooperation by announcing this at the Mess Hall and posting it on the Bulletin Board.

(signed) *George S. Fujii*
George S. Fujii, Chairman
Police Commission

The letter of Wade Head which Fujii referred to in the memorandum reads as follows:

May 5, 1943

Notice to All Residents of Poston:

Two prevalent evils existing at Poston have been called to my attention and I am writing this memorandum to you residents to ask your cooperation and assistance in eliminating them.

1. Gambling has become very wide-spread to such an extent that some drastic measures must be taken to curb it. I am sure that all well-meaning, right-thinking residents do not desire this evil to continue. We have rules and regulations against gambling and they will be hereafter enforced by the law enforcement officers and the Judicial Commission. Such rules and regulations are merely a remedy after the crime has been committed.

I am appealing to you all to help prevent the continuance of the practice of this gambling evil. I am sure that you all feel that it would be much more preferable to prevent the continued practice of this evil rather than enforcing stringent penalties after the violations have occurred. Public opinion is one of the strongest weapons that any community can employ in stamping out this continued practice. I ask for your full-hearted cooperation.

2. This other evil to which I am referring is the unauthorized misuse of motor vehicles . . .

I earnestly solicit your help and assistance in rectifying the two problems herein outlined to you.

Yours very truly,

(signed) *W. Wade Head*
W. Wade Head
Project Director

The letter of the Project Director was a posthumous warning to the gamblers. The organized and syndicated gamblers could not stand the wrath of the public; the corrupt Police Chief could not bear public censure. Both of these had gone when the letter came out. It was a warning to residents that the reoccurrence of the situation would not be tolerated and would be dealt with severely.

As of May 20, the only gambling done in the camp is again hana and poker games for nominal stakes, which are condoned. Even these players are no longer defiant and ostentatious as they were in February and March; they are playing the games secretly under cover avoiding the searching eyes of the vigilant police.

As it happened in California, public opinion was the weapon which spurred the curbing of the gambling evil after a chaotic period. It is a question whether this weapon will be exercised long enough to prevent the recurrence of gambling in the Colorado War Relocation Center at Poston permanently. This question is yet to be answered in the future.

Notes

1. As of April 28, 1943.

2. Men without dependents in this country and bachelors who were engaged in taking care of the gardens of Caucasian homes were quartered together as boarders in large houses. Each house took care of about between ten and twenty gardeners charging a set fee for room and board. It was one of the profitable businesses for the Japanese.

3. The area bounded by Ninth Street, Pico Street, Vermont Avenue, and Western Avenue.

4. The area roughly bounded by Exposition Boulevard, Adams Street, Vermont Avenue, and Western Avenue.

5. A fishing village across the channel from San Pedro, California, where about two thousand Japanese congregated, comprising about three fourths of the total population.

6. The employees of Japanese commission houses in the City Wholesale Produce Market and the Terminal Wholesale Produce Market in Los Angeles. The former was commonly referred to as "Ninth Street market," while the latter "Seventh Street market."

7. A Chinese game. A dealer grabs a handful of beans and puts them in a china bowl. He then takes out the beans by a definite number, say by sixes, until the number

of beans in the bowl is the number or less. The winner is decided by the number of beans left in the bowl. The method of betting and the odds are somewhat like roulette.

8. Another Chinese game similar to domino.

9. The southwestern suburb of Los Angeles, which included Moneta, Gardena, Torrence, Lomita, Hawthorne, and Compton. It was the center of Japanese truck gardeners.

10. The ["haul man" is a] Japanese who makes a regular round collecting farm produce on his customers' farms after their working hours. He then takes these vegetables to either one of the two wholesale markets. (In those years, these markets opened for business at 10 P.M.) He parks his truck in his stall in the central courtyard of the market and sells these products. In effect, he serves as a transfer man and as a salesman simultaneously. His fee in the 1920's was 10 per cent commission on the sale price in addition to the flat charge of five cents for a lug and ten cents for a crate. No cosigners examined his sales record and it was not difficult for him to report back to the farmers a few cents below the price and to embezzle the difference. This was the most tempting scheme for the "haul man," by which some of them were able to make more money than through legitimate means.

11. A bum without a source of income. He comes to the gambling house at the opening hour and stays until the closing time. He is fed by the house free of charge. He begs the players for some cash, dimes and quarters; when he succeeds in begging, he gambles it away.

12. In a recent interview, P. M. Kenno, the former publisher and editor of the Rafu Shimpo, or the *Los Angeles Daily News*, revealed the following facts: the *Rafu Shimpo* had the largest circulation among all the Japanese language newspapers in the United States. It had about 10,000 subscribers. This was the only newspaper in the field which could make both ends meet. At that the net profit above the expense was very meager and negligible. The *Nichibei*, the *Kashu Mainichi*, and the *Hokubei Asahi* had a circulation of about 6,000, about 5,000, and about 4,000, respectively. This was not enough to cover the operating expenses and the papers were always in the red. In consequence, it was not unusual that the rents were in arrears for several months and the wages of the employees were unpaid. It is also important to remember that they had large account payables, especially to the paper companies, long overdue. In this way the Zellerbach Paper Co. held mortgages on the *Nichibei* and the *Hokubei Asahi*; at the time of evacuation the company was operating the *Nichibei* after it was foreclosed a few years previously.

Before 1920 it was true that a circulation of 3,000 was considered enough to pay the expenses. But as the international news gained importance and the Japanese subscribers demanded more news, we had to buy the wire service from Japan at first and the UP service later. This meant rapid increase in the operating cost, and our circulation of 10,000 was barely sufficient to keep the paper going.

13. This was reported by one of the officers of the Tokyo Club.

14. The hilly stretch along the Pacific Ocean between San Pedro and Redondo Beach.

15. He was the central figure of an eviction case in Block 45. The incident is reported elsewhere separately.[4]

16. It is translated "Rifle Gang" or "Gun Men." A group of burly men who were employed by the Tokyo Club.

17. The boss of the underworld in Southern California.

18. Ample materials are available for this case and the kidnapping case that followed. The reader should refer to the *Los Angeles Times*, the *Los Angeles Examiner*, and the official record in file in the Superior Court in and for the County of Los Angeles. These cases are mentioned briefly in this paper.

19. One of these men is now residing in Poston under another name.

20. Seiichi Sumida [pseudonym] was born in Hilo, Hawaii, in 1895. He is a veteran of the World War. After the war, he worked in the Navy Yard at Mare Island until he was discharged in 1920. In the same year he came to Los Angeles, and enrolled in the Law School of Southwestern University. Since graduation he has worked for the Tokyo Club as the counselor. He was not admitted to the State Bar.

At present he is the representative from Block 45 to the Community Council, of which he is serving as the acting chairman after Sugiyama left for outside employment in the middle of May. He is also a member of the Judicial Commission and a judge of the Municipal Court.

21. Ted Haas often consulted Leighton and Spicer at the early stage of this project. In fact, Haas participated sometimes in Bureau activities such as the food survey.

22. Section 19 of the Code of Offenses reads as follows:

> *Prostitution*: No woman shall offer her body for the purpose of prostitution or solicit any man to have intercourse with her, for money, or agree to have carnal intercourse with any man for money. No person, upon any street or sidewalk, or in any room, rooming house, residence, hotel, park or other place, shall solicit any person of the opposite sex to whom he or she is not married, to have sexual intercourse with such person so soliciting.
>
> No person shall resort to any office building or to any room or rooms used or occupied in connection with, or under the same management as any cafe, restaurant, soft drink parlor, liquor establishment or similar business, or to any public park or to any of the buildings therein or to any vacant lot, or to any room, rooming house, lodging house, residence, apartment house, hotel, street, or sidewalk for the purpose of having sexual intercourse with a person to whom he or she is not married.
>
> No person shall cause, procure, induce, persuade or encourage any other per-

4. The incident is recorded in Nishimoto's sociological journal.

son to patronize prostitutes or houses of prostitution; or direct or conduct another to prostitutes or places where prostitutes may be hired or obtained; or offer or agree to provide prostitutes or solicit patronage for prostitutes or houses of prostitution; or take, offer or agree to take another person to any place with knowledge or reasonable cause to believe that such taking, offering or agreeing to take is for the purpose of prostitution, lewdness or assignation.

No person shall resort to any house, room, building, structure or place not mentioned in the third paragraph of this section, for the purpose of having sexual intercourse with a person to whom he or she is not married, in consideration of the payment of, or promise of payment of or the receipt of any lawful money.

No person shall rent, let or assign any room or apartment with the understanding or belief that such room or apartment is to be used by the person or persons to whom it is sold, let, rented or assigned for the purpose of having sexual intercourse with a person to whom he or she is not married.

No driver of any vehicle, capable of being used to transport persons for hire, shall permit any person to occupy or use such vehicle for the purpose of prostitution, lewdness or assignation, with knowledge or reasonable cause to believe that the same is, or is to be, hire, occupied or used for such purposes; nor shall such driver direct, take or transport any person to any building or place, or to any other person, with knowledge or reasonable cause to believe that the purpose of such transport is prostitution, lewdness or assignation.

23. Dr. John H. Provinse, the War Relocation Authority.

24. L. K., who was one of the first to be beaten as an FBI informer, was residing in this block before he left this camp for Denver.

25. The new double barrack building between Block 28 and the adobe school site.

26. The block in which M. N., A. S., F. F., etc., live. The residents are mostly from the Riverside section.

27. A typical expression among the Issei.

28. In the blocks other than those in the northern section and in the southwestern section there were no regular gambling establishments. Only hana and poker games were played among friends.

29. Blocks 35, 36, 45, and 46.

30. An affectionate term in addressing a stranger, literally meaning "uncle."

31. The words are of a representative of the Parents Teachers Association.

32. The description contained in this report is that of the second day, April 22.

DEMANDS

Nishimoto's Study of the All Center Conference

Introduction

This selection, on the All Center Conference, held in Salt Lake City, Utah, in February 1945, is actually the last in a set of three research reports that Richard Nishimoto wrote about the closure of Poston, which comprise more than four hundred manuscript pages. The first was a two-hundred-page study entitled "Initial Impact of the Army Announcement of Rescission of the Exclusion Orders and the WRA Announcement of Liquidation of the Relocation Centers," which focused largely on rumors and public opinion. The second was a 110-page report entitled "Developments Leading to Participation in the All Center Conference and Visit of the Representative of the Spanish Embassy." In this study Nishimoto argued that, given internal divisions, the ability of Poston's Unit I, II, and III residents to choose representatives to attend the All Center Conference in a free and open election was an indication of remarkable consensus and was in itself a major achievement in self-government.[1]

One of the key contributions of Nishimoto's corpus is that it allows us to revise our understanding of a range of daily practices that Poston researchers like Alexander H. Leighton interpreted as signs of social disorganization as also constituting forms of popular resistance to mass incarceration. A complete listing and analysis of such activities is beyond the scope of this introduction, but suffice it to say that the practice of "borrowing" needed supplies, such as wood for basic construction,[2] various forms of humor,[3] protests over objectionable construction plans,[4] and even drunkenness,[5] might be "read" in this fashion. Gary Y. Okihiro has also argued that the Issei's revival of Japanese forms of religion, culture, art, and medicine in the camps was not only often practical; it also allowed a reassertion of dignity and pride, and thus constituted a foundation for popular resistance.[6] At Poston, for example, discontent that helped produce large, organized protests was generated during the first months of confinement, when the first-generation Issei men realized that they were going to be cut out of leadership positions because of their status as "enemy aliens." Popular protest was also expressed in the form of work slowdowns and strikes, which also resulted from early dissatisfaction with wages and working conditions in Poston.[7] While some chose suicide as a solution to their anger and despair, others decided to identify and beat the spies and informers whom Poston's appointed personnel and FBI investigators on special assignment had deployed to identify the "troublemakers" they believed must be behind the labor slowdowns and strikes.[8]

In all these myriad ways, as well as others, Japanese Americans expressed their feelings about the injustices of mass incarceration. Tensions continued to build during the first year and finally erupted in the Poston strike of November 1942. The strike became so extensive and intense that on the evening of November 18 the United States Army was put on alert. Soldiers—some of whom were armed with machine guns and who were supported by an array of weapons carriers and jeeps—waited tensely outside the gates of Poston for the order to invade the camp and reassert control.[9]

Given this broad context of popular resistance, Nishimoto's three-part report, written some two years after the Poston strike, demonstrates how and why the idea of convening the All Center Conference originated in response to the War Relocation Authority's announcement in late 1944 that, with the exception of Tule Lake, all of the WRA camps would be closed down by the end of 1945. It is clear is that, while Japanese Americans did not necessarily oppose the idea of moving back out into the larger society, they were deeply concerned about their safety and their future. Specifically, many resented the fact that the proposal was yet another instance of the WRA trying to push Japanese Americans around without consulting them and without paying sufficient attention to the needs of specific groups within the overall population.[10]

It should be noted that the name All Center Conference is a bit of a misnomer, more a reflection of the goal, which was to invite representatives from all ten of the WRA camps, than the reality. In the end, representatives from only seven of the ten WRA camps attended.[11] At any rate, the representatives who attended unanimously agreed that some sectors of the Japanese American population—especially some of the Issei and the older Nisei—had been financially and sometimes psychologically broken and thus were unable to move back into the larger society without sustained assistance. The U.S. government's own publications note that "[t]his was the only time in the history of the WRA program when the agency resorted to a threat of physical force in order to complete its relocation schedule," with *relocation* in this case meaning persuading or otherwise coercing camp residents to leave.[12]

What is more, the representatives, reflecting complaints that their constituents had already raised in regard to the WRA's mandate for closure, emphasized that the nature and scope of the losses incurred by community members were in no way balanced by the WRA offer to those who complied—namely, twenty-five dollars and a free train ticket back to one's "point of origin" in the United States. The offer was hardly any incentive even for young, healthy single people, let alone families who wanted to leave camp in order to get a fresh start in life for the sake of their children.

Similarly, the All Center Conference representatives agreed that since the federal government had initiated and supervised the mass incarceration, it should take responsibility for the well-being of Japanese Americans when they returned to the larger society. In addition to those who were disabled and who would need special support, this responsibility included financial reparations to Japanese Americans for the losses they had incurred. Moreover, the representatives decided that the government should make an explicit commitment to protect the civil rights of Japanese Americans who returned, especially to areas on the West Coast.[13] Thus, after their meeting, which lasted from February 16 to 22, 1945, the All Center representatives hammered out the document reproduced below, demanding consideration of three key points: (1) monetary reparations for losses and damage, (2) special support for the elderly and needy, and (3) a full guarantee of the rights and safety of individuals.

What makes Nishimoto's research on the All Center Conference and the events leading up to it all the more significant is that, first, while it is apparent that he understood the complaints of Poston's inhabitants, he believed his role as a responsible leader was to insure that resistance did not become destructive or futile. Second, even though Nishimoto was therefore critical of popular resistance in this regard, his ethnographic analysis is thorough enough that we can better appreciate that the significance of the All Center Conference has been greatly understated in the literature.[14]

After living in the Minidoka camp near Hunt, Idaho, for three years, the Nagaishi family was subject to harassment like that shown here when they returned home to Seattle. Such incidents intensified Japanese Americans' concerns about their safety as they contemplated leaving the WRA camps to return to the larger society. (Courtesy of Visual Communications, Los Angeles)

Some authorities seem to have concluded that the venture was at best quixotic, given the political and financial pressures to which the WRA was being subjected.[15] Other accounts describe the demands that the representatives hammered out and sent to Washington, but in the final analysis they, too, minimize the significance of the gathering, perhaps because Myer and the WRA ignored the protests and essentially shut down all the camps except Tule Lake on schedule and as planned.

In contrast to interpretations that highlight the conference's ineffectiveness, Nishimoto's research is rich in detail, documenting day-to-day popular resistance and the many different expressions it found among the residents of Poston, including their participation in the All Center Conference and, by extension, their support for the resulting demands.

In short, a comprehensive history remains to be written about the All Center Conference and the light it sheds on Japanese Americans' great interest in the call for redress and reparations during the 1980s. Nishimoto's research and writings will certainly be central to further research because, although the idea for such a conference appears to have come from least four WRA camps (those in Topaz, Utah; Poston, Arizona; Heart Mountain, Wyoming; and Amache, Colorado) probably no more comprehensive database will ever be available on how this popular protest movement evolved in the camps and what its immediate and long-term implications might be.

Nishimoto's three reports thus provide the basis for two somewhat novel claims. One is that resistance to the injustices of mass incarceration and later popular support for redress had their roots in the prewar and wartime experiences of Japanese Americans.[16] Second, Nishimoto's report on the All Center Conference indicates that at least as early as 1945 a significant number of the imprisoned Japanese Americans recognized that the federal government was to blame for their wartime predicament and should therefore be held accountable.[17] This accountability included requests for monetary reparations and a guarantee of safety and protection of the Japanese Americans' rights. Regardless of the outcome, it is important to remember that Japanese Americans united behind these demands and felt passionately enough about them to send copies to WRA head Dillon S. Myer, President Roosevelt, the Department of the Interior, the Department of Justice, the War Department, and both houses of Congress.

Notes

1. These studies are available in files J 6.11 and J 6.05 in the Bancroft Library's Japanese American Evacuation and Resettlement Study Collection, University of California, Berkeley. Nishimoto estimated that 85 percent of the eligible voters participated in the election of the delegates from Poston's Unit I; Nishimoto to Thomas, February 11, 1945, JERS W 1.25B.

2. Alexander H. Leighton, *The Governing of Men: General Principles and Recommendations Based on Experience at a Japanese Relocation Camp* (1945; reprint, New York: Octagon, 1964), 148.

3. For example, the climate in western Arizona was so extreme that some wags began to refer to Poston's three units as Roaston, Toaston, and Duston; Toshio Yatsushiro, *Politics and Cultural Values: The World War II Japanese Relocation Centers, United States Government* (Ph.D. diss., Cornell University, 1954; reprint, New York: Arno Press, 1978), 476. Perhaps more to the point, "*block head* became the accepted term for block

manager, and often in a derogatory way." For this and other examples, see Paul Bailey, *City in the Sun: The Japanese Concentration Camp at Poston, Arizona* (Los Angeles: Westernlore Press, 1971), 171.

4. Bailey notes that, during the summer of 1942, Japanese Americans were unhappy about the poor conditions and lack of proper medical equipment and supplies and were horrified by the planned construction of a crematory adjacent to the community hospital. They lodged a protest with the camp authorities. See Bailey, *City in the Sun*, 97.

5. Ibid., 100.

6. Okihiro discusses this view in his essays "Japanese Resistance in America's Concentration Camps: A Re-evaluation," *Amerasia Journal* 2 (1973): 20–34; "Tule Lake under Martial Law: A Study in Japanese Resistance," *Journal of Ethnic Studies* 5 (1977): 71–85; and "Religion and Resistance in America's Concentration Camps," *Phylon* 45 (1984): 220–33. From a somewhat different angle, Thomas James argues that "[o]ften beyond the ken of administrators and teachers, invisible from the vantage point of official policy, the spontaneous mobilization of the cultural resources of the group was among the most significant educational achievements of the war years"; *Exile Within: The Schooling of Japanese Americans, 1942–1945* (Cambridge, Mass.: Harvard University Press, 1987), 107, see also 106–8.

7. Note 3 in Nishimoto's study of the Firebreak Gang, above, provides apt illustrations of this discontent early in 1942. In addition, Audrie Girdner and Anne Loftis describe how fifty-six Japanese American workers who were involved in mixing and molding adobe bricks voted to strike in August 1942 in order to obtain the pay (sixteen dollars a month) that they believed had been promised to them; *The Great Betrayal: The Evacuation of the Japanese-Americans during World War Two* (London: Macmillan, 1969), 225–26. In discussing another example of work-related popular resistance, Spicer notes the puzzlement of researchers who were trying to understand the reluctance of Poston's Japanese Americans to help local farmers in the Parker Valley to save their cotton crop. Specifically, Spicer argued that the motivation to volunteer needed to revolve around pride in the block with respect to other blocks as opposed to appealing to the patriotism of Japanese Americans in Poston as a whole. See Edward H. Spicer, "Reluctant Cotton Pickers: Incentive to Work in a Japanese Relocation Center," in *Human Problems in Technological Change: A Casebook*, ed. Edward H. Spicer (New York: Russell Sage Foundation, 1952), 41–52.

8. In a brief but explicit passage, legal scholar and political scientist Peter Irons describes the genesis of Japanese American patterns of spying and informing on each other to the U.S. government both before and during World War II in *Justice at War: The Story of the Japanese American Internment Cases* (New York: Oxford University Press, 1983), 78–79. Bailey presents an interesting, albeit somewhat vague, account of the tensions that intracommunity patterns of spying and informing generated in Poston in *City in the Sun*, 108, 111, 114–21. J. G. Fuqua (a Parker, Arizona, resident) stated

that he himself knew two or three Japanese Americans in Poston who were spying for the FBI; *Japanese American World War II Evacuation Oral History Project*, ed. Arthur A. Hansen and Nora M. Jesch, pt. 5: *Guards and Townspeople* (New Providence, N.J.: K. G. Saur, 1993), 635.

9. Major bloodshed such as occurred during the Manzanar strike and riot of December 1942 was narrowly avoided; see Arthur A. Hansen and David A. Hacker, "The Manzanar Riot: An Ethnic Perspective," *Amerasia Journal* 2 (1974): 112–57. In addition to Leighton's work on the Poston strike in *The Governing of Men*, 162–210, see Okihiro, "Japanese Resistance in America's Concentration Camps."

10. Keep in mind here that, as this announcement was made, many of those confined remembered that Milton Eisenhower, the first director of the WRA, had originally stated that the WRA camps would remain open "for the duration [of the war] plus fourteen days." In December 1944, however, with the war still in progress, the WRA authorities announced that they were going to close all the camps except that at Tule Lake during the following year, so all "residents" should prepare to leave.

11. The absence of three of the camps was due to the fact that Jerome had already been closed, Tule Lake (which had become a detention center for "renunciants") was not included, and the Japanese Americans confined at Manzanar ultimately declined to participate because they apparently believed that the WRA's policy on closure could not be overturned.

12. War Relocation Authority, WRA: A Story of Human Conservation (Washington, D.C.: Government Printing Office, 1947), 148. We need only look at some of the subsequent literature on the closure of camps to realize that the All Center representatives' fears in this regard were well founded. For a detailed case study, see James M. Sakoda, "The 'Residue': The Unresettled Minidokans, 1943–1945," in *Views from Within: The Japanese American Evacuation and Resettlement Study*, ed. Yuji Ichioka (Los Angeles: University of California, Los Angeles, Asian American Studies Center, 1989), 247–84. When the order for closure was implemented at Minidoka, Idaho, some elderly residents who were reluctant to leave had their bags packed, were forcibly taken to the train station by government agents, and were summarily sent on their way.

13. As Nishimoto notes in the document below, sometimes those who were the first to return to rural areas in California were harassed, shot at, or otherwise threatened. The war, after all, was still in progress. People had grouped together loyal Japanese Americans with the Japanese enemy, so it is understandable that the All Center representatives were instructed by their constituents to tell the federal government to take a more active stance.

14. Note, for example, that, despite his personal convictions, Nishimoto was a careful enough researcher to reproduce both the final version of the All Center Conference demands—which was softened considerably in translation by more moderate Nisei—and a side-by-side reproduction of what was obviously a much more militant version,

originally written in Japanese. Modifications were thus made by moderate Nisei, unbeknownst to the authors writing in Japanese.

15. Dillon S. Myer's account is along these lines; see *Uprooted Americans: The Japanese Americans and the War Relocation Authority during World War Two* (Tucson: University of Arizona Press, 1971), 193–95. The historian Sandra C. Taylor is similarly critical, although the credibility of her interpretation (she seems to have concluded that the All Center Conference demands were an expression of anti-American sentiment) is marred by a number of very fundamental factual mistakes; see *Jewel of the Desert: Japanese American Internment at Topaz* (Berkeley: University of California Press, 1993), 208–9, and my review of Taylor's study in the *Pacific Historical Review* 64 (February 1995).

16. This point contradicts the frequent claim that the contemporary movement for redress originated in the 1970s, as stated, for example, in Glen Kitayama's entry under "redress movement" in *Japanese American History*, 289–92. While true at a certain level, this approach totally neglects the formation of the movement for redress in the broader historical context of resistance, both at a general level and specifically in regard to mass incarceration.

17. This point contradicts previous interpretations of resistance that focus on the efforts of small groups of protesters or specific individuals (such as James Omura, Joe Kurihara, and Kiyoshi Okamoto). See William Minoru Hohri's claims in this regard in his book *Repairing America: An Account of the Movement for Japanese American Redress* (Pullman, Wash.: Washington State University Press, 1984), 29–35. My assertion is in no way intended to belittle the very real efforts of these individuals and groups, and the risks they ran in speaking up. Rather, my point is that it would be easy to minimize the extent to which members of the Japanese American community at large recognized the injustices of their situation while still in camp and that they knew full well that the federal government was responsible. Incidentally, this same fact also gives the lie to the spurious claim, repeatedly made by playwright Frank Chin, that Japanese Americans did not and do not know their own history. One example of Chin's rhetorical posturing is his argument that Japanese Americans were being hoodwinked by both the Japanese American Citizens League and the President's Commission on the Wartime Relocation and Internment of Civilians in regard to the JACL's "real" role during the war; see "Circus of Freaks," *Rafu Shimpo* (Los Angeles), August 21, 1981; and "Is Japanese America Ignorant of Its History?" *Rafu Shimpo*, January 27, 1983.

ALL CENTER CONFERENCE AND DIRECTOR MYER'S VISIT

Introduction

The announcement by the WRA of its decision to close the relocation centers on or before January 2, 1946 shattered the sense of security held in varying degrees by the evacuees at Poston.[1] They had been sheltered in the Colorado River Relocation Center for the past thirty odd months and had been convinced, rightly or wrongly, that they would be able to remain, if they so desired, in this "refuge center" for the duration. In receiving the news, only a small portion of the population was delighted in the prospect of leaving the center, for they had been obliged to remain here due to parental objection or due to other deterrents. There were a few others who took the news with submissive placidity; they believed that there was nothing that could be done to change the governmental policy. A vast number of the evacuees, on the other hand, was neither happy nor acquiescent; they reacted either in negative or in negativistic manners—varying from being violently vociferous to being passively defiant—motivated by the various sorts of fear, by the desire for economic advantages, and by other factors, which have been described previously.[2]

---

1. Japanese American Evacuation and Resettlement Study Collection, Bancroft Library, University of California, Berkeley, J 6.05.
2. See Richard Nishimoto, "The Initial Impact of the Army Announcement of Rescission of the Exclusion Orders and the WRA Announcement of Liquidation of the Relocation Centers." Japanese American Evacuation and Resettlement Study collection, Bancroft Library, University of California, Berkeley, J 6.05.

With the promulgation, the resistance to accelerated relocation and the eventual closing of the center began to crystallize in the community. The evacuees cried that they could not leave the center; therefore, the center should not be closed. They argued that steps should be taken to stop the WRA from executing its policy of closure. They shouted that they should unite against the closing of the center. Indeed, there was a great danger of emergence of an active and organized obstruction to relocation; there was a tendency that some of the residents might coercively prevent others from relocating.

On the face of the vociferous resistance, the evacuees that were planning to relocate or in favor of relocation took to cover; they became secretive about their intentions and plans for the future. In order to leave the center they prepared quietly lest they might be ostracized by their fellow residents as unduly cooperating with the WRA policies and thereby jeopardizing the chance of maintaining *status quo* for the duration.[3] The responsible evacuee leaders were quick to observe the danger of chaos, and they undertook a program, although with most of them accidentally or inadvertently, whereby: (1) those who were able to relocate were encouraged to do so; and (2) for those who could not or did not wish to relocate, they promised to do the utmost to fulfill their desire of remaining in the center for the duration. In other words, the leaders endeavored to check and keep anti-relocation agitation under control so that the free flow of egress be uninterfered.

Meanwhile, in order to satisfy the evacuees who were clamoring against the closing of the center, the Unit I Local Council as early as December 20, 1944 and the Community Council a little afterwards adopted a proposal to invite delegates from other relocation centers to solve newly created problems jointly and, if possible, to make a united stand against the policy of center closure. The Poston proposal, however, was tabled shortly afterwards, for some of the other centers had simultaneously been planning similar conferences independently of one another and an agreement had been reached so that the Community Council of the Central Utah Relocation Center at Topaz be given the sponsorship for the All Center Conference.

---

3. When Nishimoto uses the term *status quo* in this text, he is referring to Poston residents' desire to keep things as they were. This is not to be confused with the way Nishimoto and Thomas used the term *genjo-iji* in a subsequent publication to refer to an attitude of noncooperation with representatives of the federal government, including the War Relocation Authority; see Dorothy S. Thomas and Richard Nishimoto, *The Spoilage*, Japanese American Evacuation and Resettlement series (Berkeley: University of California Press, 1946), 161 and passim.

During the month of January, 1945, the resistance to relocation and to the policy of center closure seemed to have slightly decreased. To say the least, the vociferous expressions attacking the WRA and the blatant criticisms of the relocatees had greatly waned. Nevertheless, the change in the attitudes and the behaviors of the evacuees were not to be attributed to their greater acceptance of the new WRA policies; rather, no longer were they in need of such violent expressions and negativistic behaviors to assert themselves for the lack of opposition. The resistance to the WRA policies for closing of the center had become established in the *mores.* None of them disagreed or wanted to disagree with the contention that the center could not be closed and should not be closed. Every evacuee agreed that there were many evacuees who could not leave the center for the duration and the Government should provide for them here. Most of the relocating evacuees, too, were careful to explain to others that they had to relocate for special personal reasons, which did not apply to the others, although they were anxious to remain in the center to the last days; they went out of their way to assure the others that they were not in favor of the WRA policy of "forcing" evacuees out of the center. Some other evacuees made their relocation plans quietly, while at the same time arguing articulately that the center should be maintained for the duration. The Administration, too, was not willing to irritate the residents unduly; they avoided aggressive execution of the post-exclusion program. The Relocation Division employees processed relocatees quietly without fanfare.

By and large, the careful planning jointly by the Administration and the evacuee leaders had succeeded in preventing the resistance taking forms of overt and irrational agitation. Towards the end of January, the community as a whole appeared to be orderly and peaceful. Nevertheless, even the superficial observers could not fail to detect the inherent and latent resistance to the policy of closing of the center. The residents still believed firmly that the center should not be closed and they should not be forced out. The various incidents of violence and "hoodlumism" and the news of racial hatred in the Western States and elsewhere were enough to reinforce the morbid fear of the outside, and thereby kept the resistance smoldering. In other words, it was only a precarious calm that existed at the time in the community—on the surface there was no overt agitation against the WRA policy of liquidation, while below the surface the resistance remained unabated with a dangerous potentiality of bursting out at any time with disturbing stimuli.

Against this background, the Community Council received an invitation from the Topaz Community Council for participation in the All Center Conference to be held at Salt Lake City during the month of February. On January 25, the Poston Council met and voted to accept the invitation. The acceptance was immediately followed by preparations—the dissemination of the information and the selection of the delegates. The Local Councils and the Block Managers of the three Units held their respective meetings to devise the method of selecting the delegates and the platform for which the Poston residents would be pledged. Accordingly, in Unit I, a general election was approved as the method of selecting the delegates and many different demands and appeals were formulated as the platform in the block meetings, which were held during the first week of February. As described previously, many of these block meetings were tumultuous, indicating the existence of intense resistance to the WRA policies. The composite platform contained many requests for which, to say the least, the united efforts at the conference would not be sufficient to force the WRA to concede—many of them could be termed as impossible and irresponsible. For one, the delegates were to be instructed to request the WRA for the maintenance of the center in *status quo*, in direct opposition and incompatible with the newly promulgated policies of the WRA. It was true that few residents realized that such requests could be materialized at the conference; nonetheless, they were determined to instruct the delegates with the impossible platform, although in general they did not anticipate a success.[4]

In this portentous atmosphere, the most successful election in the Poston history was held on February 7, 1945; and facing a most difficult assignment Yoshitaro Katow, the Chairman of the Executive Board, and Minoru Okamoto, the Chairman of the Local Council, were elected to represent Unit I. Together with John Kubota and James Takashima, who through different methods of selection had been chosen to represent Units II and III respectively, they were ready to depart to Salt Lake City. The Community Council then approved the proposal of allowing Nobuo Matsubara, a member of the Unit I Executive Board, to accompany the delegation as their secretary.

In commenting on the platform, which the delegates were instructed to present to the All Center Conference, the evacuee leaders shook their heads in despair. They knew that the requests of the residents were impossible; they were aware of the fact that Director Myer and his subordinates would come to

4. See Richard S. Nishimoto, "Developments Leading to Participation in the All Center Conference and the Visit of the Representative of the Spanish Embassy," Japanese American Evacuation and Resettlement Study collection, Bancroft Library, University of California, Berkeley, J 6.05.

the conference to do their best to sell the program of relocation in their own terms and not in terms of the evacuees' thinking. They had forewarned the residents not to be overly optimistic as to the outcome of the conference. Yet there existed many, especially among the older evacuees, who thought that the WRA could be subdued to change its course. The leaders were faced with a responsibility of preparing the community for an inevitable disappointment so that the delegates on their return might not be unjustifiably criticized for failing to achieve the impossible task. Both Katow and Okamoto, too, were pessimistic as to the outcome of the conference. They could not promise anything but sheer determination: "We will do our best."

The Poston delegation left for Utah on February 14. On departing they issued the following message through the Japanese section of the *Poston Chronicle* (translated from the Japanese original in the February 14th issue of the *Poston Chronicle*):

> With the severance of diplomatic relations between Japan and America, the national policy of the United States decided to evacuate us, all of persons of Japanese ancestry, from California. Thus, maintaining our pride that we are the model, civilized nationals that conform to the national law, and as we were dictated by the national policy, we relocated to the center with the Nisei, citizens of the United States, who shed tears of indignation for being exiled from the places of their birth.
>
> Subsequently we have reached this day struggling desperately to establish a new society here. Suddenly the plan to close the center had been announced. Nevertheless, at the time of evacuation we had lost everything, the fruit of blood and tears of the past several tens of years. Except a small number of people, most of us are under the circumstances that we cannot leave the center easily.
>
> Therefore, it has been decided that the All Center Conference will be held at Salt Lake City. We will attend the conference taking the requests and proposals of our fellow residents. Laying the grave responsibility closely to our hearts, we are determined to do our best, though little that may be, in order to prove worthy of your expectations.
>
> On departing we beg your support.

Developments at Poston During the Conference

The All Center Conference was first conceived by the evacuee leaders and supported by evacuees at large as a means of consolidating the resistance against the newly announced decision of the WRA to close the relocation centers. They wanted to organize a united front for the maintenance of the centers in the *status quo.* However, having realized the difficulty of convincing the WRA that the centers should not be closed for the duration, they devised several conditions—primarily, more and better assistances and guarantees for safety—with which they would reluctantly consent to [leave] the center. In this manner, the initial attempt of the two pronged attack against the WRA was worked out.

In the subsequent weeks, as the WRA officials had explained the post-exclusion program fully and had begun to put it into actual operation, the evacuees leaders became aware of the futility of forcing the WRA to veer from the already announced course, at least for the present. As the realization of futility had crystallized with many of the leaders or had vacillated with others, the Community Council received the invitation to the conference. At the time, the interest for such a conference had waned; many of the responsible leaders were as a matter of fact glad that the issue of the All Center Conference had generally been forgotten. It was therefore natural that they were annoyed when they heard that the Council accepted the invitation; they did not want the dormant and latent resistance to the policy of center closure revitalized and become violent again. Unit Administrator Sumida, for example, stated in this manner: "People were getting quiet now and just getting to settle down. They were forgetting about the conference. Now that the invitation has been received and the whole thing has to be discussed in the blocks, we have to hear many nasty words about the WRA. The camp will be very noisy again for the next several weeks. It would have been all right if we didn't have this conference."

Supervisor of Block Managers Nishimoto, too, did not like to see the issue of center closure brought up on the surface again. "So, after all, they have decided to hold this conference," lamented Nishimoto. "We have worked hard enough to quiet down the community. We have succeeded in controlling the resistance. Now this conference had to come."

Nishimoto realized that the inherent resistance to the new WRA policies had not lessened. He knew that the rank and file of evacuees were still just as adamant and insistent as before in opposing the policy of closing of the center. It was evident that the resistance could flare up again with proper stimulation. "I suppose that those irrational, heckling Issei will have field day," Nishimoto added. "I guess we have to hear a lot of violent expressions and emotional statements. If we lead them right, we might be able to let them blow off some of their latent steam."

M. Okamoto and others close to the Community Council were not as enthusiastic about the conference as [when] they had first proposed it. They acted as if they had to go on with the preparations unwillingly as the responsibility had been thrust upon them. One of them remarked: "We started talking about it (the conference). I guess we have to finish it whether we like it or not."

When Chairman Okamoto presented the proposal of the All Center Conference to the regular meeting of the Unit I Local Council on January 31, it was obvious that no preparations had been made in advance for participation. The Community Council had dropped the matter early in January, and had not made any attempt to study "the wishes and demands of the people" to be proposed to the meeting. The leaders close to the Community Council had assumed that preparations would not be necessary inasmuch as the Poston residents in general were opposed to the closure policy and they would be required merely to oppose the WRA. The lack of advance planning was embarrassing to Okamoto when he was asked in the meeting by the Local Councilmen for some basic proposals with which they could conduct the block meetings. He promised to mimeograph and distribute the Heart Mountain document, which was the fruit of a long study by the leaders at Heart Mountain.[5] The document contained the various requests for the two classes of people: viz., those who wanted to remain in the center for the duration, and those who wanted assistances and guarantees in order to relocate. Thus, the two pronged attack against the WRA had been embodied in the document, and suited the trend of thinking of the evacuees at Poston. The block meetings quickly adopted those demands in the document as their own, and the Poston platform was formulated with a few additions and modifications.

It was easy to formulate those demands, but to obtain concessions from the WRA for those demands was entirely another matter. The document contained demands, which the WRA would not concede in any way at this stage. Many of the evacuees realized the difficulty of getting even a minor concession, but they were not hesitant in making many unreasonable demands. A sophisticated urban Issei characteristically remarked: "Well, is there any harm in asking? Unless you ask, you can't get it."

Another Issei stated similarly, representing the prevalent attitude: "If we can't stay in the center, we might as well try to get most out of the WRA. It is to show the WRA how difficult it is to close the center."

---

5. Heart Mountain was a WRA camp in Wyoming.

The leaders, were, however, worried over the presence of many evacuees in the community who wishfully expected that the crux of the present post-exclusion program could be reversed as a result of this conference. Some of the PTA members were especially guilty of hoping that the policy of closing the schools could be reversed by appealing to the WRA through the delegates (*infra*, pp. xxx).[6] Against the optimism the responsible evacuees issued warnings repeatedly. They publicized that the main purpose of the conference was to exchange information and ideas among the delegates from the various centers and reach some agreements as to their future course in jointly championing the interests of evacuees. The Supervisor of Block Managers, too, warned the Block Managers and instructed them to caution the residents against wishful thinking.

In the regular meeting on February 13, Supervisor Nishimoto informed the Block Managers that an arrangement had been made with the delegates for transmission of daily reports from Salt Lake City. The Supervisor would prepare copies of the reports as soon as they were received and distribute them to the blocks, he said. The Managers were in turn asked to keep their respective residents informed of the proceedings of the conference. Nishimoto again reminded the Managers that the residents ought to be cautioned against optimistic anticipations as to the outcome. He went on to say as follows:

> I have warned you again and again not to expect any definite concession from the WRA out of this meeting at Salt Lake City. The delegates are entrusted with an impossible task of asking the WRA to maintain the center in *status quo* and to provide the relocatees with more assistances and guarantees. As I have said often and I am sure you will agree with me, the outcome will not be anything which will satisfy the wishful thinker or the 'sit-tighter'. Please inform them whenever you have an opportunity that this is the first conference of this sort and we cannot achieve anything beyond mapping out our future course for opposing the WRA and its policy of center closure. The delegates did their job well if they had succeeded in laying a foundation for future conferences to pursue the fight to achieve the ultimate aim of these residents here: that is, the maintenance of the center for the duration.

6. As noted in the Note on Transcription and Terminology, cross-references like "*infra*, p. xxx," with the page number left unspecified, are probably to two other lengthy reports Nishimoto wrote as background to his All Center Conference study. They are reproduced as they appear in the archival copy of this document.

> You will receive reports from the delegates at Salt Lake City. I am asking you to utilize these reports to the fullest possible advantage in educating the people that all of us, let alone the delegates to the conference, are faced with a tremendous job before we can make the WRA concede that the center should not be closed.

After Nishimoto's speech, one of the Managers reported that most of the residents had participated in the block meetings and the election as a method of demonstrating against the WRA and that they as a whole were aware of the difficulty. Several other Managers, on the other hand, argued that there were many evacuees whose outlook on the outcome were not realistic. They argued that the Managers should do their best to convince these evacuees of what this first conference could accomplish.

Thus, the channel of communication from the delegates at Salt Lake City to the residents at Poston was established. The use of propaganda through the communication system to prepare the residents for the return of the delegates to Poston was planned. On February 16, the first telegram was received from the delegation at Salt Lake City. It read as follows:

SALT LAKE CITY UTAH FEB 15, 1945.
ARRIVED IN SALT LAKE AT 630 PM. ALL FEEL FINE. WEATHER VERY COLD. CONVEY OUR BEST REGARDS TO ALL POSTON DELEGATES
9:21 A.M.

The Community Council made copies and distributed them to the Unit Administrators, the Supervisors of Block Managers, the Local Councils, and the Executive Board of the three Units. The Supervisor's office in Unit I in turn made more copies and sent them to the Block Managers. The Managers then read them to the residents in their respective Mess Halls at meal time.

Early in the morning of February 17, evacuees in the administrative area were excited over the news of shootings and the burning of a Nisei's home in the Fresno district. Wild speculations and interested discussions started quickly when a Nisei had reported that he had heard the news over the radio station KNX in Los Angeles the night before. About 10 o'clock in the same morning, the Los Angeles newspapers reached the project; the editions carried the news spectacularly. The newspaper stories further accelerated the spreading of the news throughout the community. The *Los Angeles Times* of February 17th, for instance, printed the news on the front page accompanied by a picture of the burning house, 4 1/2 inches long and four columns wide, under the headline "Fresno Shotgun Squad Hunted in War on Nisei".[7] It reported that a group of unknown assailants "blasted hundreds of pellets into a house occupied" by S. J. Kakutani, "returned American-born Japanese". It also reported that about the same time on the night of February 15 the home and furnishings of Bob Morishige in the nearby town of Selma were destroyed by the fire set by unknown incendiarist. The article mentioned at the end that "four days ago three shotgun blasts struck the home of Frank Osaki, who returned from an Arizona relocation center three weeks ago." On an inside page in the same edition of the *Los Angeles Times*, another article was printed reporting the same incidents.

The surprise and interest of evacuees at Poston over the news of three incidents which took place in rapid succession were great. They were surprised because they had believed that the Central California areas were free from rabid racial hatred and the potentiality of racial disturbances. They were greatly interested in the news, because their contention that the outside world was not friendly to the evacuees was vindicated. They were amused, because Central California now had to be included among the "danger zones" together with Imperial Valley, the Salinas-Watsonville area, Orange County, Lancaster, and Gardena. The young and the old expressed alike that it was premature to return to California at this time. Some of them went further to reason that the WRA might be convinced of the advisability of keeping the centers open beyond the announced date.

The most prevalent reaction was expressed by a Nisei evacuee from Delano, about twenty-five years of age, in this manner: "I knew that it was too early for those people to return to California. We should wait for a long while before we plan to go to California. It isn't safe yet. You can't tell what might happen."

A Hawaii-born Nisei, evacuated from Los Angeles, about thirty-five years of age, said that he had known such incidents would occur at the beginning. He returned to Poston to take his family out having prepared to farm in New Mexico. He stated:

> I knew that. I knew things like that will happen. Sure, I want to go back to California. But not for a while. I don't want anything to happen to my family

7. In the edition available on microfilm, this story appears in pt. 1, p. 3, under the headline, "Gang Terrorizes Returning Jap Evacuees."

> out there. That's the reason I went out to New Mexico to look around for a farm. I found a place. People were nice out there. I didn't notice any race discrimination. I am going to take my family to New Mexico. It's near Albuquerque. I am going to farm for one year or so. I don't know if I can make money or not. That's one of those things. Probably I will return to Los Angeles after one year or so.

A Nisei of Zoot-suiter type, about twenty years old, expressed forcefully: "Hell, that's what you get for going back to California. Why go to California?"

Another Nisei remarked: "California? Not me! I'm going back East somewhere."

An Issei, a resident of the block with urban evacuees, probably about fifty years old, stated: "They are telling us to relocate. How can we? This is a good proof. It's not safe for us to relocate. The WRA should realize that. No, I'm going to stay here until the war ends."

Another Issei, apparently a farmer in the pre-evacuation days, had this to say: "California has been opened. But what is the use? We can't go back there. This is wartime. It's natural that those people are mad about the Japanese and want to harm us. It was bad enough before the war. I can't see how situations are better in California right now."

An Issei rural evacuee was resentful over the fact that many evacuees were planning to return to California: "Many guys trust the WRA and believe what it says. They believe that the WRA is really going to close the center this year and get excited. They are scared of being forced out by the WRA and are planning to relocate. I know most of them are going to California. They are fools. Let them go back to California if they want. The same thing will happen to those fools."

An Issei about sixty years old wished that more incidents of this sort would aid those that were planning to remain here for the duration. He stated: "I want more incidents like that. The more the better. Then the WRA will be convinced that they should not close the centers. The WRA will change its mind and will say that we better stay in the centers for the duration. We all know that the centers are the safest place for us, but the WRA doesn't know that yet."

A middle aged Issei remarked sarcastically in English: "Good old California! Same old gangs of racists!"

A member (an Issei) of the Community Council recounted the experience of Itaru Kubota, the former Chairman, who received "uninvited guests" of hoodlums one night to intimidate him when he visited Fresno. Kubota subsequently returned to his home in Fresno in order to "blaze the path for others to return safely," according to one of his friends who quoted him. Kubota believed that the only way to combat the racial discrimination was to have more Japanese return and "educate the Caucasian". The Issei who narrated Kubota's experience added: "I knew that incidents like these would happen soon. Many people said that Central California is all right for Japanese, but I didn't believe it. Kubota told me that things were not so good out there. It was already in the air when Kubota visited Fresno last month. After all, we, Issei, can't go to any place but to California. So, I think it is wise to stay here and watch how things will turn out in California."

Unit II Administrator Uyeno wondered whether his erstwhile enemy, Setsugo Sakamoto, the Chairman of the Unit II Local Council, would go through with the plan of returning to his former home in Fresno in light of these incidents. The Unit Administrator, a Kibei in his early thirties, seemed to be amused over the situation. Sakamoto had been making plans to direct the return of his friends to their former homes in the Fresno area; Uyeno reported that Sakamoto had persuaded "more than a half of Block 224" to leave the center with him.

In receiving the news story, Corlies Carter, the Relocation Program Officer, too showed a great concern. He was worried, because he believed that the incidents would greatly increase the already present feeling of insecurity and the fear of the outside, let alone California, and would further retard the slow progress of relocation. He was disturbed over the prospect that the interest and awakening enthusiasm of many evacuees in Unit II, especially, for returning to Central California in the near future might abruptly be halted. With the aid of Mrs. Pauline Brown, the Reports Officer, he sent a telegram of inquiry to Robert Cozzens, the Director of the WRA office at San Francisco. However, when he received a telegram from the San Francisco office the next morning confirming the newspaper story, he was a dejected man. He said in a tone of low spirit that he could only hope for the best.

Likewise, the evacuee leaders showed a great deal of anxiety over the news. As the news was discussed widely in the community, they agreed to send an instruction to the delegates at Salt Lake City that the "guarantee of life and property" for the relocatee, one of the Poston requests, be strongly presented to the WRA officials at the conference. Together with a copy of the February 17th edition of the *Los Angeles Times*, the instruction was dispatched to the delegates via air mail. It is interesting to note that about one week afterwards the rumors of new shootings in the same area were widely circulated in the community. However, upon investigation these new stories were found to be baseless.

During the same turbulent day, February 17, the Community Council received the second telegraph from Salt Lake City.

SALT LAKE CITY UTAH FEB 16 1945
CONFERENCE OPENED 10 AM. 27 DELEGATES OF SEVEN CENTERS ATTENDED. PROPOSAL OF CENTERS READ AND DISCUSSED. OUR DELEGATES ARE DOING THEIR BEST. ADVISE RICHARD NISHIMOTO AIR MAIL POSTON PROPOSALS FORTY COPIES.
[MATSUBARA] 9:06 A.M.

From this [night] letter it was evident that the Poston representatives wanted to distribute the proposals of the Poston residents among the delegates from other centers.

On February 20, Secretary Matsubara air mailed the following report, (translated from the original in Japanese):

ALL CENTER CONFERENCE

The Names of Representatives

1. Gila: Hiroji Nishimura, Shigeichi Mitsuyoshi, Mitsuru Fukuzawa (Nisei), and Yoriyuki Sato;
2. Granada: Sakae Kawajiri (Nisei), Shinichi Furuya, and Eiji Uragami;
3. Heart Mountain: Kaoru Akashi, Minejiro Hayashida, Minokichi Tsunokai, Kumezo Hachimonji, and Shigeichi Kawano;
4. Minidoka: Yoshito Fujii, Genji Mihara, Tohru Ogawa, and Iwao Oyama;
5. Poston: Yoshitaro Katow, Minoru Okamoto, Minoru Kubota, and James Katsumi Takashima;
6. Rohwer: Chuji Fujino, Shitaro Ito, and Shuzo Shingu;
7. Topaz: Tsuna Watanabe, Shizuo Sasaki, Kiichi Nodohara, Ichiji Sugiyama, Masaru Narahara (Nisei), and Susumu Yamashita (Nisei)

Secretaries: Shintaro Murakami, Toshiko Yamamoto (Nisei), and Mitsuye Endo (Nisei).[8] All these three from Topaz.

8. Mitsuye Endo is listed as one of the two All Center Conference English-language secretaries here, as well as throughout the official All Center Conference report. This is the same Nisei woman who was at the center of the Ex Parte Endo case. For an outline of the technical dimensions of this important court case, see the entry "Endo, Ex Parte," by Glen Kitayama, in *Japanese American History: An A-to-Z Reference from 1868 to the Present*, Brian Niiya, ed. (New York: Facts on File, 1993), 134–35. When asked for an interview regarding her participation and memories, however, she wrote in reply on February 8, 1993:

Report No. 1

The Salt Lake Conference was opened at 10 A.M., February 16, at a room of the Y.W.C.A., Masaru Narahara, the Chairman of the Topaz Community Council, which sponsored the meeting, having been installed as Temporary Chairman. 27 delegates were present.

The business was taken up after the election of Chairman and Vice Chairmen. The business discussed and the matter decided were as follows:

1. The reason of Manzanar for not participating. Chairman reported "they could not see the importance of this conference . . . " A motion was carried to send a telegram asking again for participation.
2. It was decided that both Japanese and English be used during the conference.
3. The Poston proposal: to submit invitations to different organizations to send representatives to this conference. It was discussed and passed.
4. The selection of the Program Committee (for formulation of agenda): Mitsuru Fukuda (Gila), Tohru Ogawa (Minidoka), Kumezo Hachimonji (Heart Mountain), Shinichi Furuya (Granada), Shuzu Shingu (Rohwer), Minoru Okamoto (Poston), and Kiichi Nodohara (Topaz).
5. The selection of the committee to arrange proposals: Yoriyuki Sato (Gila), Iwao Oyama (Minidoka), Shigeichi Kawano (Heart Mountain), Eiji Uragami (Granada), Yoshitaro Katow (Poston), Ichiji Sugiyama (Topaz), and Chuji Fujino (Rohwer).
6. The resolutions of the various centers were read by their respective delegates and were explained.

(The meeting was adjourned at 5:25 P.M.)

Among those discussed on this day, discussions were tumultuous on (1), (2), (3), and (4). Especially on the question of inviting the Spanish representative,[9] the delegates were divided pro and con sharply and exchanged heated

"At the conference, all we [the two English-language secretaries, Endo and Mary Yamamoto] were asked to do was to take down Dillon Myer's opening remarks, after which Mary and I went back to our hotel room to transcribe it. We did not stay for the rest of the conference proceedings and were not involved in any other way. I did not know any of the others involved.

"There is no need for an interview as this is all I remember about the conference."

9. Since the Issei were Japanese nationals and since Japan did not maintain diplomatic relations with the United States during World War II, the Issei were allowed to report their grievances to the Spanish consul. As pointed out, the situation was especially bad for Issei in the Justice Department camps in the beginning and involved "abuses, threats of physical harm, physical beatings, shootings, and actual killings." Over the course of the war, Japanese nationals were increasingly able to defend themselves against outright abuse by citing the articles of the Geneva Convention in their protests against unjust treatment. See Tetsuden Kashima, "American Mistreatment of Internees during World War II: Enemy Alien Japa-

opinions. In addition, during the afternoon conference, the photographer of the *Salt Lake Tribune* rushed into the conference room without permission and flashed a picture. As a result of vigorous protest, he agreed to expose the film; in return, he asked for a permission to take pictures of the group. At the same time, he asked for the release of news stories. After discussion on these matters, the requests were granted.

The Conference—Second Day—from 9:00 A.M. to 5:35 P.M.

The important subjects discussed or resolved during the day included the following.

1. Report of the Program Committee.
2. The committee on resolutions from the centers met to arrange and consolidate the proposals.
3. No news release will be granted unless approved by the conference. This will include the newspapers of the centers.
4. The minutes of the meeting and the resolutions will be printed.
5. The conference expenses will be equally shared by the various centers.
6. It was decided to choose one spokesman from each center during the session with Director Myer.
7. To establish Resolution Committee.

Among these, the selection of personnel for (6) and (7) were carried over to a meeting in the future.

> "From tomorrow, February 19, we go into the main conference. Since the proposals from the various centers are to be deliberated, heated arguments are again expected. Discussions on the floor will be lively."

The letter in Japanese from Matsubara was immediately mimeographed and distributed to the blocks. (No copies in English were made.) It was reported by some of the Block Managers that many residents, especially the Issei, read the report with much interest, for "they had been waiting for news from

---

nese," *Japanese Americans: From Relocation to Redress*, ed. Roger Daniels et al. (Seattle: University of Washington Press, 1991), 52–56.

Salt Lake City." One of them said, "Their reactions are very good. There is no heckling or irresponsible expression. They seemed to be satisfied with what the delegates are doing."

Telegrams continued to arrive from the delegates. The report received on February 21 read as follows:

SALT LAKE CITY UTAH FEB 20 1945
DISCUSSION ALMOST CONCLUDED. DRAFTING RESOLUTION. MEET MYERS TOMORROW MORNING. OPEN SESSION WITH DISTINGUISHED GUESTS AFTERNOON. WILL REMAIN UNTIL SATURDAY NOON. THANKS PROPOSAL COPIES.
MATSUBARA 9:24 A.M.

The telegram received on February 22 read as follows:

SALT LAKE CITY UTAH FEB 21 1945
MYER MADE SPEECH ON WRA POLICY. DISCUSSIONS FOLLOWING IN OPEN MEETING WITH REPRESENTATIVES OF FRIENDLY ORGANIZATIONS. CONSTRUCTIVE SUGGESTIONS REMARKS PRESENTED.
MATSUBARA 9:06 A.M.

The night letter received on February 24, 1945 read as follows:

SALT LAKE CITY UTAH FEB 25 1945
CONFERENCE CONCLUDED TONIGHT WITH FAREWELL PARTY. COMMITTEES STILL WORKING ON RESOLUTIONS AND OTHER BUSINESS. EXPECT TO LEAVE HERE TUESDAY.
MATSUBARA 9:07 A.M.

The telegram received on the same day stated as follows:

RESOLUTIONS ADOPTED. FURTHER DISCUSSIONS ON RESPECTIVE CENTER PROBLEMS CONTINUING. CONFERENCE WILL BE CONCLUDED TONIGHT.
MATSUBARA 2:14 P.M.

Copies were made of each telegram and each block received one copy of every telegram. In the usual manner, the Block Manager informed his block residents of the content of each telegram at mealtime.

On February 25, the Community Council received the second detailed report via air mail. Secretary Matsubara wrote as follows (translated from Japanese): February 19—the Third Day of The Conference

Begun at 9:30 A.M. at the Japanese Christian Church

The matters decided today:

1. The method of voting—A motion granting each center one vote was adopted.

2. The selection of the Public Relations Committee. In order to avoid wrong reporting in the newspapers, the Committee is delegated with the duty to release correct news. At the same time, the Committee is to handle all matters pertaining to public relations.

The Committee is composed of one member from each center. John Kubota was selected on the Committee from Poston.

3. Discussions on compilation of the resolutions from the various centers.

Heated discussions were carried during this session on the request of those who wished to relocate and on the reasons of those who could not leave the center.

Adjournment at 6:15 P.M.

(February 18—sightseeing trip to the Mormon church in the morning and to Tooele in the afternoon.)

February 20—the Fourth Day—from 9:30 A.M., at the Y.W.C.A.

In the morning, the proposals of the various centers were deliberated one by one. In the afternoon, the Resolution Committee was selected. From Poston, Katsumi Takashima became a member of the Committee.

Following this, the delegates discussed matters to be presented to Director Myer in a closed session tomorrow. (Again they argued among themselves considerably.)

Adjournment at 5:30 P.M.

February 21—the Fifth Day

In the morning, the delegates met Director Myer in a closed session.

In the afternoon, an open meeting was held among Director Myer, the delegates, the representatives of the organizations which had been invited, and other public officials. (This is one of the most valuable achievements of this conference.)

February 22—the Sixth Day.

In the morning, Rev. Nugent, a Protestant minister, attended the meeting and gave a speech of encouragement.

Then the delegates debated on the question of to whom the resolution and its copies be mailed. This subject, too, caused the delegates to argue heatedly.

In the afternoon, it was resolved to establish a central organization in order to attain the objectives of the residents of all the centers. It was also resolved that Manzanar be asked to cooperate with other centers in the future so that mutual problems be solved together. It was agreed unanimously that the resolution be submitted to the Director of the WRA. The Poston delegates worked hard and well, and most of the Poston proposals were adopted in the main conference.

In the usual manner, this air mailed report was mimeographed and distributed to the blocks.

On February 26, the final night letter was received from Secretary Matsubara. It read as follows:

SALT LAKE CITY UTAH FEB 25 1945
FINAL MEETING OF COMMITTEE HELD SATURDAY NIGHT.
CORRECTIONS MADE ON RESOLUTIONS. MAILED CORRECTED COPY
TODAY. DISREGARD PREVIOUS ONE. EXPECT TO LEAVE HERE
MONDAY NIGHT.
MATSUBARA 9:24 A.M.

Thus, the conference was concluded and the delegates sent the words that they were returning to Poston. At the end of February, the interest of evacuees at Poston in the All Center Conference and other means of protesting to the WRA against its policy of center liquidation had decreased. Rarely did they mention the conference, although they read the distributed copies of the information sent from Salt Lake City. Most of them had reached a realistic estimate on the outcome of the meeting; they stated that they could not expect the WRA to announce the reversal of its policy at this time. Some of them remarked that they were satisfied with the conference, because "most of the Poston demands" had been embodied in the final resolution of the conference. They knew that the WRA would probably reject all the demands, they said. As one Issei commented, many residents believed that the fight had just begun: "The conference is our first step. We can't expect to succeed in getting what we want from the beginning. Time will come when the WRA must change its policy. We don't have to worry."

Indeed, very few except leaders talked about the conference. The residents in general believed that the WRA could not close the center while thousands of evacuees remained here. They were convinced that circumstances would compel the WRA to reverse its stand at some future date. Many of them thought that the conference was serving the purpose of calling the attention of the WRA that they could not leave the center. There had been nothing since the announcement of the liquidation policy to disturb their contention that the center could not be closed. On the contrary, the subsequent developments corroborated the evacuees' reasoning and arguments. The outside world, especially California, as seen through first hand reports and the newspapers, was hostile to them. The progress of relocation had been much below the estimates of many observers; many residents were surprised, they said, that more people had not left the center. A little more than 200 persons had relocated during January and about the same number of persons would have relocated by the last day of February. The slow progress of relocation assured many that they need not worry about the center closure; it alleviated the feeling of insecurity created by the policy promulgation. An urban Issei evacuee summarized the situation well in the following words:

> The delegates are telling the WRA that we cannot leave the center as easily as the WRA claims. It is backed up by the rate of relocation. Not much people are leaving. I am surprised, though. I thought more people would go out.
>
> There are plenty of people here. The WRA cannot kick us out of here. As long as there are so many of us here, we are all right. The WRA will change its policy. But I don't believe the WRA will announce the change until the last minute.

There were, on the other hand, some evacuees who awaited the return of the delegates anxiously. Supervisor Nishimoto received several inquiries as to the date of their return. One of them characteristically stated: "They might bring back some interesting news. It is always important to find out how other evacuees at other relocation centers are thinking. Because of the conference sessions, the delegates may have some valuable estimates for the future."

Another Issei, a member of the Unit I Local Council, remarked: "After we hear the inside stories of the conference we will know what to do next."

The community had regained most of the complacent composure of the days previous to the announcement of the policy of center closure. People were in general not expectant for a successful and satisfying report from the delegates; many of them were quite indifferent as to the outcome, although some showed curiosity for the news. The evacuee leaders had greatly contributed in informing the public that "this was the beginning of a long pull, and the beginning will be hard and disturbing." To this seemingly calm community, the delegates were returning.

The Reports of Delegates

Late on the night of February 27, 1945, Yoshitaro Katow, Minoru Okamoto, John Kubota, and James Katsumi Takashima, the four delegates who had represented the evacuees at the Colorado River Relocation Center in the All Center Conference at Salt Lake City, and Nobuo Matsubara, the Secretary who had accompanied the delegation, returned to Poston. In the morning of February 28, evacuee political leaders scurried around in the administrative area passing the information that the delegates had returned. Many evacuees were anxious to learn of the news on the conference and sought these delegates in their respective offices, although none of them reported to work. Sensing the advisability of presenting the delegates to the Council as early as possible, G. Iseda and S. Yoshikawa, the Chairman and the Public Relations Coordinator respectively, busied themselves with notification to the members of the Council and other preparations for holding a special session of the Community Council on March 1 to hear reports from the delegates.

In the meanwhile, Project Director Mills had heard that the delegates were back. Through Assistant Director John Powell, Mills asked Supervisor Nishimoto to arrange an interview with Katow. It is interesting that Mills did not desire to see Okamoto, whom he distrusted. Although Katow had not been acquainted with Mills and other recent arrivals high in the Administration because he had confined himself in the isolated sphere of the Community Enterprises for more than one year before he became the Chairman of the Executive Board, he was generally well regarded among the appointed personnel due to the verbal "boosting" by Powell and others older in the point of service here among the staff members.

Answering the call from Nishimoto, Katow came to see the Supervisor on the afternoon of February 28. The delegate immediately gave a brief description of the conference. The meeting at Salt Lake City, in his opinion, was disorganized and irresponsible. Only did the presence of the capable Nisei representatives save the conference from becoming a chaos and failure. Katow accused the older representatives of emotionally unbalance and unrealistic; the Issei delegates were prone to argue on the points of the international law and to rely on the Japanese Government as a panacea for the evacuee problems in America.

"Issei are no good," Katow lamented. "They are too old. They don't know who they are. They forget that they are enemy aliens. Every other words they must say something about asking the Japanese Government to do this or that. They get excited and make impassioned speeches. And when the speeches are concluded, we don't know what the speakers are talking about. It's awful. Don't send Issei to any of conferences of this sort. It's a shame for the whole Japanese population in America. At least, the delegates should remember that we have been in America for more than thirty and forty years and lived here as law abiding residents. We must live in America after the war. There is no mistake about that. I don't care what people say about going back to Japan after the war. They can't kid themselves forever. It will be only a small number of people that will return to Japan. Most of us are going to remain in this country. So, we should act accordingly. We should continue to act like law abiding residents. We must avoid irrational acts and expressions. We must not act like a bunch of people who are not grateful to America for what she had provided in the past. We must forget Japan when we are dealing with the WRA problems."

"These Issei delegates acted like they were presenting requests to the Spanish Consul or somebody like that," Katow continued to express his disgust. "Many of these Issei were a kind of fools we are familiar with in the centers. They think that Japan is all mighty and before her the world will shrink with fear. They believe that America will do anything if Japan tells it to do so. Those delegates can't think; their heads are outmoded. It is dangerous for the whole Japanese population to entrust them with such a grave responsibility. We must avoid that in the future.

"Some of the requests which they asked to be embodied in the resolution were foolhardy and irrational. A copy of the resolution is to be sent to the President of the United States. We could not stop them from embodying those crazy requests in the Japanese original. But when our committee worked overnight in translating them into English, we deleted all the objectionable points without the knowledge of other members of the conference. People on the outside will think we are crazy if we included those things in the English version. Those Issei don't know that we changed the content in the translation.

You will understand what we were up against. For instance, we changed 'demands' in the Japanese original to 'petition' and 'recommendation' in the English version. Those old people don't realize the seriousness of demanding anything from the government of a nation. They are fools. There are other revisions in the English resolution. If you compare them, you will see what we deleted. Of course, this will meet with your approval."

Regarding the interview requested by Director Mills, Katow was reluctant. He reasoned that he had not reported to the "people" of Poston yet, whom he had represented at the conference, and questioned the propriety of seeing Mills in advance. "After all, we were paid by the people," Katow said. "We didn't get paid by the WRA; the WRA had refused to pay our expenses. It's people's money that we have spent. So I believe we should report to the people first."

After he was persuaded and assured that the interview would be treated confidentially, he acceded in going to see Director Mills in the company of Nishimoto. First, Mills was warned that the interview be kept confidential, for the delegates had not made reports to the community. Then Katow began to explain, "We gathered facts and studied facts." He reported that the delegates from other centers had brought tangible information or statistical data analyzing the deterrents to relocation. It was obvious, Katow explained, that the problem of center liquidation was regarded more serious than at Poston and extensive studies had been made in advance of the meeting. In deliberating on these "facts", Katow was surprised that the deterrents presented did not vary appreciably from one center to another; evacuees at the various centers were confronted more or less with identical problems in leaving the centers.

According to Katow, these problems were arranged and studied further by the Agenda Committee, on which he served as a member. In studying these problems, it was found that the center population could be divided into three groups, viz.,

1. Those who are able to relocate in the near future. Some of them are able bodied and can seek employment on the outside. Some others have property. Still some others have children that have relocated and reestablished themselves.
2. Those that desire to reestablish themselves and their families on the outside, but they are fearful for themselves and their families because of the economic losses which they had incurred at the time of evacuation and age, dependents, and other reasons. These people can be relocated with more help and better assistance from the WRA.
3. Those that wish to remain in the center until the end of the war.

The available data proved that residents belonging to the first and second groups comprised more than the majority of the population in the various centers. As an example, the Heart Mountain delegates stated that more than 85 percent of their people could not relocate with the present provisions of the WRA or wanted to remain in the center for duration. The Rohwer data revealed that more than sixty-five percent of the center population belonged to either the first or the second group. The percentage for Poston was estimated at 75–80 percent by Katow. In the opinion of the Poston delegates, the majority of residents in every center was found in the second group; they wanted to leave the center, but could not do so with the grants and guarantee provided by the WRA at present. All in all, the number of persons that could not leave the centers with the present provisions was found to be between 65 percent and 70 percent of the total number of evacuees now remaining in the centers, estimated to be about 70,000. In Katow's opinion, most of these evacuees could be persuaded to leave the centers if the WRA were willing to provide them with more assistance and tangible proofs of guarantee. "They don't want to live in the centers. Those that must remain in the centers are very small in number. Most of them want to reestablish themselves on the outside again, but they believe they cannot do so with the present provisions such as twenty-five dollars grants, train tickets, and so on. They are not adequate to go out and start their lives all over after they had lost what they had."

"Facts presented by the delegates from the various centers substantiated these contentions," Katow again stressed the point that the discussions of the delegates had entirely been based on the interview material and statistical data. "For example, the committee of Councilmen at Rohwer sat with WRA interviewers and counseled evacuees to find out why they could not relocate. These interviews were beneficial in finding out the real reasons why people cannot relocate. Many unknown reasons were uncovered, because the evacuees interviewed cooperated. The committee then compiled the results of these interviews and the Rohwer delegates presented the findings of the committee to the conference. At Heart Mountain, too, they did the same thing."

"We presented these facts to Mr. Myer," Katow continued to explain to Director Mills. "We did not say to Mr. Myer that the centers should not be closed. We said that we cannot leave the centers under the present WRA system of assistance. We don't want to obstruct the government policy. We want to cooperate with the WRA. Mr. Myer promised that he would do everything possible to help these people who want to leave the centers. But he said that has to be on [an] individual basis."

On questioning by Director Mills, Katow continued to explain the content of Myer's speech before the conference. He reported in detail about the five points given by Myer as the reasons that the centers should be closed at the end of this year. "He gave a very good speech," Katow summarized. "He is a very fine man."

"We met a man they called Judge Wolfe. He is a judge of the Utah Supreme Court. He was very sympathetic towards our problems. He said he would do everything possible to help us, and told us to help the WRA program as much as possible. He seemed to have known Myer before."

Katow concluded his report with the following illustrations on how some of relocatees were doing in the Salt Lake City area. "I can't say for sure whether those people who have relocated are happy there. They are very busy working, and don't have time to think of anything else but their works. They said they haven't saved anything. You can't save now; things are very expensive. They are living in awful places. Places I saw—there were five persons in one small room—there were a couple and two children sleeping in one room at another place. That's just an example about housing. Life outside is not easy."

Katow reported that he had met an evacuee who relocated from one of the centers and attempted to obtain a business license in the city of Leyton. The city, however, refused to issue any business license to persons of Japanese ancestry. The Nisei applicant contested the denial and filed a suit in the court. He was required to hire attorneys to represent him from each of the two warring factions in the city in order to have any fair chance of winning in the trial. The case was now transferred to the court in Salt Lake City having been granted the motion to change the venue. As Katow was told by the Nisei, the cost of the trial had run up to approximately $7,000. "That was the main reason among other things that the matter of business license was made a major issue during the conference," Katow concluded.

After the interview in Director Mills' office, Katow had an intimate private conversation with Supervisor Nishimoto. The delegate again spoke disdainfully of the Issei at the conference, and cautioned to send younger men as delegates to future conferences. The Issei delegates were unreasonable and irrational from the first day, Katow related. They were argumentative and boisterous; they refused to listen to or grasp the points advanced by other speakers. "I thought the conference was going to be split up on the first day because of arguments and quarrels. They fought and fought," Katow reminisced.

In Katow's opinion the delegates was not aware of the fact that they represented all the evacuees remaining now in the centers. Instead, they advanced their points solely from the interests of the residents in their respective centers. Especially on the question of whether to invite the Spanish representative to the conference, the discussion was sharp and tumultuous. Many of the Issei delegates refused to listen to the argument of the Nisei delegates that the Spanish representative ought not to be invited. "These Issei argued and argued as if they wanted to carry the issue of center closure direct to the Japanese Government. After a long, quarrelsome debate on the issue, the cool heads won out. It was decided that this was a domestic issue and we should deal directly with the American Government and not with any foreign government including the Japanese Government. I admired the guts of the Nisei delegates on this issue. The Issei have lots to learn from the young men. For a while, I thought we were going to pack up and go home."

As Katow put it, Myer would try to close the centers by the end of this year. He was interested in the welfare of the younger people remaining in the centers. "They are American citizens, and it's natural that Myer is worrying about these people. I don't think he or the American Government cares much about the Issei. We are enemy aliens and we can't complain about that. We are fortunate that we have children born in America."

As one of the five reasons why the center should be closed, Myer placed the welfare of these youngsters first and foremost. In Katow's opinion, there was hardly a chance that the schools would be opened this fall. "Myer wants all the school children go to schools on the outside this fall. He is convinced that to keep them in the center schools or in the centers any longer is not good for them."

Myer insisted, as Katow reported, that the center would be closed; he refused to acknowledge a probability that thousands of evacuees would be left in the centers on the closing date. "In spite of his strong statements, he gave me a feeling that he has some alternative plan when so many thousands are left here. I am sure he knows that he cannot relocate all of us in one year. At one point, however, he gave me an impression that he believed all of us, maybe most of us, will relocate if he gave us more assistance. He hinted that something will be done to give us more financial assistance, but he refused to commit himself on that. He said that he could not reveal his future plan because of the Congress and the public."

Speaking of Myer, Katow reported that he was embarrassed when Eisenhower's statement that evacuees would be detained in the relocation centers for the duration and fourteen days. At the conference he evaded the issue by saying that such a statement as made by Eisenhower must necessarily be changed as time changed government policies. "But he sure looked worried about it. He said, 'Even though Mr. Eisenhower said it, I know you wouldn't want to remain in the centers.' One of the delegates from Granada[10] told me that Myer refused to believe it when he was told of the statement by Eisenhower in the little pamphlet during his (Myer's) visit at Granada. Myer said that it must be *dema*,[11] and said that he wanted to see it in writing. So one of them brought out the pamphlet and showed it to him. Myer read it, but refused to comment on it except 'The conditions changed, so policies too must change.' There is no question that Myer is worried about that statement. It's same as the Government lying to us."

The delegates at the conference made an arrangement to form a permanent organization to coordinate the activities of the various centers to further the interests of the Japanese in the United States. It was aimed to carry the program much beyond the present goal of obtaining more assistance and better guarantee from the WRA and of fighting for the maintenance of the centers in the *status quo.* The newly created organization intended to look after the welfare of the Japanese when and after the centers were closed. It planned to establish offices in major cities in the country to carry out its program. "We want to use the conference as the starting point. We decided to establish the headquarters at Topaz for a while. We are going to grow gradually. These things are not in the official minutes of the conference, but we discussed a lot about this. People (the delegates) talked against the JACL [Japanese American Citizens League]. They were not satisfied with the JACL. They wanted to form a bigger and better organization than that. They don't trust the JACL. This organization will include not only the Nisei but also the Issei. It is going to treat both Issei and Nisei alike as the Japanese."

This organization, according to Katow, would meet whenever necessary as the Topaz headquarters directed it. It was, however, agreed that at first such a conference would be called every six months. The discussion on the permanent organization carried much further into the future; the delegates made a tentative plan to send an observer to "the peace conference between the United States and Japan."

"We are thinking far ahead," reported Katow proudly. "Everybody agreed

---

10. This camp, also known as Amache, was in Colorado.

11. A false or groundless rumor.

that a representative ought to be sent to the peace conference. The representative should present to the conference the matter of losses and damages incurred by the evacuees as the result of evacuation. There is no question that matters vitally concerning us will be discussed at the peace conference, and it will be valuable for us to have someone representing our interests. Of course, that's not in the record."

Katow believed that the Poston delegates had done creditable work at Salt Lake City. Except on a few occasions, they were united and worked harmoniously. In Katow's appraisal, Okamoto was the worst member. Sometimes he refused to act in accordance with the previous arrangements which had been agreed among them. On other occasions, he argued in the extreme presenting such contentions as those that would be advanced likely by the irrational, irresponsible Issei. "Okamoto was no good. He had no head. As usual, he tried to bring out 'the Japanese Government' to strengthen his arguments. With him, it's always the Spanish Consul or the Japanese Government. On several occasions we were embarrassed by him. Besides, he heckled from the floor when other delegates were speaking. I heard him say more than several times, 'Shut up,' or, 'That's enough. You have spoken more than five minutes.' He is a regular *yaji* (irresponsible heckler)."

Katow thought that the delegates from Heart Mountain showed a shameful lack of unity among them. It appeared to him as if of the five delegates from Heart Mountain represented each of as many different warring factions in the center. He noticed that the Heart Mountain delegation was the most disorganized group; they presented divergent views at the same time and quarreled among them on the floor. On one occasion, Hachimonji made a certain statement and alleged that it was the opinion of the residents of Heart Mountain. The other delegates, however, challenged the authenticity of the statement and insisted that he should make a correction that it was merely an opinion of his own and not of the residents of the center. After heated debate Hachimonji apologized to the body.

Cohesion and unity were evident among the members of the Gila delegation, those of the Granada delegation, and those of the Rohwer delegation. The Rohwer delegation was the most organized and unified group. Both Shingu and Fujino from Rohwer were very capable; Fujino was considered as the chief of the delegates from Rohwer. He acted very dignified; he let the two younger delegates do the actual work, while he remained "behind the scene" and counseled them.

Katow concluded his informal conference with Nishimoto by stressing the importance of forming a group at Poston to study the real deterrents of the residents for relocation. He emphasized the necessity of compiling the statistical data through the interviews initiated by evacuee leaders. He deplored the present condition where the leaders were indifferent with the relocation problems of the Poston residents.

On March 1, 1945, from 1:30 o'clock in the afternoon, a special meeting of the Community Council was held in its office to hear reports on the conference from the four delegates. To this meeting the evacuee leaders in the administrative positions were invited as special guests. Those present as guests were Unit [I] Administrator Sumida, Unit II Administrator Uyeno, Unit III Administrator Yoshimine, Unit I Supervisor of Block Manager[s] Nishimoto, Unit III Supervisor of Block Manager[s] Nishi, and Unit III Assistant Supervisor Uyeki. G. Iseda, the Chairman presided over the meeting.

First, mimeographed copies of the conference resolution addressed to Director Myer, both in English and Japanese, were distributed. By the request of those present, Iseda decreed that the copies in Japanese be used for discussion at this time. Nobuo Matsubara, the Secretary attached to the delegation, read the resolution in Japanese word by word. As Katow had warned, there were discrepancies between the Japanese original and its English translation. It is significant to remember that the English version was presented to Director Myer, and the Japanese version was read to the members of the Community Council. Below, the two versions are printed side by side for comparison.

Dear Mr. Myer:

English Version	Japanese Version
February 24, 1945 Mr. Dillon S. Myer, National Director War Relocation Authority Washington, D.C. We of Japanese ancestry residing within these United States feel that the people of this country, generally, have accepted us on the strength of our record as law-abiding residents during the past fifty and more years. We have engaged in farming, com-	

merce, fishing industry, etc., as operators and laborers, and so had established solid foundations in this country.

The outbreak of hostilities between the United States and Japan in 1941, was followed, in 1942, by the War Department's order that all of us who resided within the west coast area, inclusive of American citizens as well as Japanese nationals, be forcibly evacuated. We suffered extreme shock and mental anguish, as well as substantial material losses. The foundations we had created by years of toil were almost completely wiped away. We have existed these past almost three years within the confines of barbed wire fences, within camps located in desert wilderness.

. . . The foundations, the results of hardships and toil for the past half century, were completely uprooted from the bottom. We have existed with perseverance almost three years . . .

On December 17, 1944, the Western Defense Command announced the rescinding of the exclusion order. At the same time the War Relocation Authority announced that all our camps would be closed by not later than January 2, 1946.

Surveys of general opinion among center residents as a result of the foregoing dual announcements disclosed the fact that due to their present economic status, their fear of violence and discrimination on the outside, etc., the majority were not in a position to make plans either for relocation or for return to their former homes on the west coast, under present conditions and under currently available facilities and assistance provided by the W.R.A. and other agencies.

As a natural consequence, this, the All Center Conference, was decided upon. Delegates representing seven relocation centers met from February 24, 1945, at Salt Lake City. After serious deliberation, mindful of our grave responsibility to do our utmost for the best welfare of 75,000 people, we now make the fervent appeal that the WRA centers be kept open for the duration of war and for some time thereafter as may be needed and, further, be operated with a view to providing residents with necessities, facilities and services on at least an equal level as in the past.

. . . for the duration and until such time thereafter when they can relocate freely . . .

We, hereinunder submit a statement of facts and recommendations with the request that you will accord them your full and sympathetic consideration.

Respectfully submitted,

/s/ Masaru Narahara
Masaru Narahara, Chairman
All Center Conference

approved:

/s/ H. Nishimura
Delegate for Gila Project
/s/ S. Kawashiri
Delegate for Granada Project
/s/ G. Mihara
Delegate for Minidoka Project
/s/ M. Hayashida
Delegate for Heart Mountain Project
/s/ G. Katow
Delegate for Poston Project
/s/ C. Fujino
Delegate for Rohwer Project

/s/ I. Sugiyama
Delegate for Topaz Project

Copy: Harold Ickes,
Secretary of Interior

Statement of Facts

1. Mental suffering has been caused by the forced mass evacuation.
2. There has been an almost complete destruction of financial foundations built during over half a century.

   There has been a complete destruction . . .
3. Especially for the duration, the war had created fears of prejudices, persecution, etc., also fears of physical violence and fears of damage to property.
4. Many Isseis (average age is between 60 and 65) were depending upon their sons for assistance and support, but these sons are serving in the United States Armed Forces. Now these Issei are reluctant to consider relocation.

   The Issei are well on in years and their sons are serving in the armed forces and there is no one to support their families. The insecurity of livelihood due to these facts.
5. Residents feel insecure and apprehensive towards the many changes and modifications of W.R.A. policies.
6. The residents have prepared to remain for the duration because of many statements made by the W.R.A., that relocation centers will be maintained for the duration of the war.

   Because of the statement in the pamphlet distributed under the name of Mr. Eisenhower (line 29, page 8), "It is required to enlist in the work corp of the relocation center for the duration and fourteen days," the evacuees have lived with the understanding.
7. Many residents were forced to dispose of their personal and real

properties, business and agricultural equipment, etc. at a mere trifle of their cost; also drew leases for the "dura tion", hence have nothing to return to.	
8. Practically every Buddhist priest is now excluded from the West Coast. Buddhism has a substantial following, and the members obviously prefer to remain where the religion centers.	Practically every Buddhist priest is now excluded from the West Coast. The Buddhists cannot obtain the services of the priests when they return to the coast. There is no complete freedom of religion.
9. There is an acute shortage of housing, which is obviously a basic need in resettlement. The residents fear that adequate housing is not available.	The W.R.A. has no concrete plan for solution of the housing situation, which is most vital to relocation. The fear of housing situation due to the fact that evacuees alone must solve the problem.
10. Many persons of Japanese ancestry have difficulty in obtaining insurance coverage on life, against fire, on automobiles, on property, etc.	

Recommendations	Demands
We recommend:	
1. That special governmental agencies or units be established solely for providing assistance to evacuees who might require funds in reestablishing themselves. a. Resettlement aid (grants) b. Loans	. . . We request that these agencies be maintained for a reasonable time after the closing of centers.
2. That the present relocation grant be increased. It should be given to every relocatee. The penalty clause on the present form should be deleted. We further recommend that federal aid be granted according to every individual's particular need	That the present relocation grant be increased. It should be given to every person irrespective of the amount of funds in his possession . . . We further demand . . .

until such time as he is reestablished.

3. That long term loans at a low rate of interest be made available, without security, to aid the residents in reestablishing themselves as near as possible to their former status in private enterprises, such as business, agriculture, fisheries, etc.

4. That the W.R.A. use their good offices so that consideration may be given on priority by O.P.A. Because of evacuation, residents were forced to dispose of their equipment, tucks, cars and etc., many of which at present require the approval of an O.P.A. Board. These equipments are essential to many residents in order to reestablish themselves in former enterprises.

That the W.R.A. use their good offices so that consideration may be given on priority by O.P.A. Because of evacuation, residents were forced to dispose of their equipment, trucks, cars and etc., many of which at present require the approval of an O.P.A. Board. These equipments are essential to many residents in order to reestablish themselves in former enterprises.

5. That the W.R.A. make every effort to obtain a return of property for evacuees who, due to evacuation and consequent inability to maintain installment payments, have lost the same; further, in order to prevent loss of property, to obtain some definite arrangement for the granting of government aid, as may be necessary, to evacuees unable, as a result of evacuation, to maintain installment payments.

The evacuees have lost the real property purchased on installment plan at the time of evacuation due to the lapse of payments. We demand that aid be given to the efforts to reestablish the right to the property which has been lost.

6. That the W.R.A. give financial aid to residents with definite plans, for the purposes of defraying the expenses of investigating specific relocation possibilities.

That the W.R.A. give financial aid to residents leaving on short term leaves with definite plans, for the purpose of defraying expenses of investigating specific relocation possibilities.

7. That the W.R.A. establish adequate staffed offices in important areas and employ persons of Japanese ancestry since they understand Japanese psychology; and also establish in these field offices, legal and employment departments.

   That the W.R.A. establish branch offices in important areas and employ persons of Japanese ancestry in order to aid relocatees. In these field offices, legal department and employment division should be established.

8. That the W.R.A. continue the operation of evacuee property offices for the duration to fulfill the needs of relocatees.

   The W.R.A. should continue the operation of evacuee property offices for the duration to fulfill the needs of relocatees.

9. That the W.R.A. accept for reinduction into centers those who relocate and who find themselves unable to make satisfactory adjustments.

   That the W.R.A. accept for reinduction into centers those who relocate and who find themselves unable to make satisfactory adjustments.

10. That the W.R.A. arrange for the establishing of hostels and other facilities in various areas; and furthermore, build new housing through the F.H.A. with W.R.A. assistance.

    That the W.R.A. arrange for the establishment of hostels and other facilities in various areas; and furthermore, build new housing through the F.H.A. with W.R.A. assistance.

11. That the W.R.A. provide transportation of evacuee property door to door.

    That the W.R.A. provide transportation of evacuee property door to door.

12. That the W.R.A. negotiate for the establishing of old people's homes exclusively for persons of Japanese ancestry.

    We demand that relocatees after their return or relocation be guaranteed of their livelihood by the Soldiers' family assistance system, the unemployment insurance, or the relief fund for the people dislocated by the war, which has been established by the Congress, until such time as they can reestablish themselves firmly.

13. That the W.R.A. make negotiation to arrange (1) so that evacuees formerly civil service employees will be reinstated and (2) so that persons of Japanese ancestry will be

able to secure business licenses as formerly.

14. That short term leave regulations be changed to permit an absence of two months with one month extension privileges. Also, that the evacuee investigating relocation possibilities be permitted to become employed without change of status.
15. That when an evacuee relocates or returns to his former business or home, W.R.A. should make every effort to release frozen assets (blocked accounts) both in cases of individuals or organizations.
16. That the W.R.A. negotiate for the concluding of arrangements where under alien parents may be able to operate or manage properties with powers of attorney issued by their children, particularly by sons in the United States Armed Forces.
17. That the W.R.A. arrange to secure outright releases for parolees who relocate.
18. That the W.R.A. obtain the establishment of some avenue of governmental indemnities for relocatees who may become victims of anti-Japanese violence in terms of personal injuries or property damage.
19. That the W.R.A. arrange for adequate government compensation against losses to evacuee property by fire, theft, etc. while in government or private storage or while in transit.

We demand proper restitution for the losses to evacuee property by fire, theft, etc., intentional or accidental, while in W.R.A. or government storage or while in transit.

20. That the W.R.A. arrange to pro-

vide students of Japanese ancestry with adequate protection in case of need, and opportunities equal to those enjoyed by Caucasian students.

Suggestion

The foregoing is a partial list of appeals emanating from center residents, and each item is founded on factual cases. We make the suggestion that the W.R.A. should verify the existence of these problems, possibly by adopting some such procedure as follows:

The W.R.A. should conduct a more accurate and intensive relocation survey than at present, with intent to determine what are the actual needs of the residents, in terms of making their relocation possible. This Survey might be conducted in every project, by interviewing a number of evacuees selected from among those unable to make relocation plans, and further selected with a view to obtaining an accurate cross-section (occupations, location of former homes, etc.) The assistance of interpreters recommended by the Community Councils might be enlisted.

Note: The suggested survey should, perhaps, be conducted so that all center residents will be interviewed; however, as a first step, we recommend the interview of lesser numbers, in the interest of expediency, because we desire the earliest possible acknowledgment of the conditions, and establishment of adequate policies for the furthering of relocation.

However, the Japanese version, in addition, included the following resolutions passed in the conference:

Resolutions

No. 1 Resolution Regarding Coordination Among the Centers

We resolve to coordinate our activities constantly among our centers and to exchange information on the trends of people in the various centers for the purpose of fulfilling the aims of this conference. If deemed necessary, a second conference may be called.

Note: The headquarters shall be established at the Topaz Relocation Center. In case the second conference is to be called, the various centers shall exchange their respective proposals and agenda in advance among them in order to facilitate the discussions of the matters during the conference.

February 22, 1945
All Center Conference

No. 2 Resolution to The Manzanar Center

In the name of the All Center Conference, the following resolution was unanimously passed so that it be submitted to the Block Managers Assembly at Manzanar:

We believe essential to have all the relocation centers keep in step and move forward in order to fulfill the aims of this conference. Therefore, in the name of this conference we resolve to report to the Manzanar residents, who did not participate in this conference, the policies and resolutions decided by us in order to carry out the aims. At the same time, we recommend that they agree with the purpose of this conference and that they hereafter participate in the conference in order to keep in step.

February 22, 1945

All Center Conference

Recommendation

Having attended the All Center Conference, we have observed that the Community Councils or the Special Study Committees had earnestly been studying the problems arising from the closing of the centers and the problems for relocations for a considerable length of time. We, therefore, recommend that such a Special Study Committee be established to investigate and study constantly these problems, which are vital to all the residents at Poston, in order to fulfill their wishes.

February 25, 1945
The Poston Delegates to the All Center Conference

When Nobuo Matsubara finished reading these pages of the resolutions and recommendations passed in the conference, City Manager Minoru Okamoto commenced to give his verbal report briefly. He explained the five reasons as given by Myer that the centers should be closed this year. During the question-answer session with Myer, Okamoto reported, the Director was asked what he would do with those still remaining in the relocation centers on the closing day. Myer replied that he did not expect any evacuee left on the last day; he believed that no one wanted to remain in the centers and everyone would leave before the deadline. Okamoto believed that the WRA would go out of existence after this year, but he could not conceive that every evacuee would leave the center. He thought that Myer would realize the impracticability of the present closure policy by the end of this summer and would decide to resign from his office. "He didn't say so, but he hinted that," Okamoto stated.

To the question whether the delegates received any answer to the requests of the conference, Okamoto believed that the document had not reached Director Myer yet. He explained in detail as to how much time had been consumed at the conference in deciding which request should be included in the final document, because the delegates of a center naturally wanted to have their proposals incorporated. For another reason, there was a considerable debate among the delegates as to the advisability of presenting the resolution to Director Myer during the conference. Many of them were afraid that Myer would be able to answer all the requests before the body without hesitation and that all his answers would be unfavorable to the evacuees. In the end, they decided to present the document after the meeting with Myer so that he would be compelled to reply in writing after the delegates returned to their respective centers. "If Myer replied [to] the requests one after another at the conference and gave unfavorable answers, which were more than likely, we wouldn't be able to return to the centers and face the residents," Okamoto confessed. "Besides, we weren't quite ready with the formulation of our demands when we were scheduled to meet Myer. We thought it would be better that Myer answered the resolutions by writing to the various centers. But Myer will be getting the paper today or tomorrow. He is visiting Gila now. By the time he comes here and speaks to the community, he will have all the answers. I am afraid that he will cover every point in it when he speaks to the people here."

Okamoto then went on to explain that many organizations sympathetic to evacuees had been invited to attend the conference, but only a few of them were able to do so due to lack of time. There were, however, Okamoto reported, several important organizations present. Among them a Jewish and a Negro delegates were conspicuous and very sympathetic to the problems of evacuees. In Okamoto's opinion, Judge Wolfe of the Utah Supreme Court was the most significant guest; he understood the various complicated problems of evacuees and appreciated their plight. "He had very good knowledge of the Japanese problems," Okamoto reported. "He was our real friend. In the morning, Judge Wolfe stated that he thought something could be done with the Congress so that the centers be maintained for many of us who want to remain. He seemed to be a friend of Mr. Myer. They went out for lunch together, and came back after more than one hour. In the afternoon, Judge changed his mind slightly and said that it was best for evacuees to relocate as soon as possible. Myer must have told him something during the lunch hour. Judge said that he sympathized with Myer's position; he said he was having hard time placed between the Congress and the evacuees. He said that he understand the difficult position the delegates were in; the delegates were sandwiched between the WRA and the evacuees, he said. He believed that the delegates should encourage the relocation program when they returned to the centers. He told us to help Mr. Myer, because he had our interests at heart and was fighting for us against all kinds of odds."

Okamoto concluded his report by saying that he believed Myer had some alternative plan when it became obvious that the present closure policy would fail. Myer hinted that he had some plan to increase the present relocation grants and to improve the present assistance. However, he refused to reveal the plan for the obvious reason that it might be obstructed if it were known to the Congress or to the general public too far in advance.

Following Okamoto, Y. Katow gave his verbal report. He emphasized as usual that the facts present by the various delegations had been studied and the requests had been devised from the study. The study of these facts revealed that the residents now remaining in the centers could be divided into the three groups: viz., those who would relocate in the near future, those who wished to relocate, but could not do so with the present provisions given by the WRA because of their economic conditions, and those who could not relocate at all due to physical or financial reasons. The people who belonged to the second class constituted the vast majority of the present population, Katow reported; the number of persons belonging to the third class was found to be very small. Katow believed that those who now claimed that they would not or could not relocate would do so if they were given more and better assistance by the WRA. "I know that many people are saying now that they wouldn't budge. But I believe they will leave the centers if they received something by which they can reestablish themselves on the outside. With most of them it's a question of better financial aid. But Mr. Myer made it clear that he would not give everyone more money. He said that if he gave $300, we would ask for $500. Then if we succeeded in getting $500 per person, we would be asking for $1,000 next time. He said that it would not be good for us to get more money. He said he was willing to give money to any individual if he could prove to the satisfaction of the WRA that he needed the money justifiably in order to reestablish himself on the outside. This, however, must be decided on the merits of the individual case. Myer made it clear that he was against the general hand outs of money to evacuees."

Delegate Katow was of the opinion that Myer had other plans to assist rehabilitation of evacuees and to facilitate the eventual closing of the centers. As for example, Katow claimed, the Director inferred during an informal discussion that he had some drastic plans to solve the housing difficulties of relocatees, but he refused to reveal the nature of these plans. (Some weeks afterwards, Corlies Carter intimated that such drastic plans were being schemed in the WRA office at Washington [see *infra*, p. XXX].) In the formal meeting, however, Myer insisted that the WRA would not assume the responsibility of "house hunting" for the relocatees. As Katow put it, Director Myer insisted that the burden of solving the housing problem rested with the relocatees. "The way Mr. Myer said it was this way. He said that the WRA doesn't know what kind of house a relocatee needs. One relocatee may want a house with two rooms for the monthly rental of, say, thirty dollars, while a next relocatee may want a house with five rooms. Again one relocatee may want to live in one section of town, while another relocatee may not be satisfied with the location of the house. He said that each relocatee should look for his own house himself. The WRA cannot be expected to handle such an enormous task. He agreed that the housing problem is tough, but he was sure that it could be solved if the relocatees tried hard enough."

Katow touched upon the five reasons that Myer had advanced for the closing of the centers. "I believe that Mr. Myer really thinks it will be for the best interests of the Japanese that the centers be closed. He is really fighting for the future of our people. So he will push this program with everything he's got. He told us that he has no plan at all for the people who will be left in the centers at the time those centers will close. He was emphatic in saying that he did not expect any evacuee remaining in the centers on January 2, 1946."

At this point, Minoru Okamoto, who was sitting next to Katow at the speakers' table, interjected, "Mr. Myer said that he did not ask the Congress for the budget to run the centers beyond this year. He told us that the WRA did not have money to operate these centers after January 2."

"Yes, that's what he said," Katow continued with his report. "He insisted that there will be no more WRA after this year. But at one point he dropped a hint that he realized there would be some people left in the centers after this year. In spite of his confident speech, I believe he knows that every one cannot relocate within this year. I am sure that he has some plan for these remaining people, although he will not admit it right now. (Nobuo Matsubara, too, corroborated this conjecture in an interview with Nishimoto.) One thing I'm sure though. That is, there will be no more WRA. I don't know whether Mr. Myer will resign this summer or not. But some change will be made about this summer. This is one of the most valuable fruits of this conference."

In contrast with Okamoto's contention that he was certain that Dillon Myer would resign before the WRA could change its policies, Katow was of the opinion that the WRA could modify its course without Myer's resignation. "In the informal meeting, Myer mentioned that he would have to resign if the present policies failed. But I doubt it. Without resigning Myer can modify the WRA policies so that they would be more realistic and more adoptable to the condition that there would be many thousand people left in the centers."

Katow then narrated the difficulty of the Agenda Committee, on which he served as a member, in formulating the final resolution. For example, the residents of Poston in general were concerned with the maintenance of the centers for the duration and the delegates had been instructed to propose this request, Katow explained. In the same manner, the delegates from Gila argued in the conference that the resolution should aim at only one point, exclusive of all others—the maintenance of the centers in the *status quo*. The Gila delegates were adamant in insisting that it was not to include any requests or conditions by which the evacuees would leave the centers. They said that they came to the conference to fight the WRA policy of closing the centers. They stated that they were not interested in anything else but that.

According to Katow, the delegates from Topaz, too, proposed similarly that the resolution should cover only the opposition to the WRA policy of center closure. The Topaz delegates, however, argued from a slightly different reasoning. One of the Topaz delegates explained that the resolution should be planned in two steps—the first resolution should ask only for the maintenance of the centers for the duration and a reasonable time thereafter; and when the first resolution was rejected, a second resolution should be sent to the WRA asking for the various conditions for relocation as they had been embodied in the platforms of the various centers. In the end, however, an agreement was reached whereby a resolution was passed asking for the maintenance of the centers stating the "facts" why the evacuees could not leave the centers, and attaching the various conditions of assistance and guarantee for relocation. "It means that we cannot relocate under the present circumstances, but if these conditions were granted, we will leave the centers."

Katow went on to report that in all probability the present resolution would be rejected by the WRA. "I don't believe that the WRA will give us those conditions of assistance and guarantee," Katow commented. "But we presented the resolution to the WRA anyway. It was our contention that the first resolution should be presented to our direct superior, that is, the WRA. When the WRA rejects it, we have a right to appeal to a higher authority. So, as our next step, we will present our second resolution to the Secretary of the Interior. It is going to be worded stronger than the first one. When that fails, we are going to appeal direct to the President. It's going to be worded much, much stronger than the first paper. We have planned the fight way into the future."

Delegate Katow then reported on the formation of the permanent All Center organization, which would coordinate activities among the centers to promote the welfare and to safeguard the interests of the evacuees. He again mentioned the hope of these delegates for participation in the peace conference. He also emphasized the necessity of conducting a survey, initiated and operated by the evacuee leaders, in order to determine the difficulties and problems confronting individuals for leaving the center. "I was really ashamed that we had not prepared for this conference. Conferences are going to be called in the future, so we should be prepared. We can't do anything without facts and data."

On questioning, Katow replied that the Spanish Consul was not invited to the conference. He explained that the question at issue was solely between the WRA and the evacuees, and did not concern at this stage neither the Japanese Government nor the Spanish Government, its Protecting Power. He added that there were several Nisei among the delegates, and it was agreed that they should not be embarrassed by being compelled to discuss the subject with the Spanish representative. As Katow put it, it was not time to draw the Spanish representative in the issue; such time would come in the future, when the final appeal to the President was rejected. In preparation for such an eventuality, Katow pointed out, it was agreed that the copies of the minutes and the resolution be sent to the Spanish Embassy unofficially. The transmittal of the copies to the Spanish authorities was not recorded in the minutes of the conference.

At this point, the reports by the delegates were declared concluded. Chairman G. Iseda thought that there was nothing to be done except distributing the mimeographed copies of the resolution to the community. He pointed out that they could only wait for Myer's reply.

Okamoto, however, stated that the residents would hear answers to all the points in the resolution when Myer visited Poston in a few days. "This is the last center he is visiting. He has practiced his speech all he wants by this time. He is an eloquent speaker. I think he will rattle off answers to all the points. We can't help that. But we want his answers in writing; and that's important in order to move to our next step."

The general reactions of those present in the meeting of the Community Council were mild and sympathetic. One of them stated: "We are thankful of the efforts of you delegates. We know that your task was very difficult. You have, indeed, acted nobly and acquitted yourselves well. We, the residents of Poston, are grateful for your endeavors."

Another member of the Community Council commented: "We are fighting the WRA right into their face. We are trying to force the WRA to do something directly opposite of what they have planned. On top of that, you had to face Myer. It is tough to fight Myer. He is suave and elusive. I believe the job was well done."

Another Issei in the audience stated: "People as a whole do not expect a successful result from the beginning. This is about the best we [could] have expected."

Sumida, the Unit I Administrator, said: "It was a good thing that these delegates from the different centers got together and discussed the common problem. It is always important to find out about the people in other centers. In that sense, this conference was meaningful and significant."

Chairman Iseda added: "It is a foregone conclusion that Myer will say 'no' to all of them. It's no use to ask Myer. We must go over his head."

Then, he added: "There was a request as I remember that the delegates report on the conference from the Block 4 stage (*supra*, p. XXX). I don't think we need to have such a gathering. What do you think?"

Okamoto replied that such a meeting should be dispensed with, because Myer within a few days would cover the same ground as he had done in the conference. In such a public meeting, Okamoto reasoned, the information as given before the Community Council could not be revealed. Aside from the "inside story", there was very little to report until Myer's formal replies were received. As Okamoto put it, the fruits of the conference had been embodied in the resolution, and its mimeographed copies were being prepared in order to be distributed to the blocks.

Supervisor Nishimoto, however, pointed out that some caution should be exercised to inform the community that the resolution was not the end by itself. The permanent organization resulting from the conference "will begin the work from there. When the copies are distributed to the blocks, I am sure that people will ask, 'What did Myer say to these?' Publicity should be handled adroitly so that they will know that this is just the beginning."

They agreed that some means should be worked out by the Community Council to inform the residents as to what had been accomplished in the conference and what were to be expected in the future. With this arrangement, Iseda presented for discussion the program of Myer's visit and the strategy of meeting with the Director (see, *infra*, pp. xxx–xxx). The meeting of the Community Council was adjourned at 4:00 P.M., after two hours and half of discussions and reporting.

The delegates were obviously uncomfortable and defensive about their accomplishment at the conference. Their attitudes were gauged from the following bits of informal conversation they had after the session with various individuals. Okamoto, for instance, was heard telling one of his friends, "You can't expect everything in the way you want. We are bucking up against something big this time."

Katow told another Issei, "We tried the best we could. It was a very difficult job. We are just beginning. And we must get together and keep on fighting. I feel that my job is from now."

Kubota was heard saying in one corner of the room, "I don't know if this will satisfy people. I hope they didn't expect too much from this conference."

To Kubota's remark, James Takashima interjected, "Hell! If they don't like it, I will give them back the money [the traveling expense defrayed by the Community Council]. What do they expect anyway?"

Supervisor Nishimoto realized that the residents would not be satisfied with the distributed copies of the resolution; he saw the importance of disseminating more detailed information on the accomplishment of the conference, because Myer had not replied to the resolution and because the public meeting as planned previously had been dispensed with. He was convinced that the people should be told of the difficulties which the delegates had faced in the conference and the plans for the future which they had worked out. The community had learned of the return of these four representatives and was anxiously awaiting the report on the conference. Nishimoto was apprehensive of the lack of understanding of the community on the part of the members of the Community Council. As he told it to one of the Block Managers, they believed that there was no need of these delegates to report to the residents. "They think they are big shots. They have heard the reports, and are satisfied now. They think that's the end of it. They don't realize that the community will start clamoring to find out what happened at the conference. The people will begin to shout why they aren't told of what happened. They will accuse the delegates and condemn them for failure to report. All kinds of rumors will fly around discrediting these men."

In line with his reasoning, Nishimoto called for an emergency meeting of the Block Managers of Unit I on the afternoon of March 2. On the face of the stand of the Community Council that no public meeting be held, the Supervisor planned to inform the community through the Block Managers. The Unit I delegates—Katow and Okamoto—and Secretary Matsubara were invited, and they in turn gladly accepted the invitation. This meeting, however, turned out to be bombastic and chaotic; it became unexpectedly significant and far reaching in its consequence. It brought out the dormant schism between these three individuals, and clarified where each of them stood. In this meeting, Okamoto revealed a complete change of his conviction and came all out for relocation and the WRA policies. Only two months previously, the same Okamoto was reported to have had a heated quarrel with Itaru Kubota, the then Chairman of the Community Council, over the question of relocation. Having heard that Kubota was planning to return to his former home in Fresno, Okamoto accused him of unduly cooperating with the WRA and thereby jeopardizing the "welfare" of the evacuees, who could not leave the center. He was reported to have said in the end (quoted by Unit Administrator Sumida, who was present in the room at the time), "You are a sap falling for the lines fed by the WRA. The center isn't going to close. Guys like you are spoiling the chance of these people in the center. You are the Chairman of the Community Council. It is your duty to remain in the center and fight for getting what these people want. Instead, what do you do? You plan to relocate at the first chance before these people know what this policy of the WRA is all about. Hell! Get the hell out of here, if you want. We have no use for a guy like you."

This same Okamoto appeared often in the capacity of the Chairman of the Unit I Local Council or the City Manager before the public and in meetings and declared that the center should not be closed. He accused the WRA of causing unnecessary human sufferings by "pushing everyone out of the center." It was this Okamoto, who wanted to appeal to the Spanish Consul so that the WRA reverse its stand of closing the centers. It is especially significant to note that Okamoto's original political strength had been drawn from the people who believed in the ultimate Japanese victory. In the light of his previous conviction, rumors pertaining to a change of his conviction, which were heard in limited circles a day or two prior to his trip to Salt Lake City and after his return, were meaningful and indicative of what might happen with other leaders. These rumors reported that Okamoto had been in [an] argument with his fellow block residents or had quarreled with his *Go* playmates over the outlook of the war in the Pacific. His friends had been ired by Okamoto's contention that Japan would lose the war and her end would come within this year. As one of the rumors put it, Okamoto believed that Japan would capitulate before this September.

On the heel of these rumors reporting the change of his estimate on the war, Okamoto committed himself for the first time in public, before the Block Managers, that he favored the WRA policies for closing the centers. The City Manager let it be known that he reversed his stand and irrevocably committed all out for relocation. "What the hell are you guys doing in [a] dump like this? You shouldn't stay here. You should get the hell out of here." These statements made by Okamoto unexpectedly out of the clear sky caused consternation among the audience; and on these statements the later events surrounding Okamoto developed.

This meeting of the Block Managers was held from 1:30 o'clock in the afternoon in the Unit Conference Room. As the notices specified that the delegates would be present, the interest of the Managers was high; they gathered well in advance of the appointed time and there was no absentee. Supervisor Nishimoto presided, and opened the meeting with a brief statement that the delegates had returned from the All Center Conference with successful accomplishments. He reminded the body that the task was difficult, but the outcome was better than what had been expected. He then passed copies of the Salt Lake resolution among the Managers, and asked them to read them.

After an interval of several minutes, Katow explained the difficulties which the delegates had faced in formulating the resolution. He again related the various arguments advanced by the delegates of different centers whether the stand against the center closure should come first and foremost or whether only the various conditions of assistance and guarantee should be treated as more important. Katow then went on to explain in detail the permanent organization established as a result of this conference.

After Katow, Okamoto reported on Myer's five points for closing the centers. "Mr. Myer will do everything in his power to close the centers at the end of this year," Okamoto stated with a tone of conviction. "He will probably do something in the meanwhile to help out those people who need more help. But he is dead set on the closing policy."

The City Manager recounted the open session with the representatives of the various organizations sympathetic with evacuees. He again related the statements made by Judge Wolfe.

One of the Managers then asked whether there was any answers to the resolution when Myer spoke before the body. Okamoto explained why the delegates decided to present the resolution after Myer's speech, describing the same inside planning as he had told the Community Council. "Mr. Myer is coming next week, and he will cover all these points. He is a good speaker, and I won't be surprised if he gave very good answers to them."

At this point, Supervisor Nishimoto announced that Myer would be here on March 6 and 7, and gave the date and time of Myer's speech before the residents from the Block 4 outdoor stage and of his meeting with the community leaders in the Elementary School Auditorium. He added, "You have heard the reports from the delegates, and before we go into 'question and answer', I want to say just a few things." With this opening, he reminded the Managers that he had warned them often not to expect too much from the conference. He repeated the same grounds as he had repeated argued in the Managers' meetings before the conference. "As I see it, there are still some people who think the delegates are all mighty and can change a governmental policy by their say so. It is your job to straighten [out] these people. I am asking you to take the reports of these delegates back to your blocks and inform your block people. There should be no dissension to the contention that our delegates have done their job well, and I want you to tell the people so."

After Nishimoto instructed the Managers how the residents should be handled and what they should be informed of, he allowed the Managers to ask questions. The first question came from the Manager of one of the blocks occupied by Orange County evacuees. (Perhaps he is a repatriate.) "I understand well as to what you have done for those people who are to remain in this country after the war. We are thankful for what you have done. But I would like to know what you have done for people like us. We have no desire to remain in this country after the war. We have given up any desire of staying in this country. We are only thinking of going back to Japan. The sooner, the better it is. Have you done anything for us at the conference?"

"No," replied Katow. "We did not discuss the problems of those people who had applied for expatriation or repatriation. The WRA wants them to leave the center just like anyone else, unless they are on the Army stop list. So, their problems become same as those of the rest." (John Burling, the special representative of Attorney General Biddle attached to the Assistant Secretary of the Interior Chapman, who visited Poston in the latter part of March, 1945, contested the legality of this particular phase of the WRA post-exclusion program (see, *infra*, p. XXX).

Katow, nevertheless, added cryptically, "Your problem should be simple. You have made up your mind. There shouldn't be any worry."

The inquiring Manager, however, continued, "That means the conference was no value to us. The WRA is telling us to get out of here and await exchange ships on the outside. I don't think that's right."

"I don't believe that discussion of those people was our job . . . " Katow probably wanted to say that the conference had been held for the purpose of solving the problems of the people who wanted to remain in the United States after the war. He had intimated that the conference adopted the stand that the remaining evacuees in the centers wanted to relocate, but could not do so unless they were provided with better propositions. Supervisor Nishimoto, however, feared that the discussion might lead into futile arguments, and stopped it by saying, "The problems of expatriates and repatriates are special problems affecting a small segment of the population. They do not affect the residents as a whole. The expatriates and repatriates can take the matter up directly with the WRA."

As Nishimoto asked for more questions, another Manager queried, "How were the delegates from other centers?"

"We have pledged not to mention the names of centers, when we are called on to make these reports," Katow replied. "But there were several centers who presented their points aggressively. There were at least three centers, which argued that the resolution to Myer should ask only the maintenance of the centers in the *status quo*." Then he continued to say how other centers had been well prepared as the result of surveys and interviews that they had conducted before coming to the conference, and emphasized the importance of conducting a similar survey at Poston in order to ascertain "the real difficulties of people for relocation". He stressed the point that no representative could champion the cause of people without knowing their real conditions.

At this point, Okamoto mentioned the fact that the delegates from Rohwer and Granada appeared as if they supported the post-exclusion program of the WRA. They were in favor of cooperating with the WRA program, and argued that evacuees should endeavor to relocate while the WRA was providing the facilities to assist relocation. In Okamoto's opinion, for Myer had visited these two centers prior to the conference, the delegates had been "indoctrinated" and were very sympathetic to the WRA.

Then, Nishimoto asked the delegates to discuss their outlook for the immediate future. Here Okamoto commenced to give the unexpected, dynamic speech. "The WRA will close the centers by January 2, 1946. There is no question that it will carry out its program as they announced. You are talking about *ganbaru* [sticking with it] and staying here until the last day of the center. I don't know how many of those people will be here until the last day. They may be saying to *ganbaru* today, but they may relocate tomorrow. That's happening everyday. You can't depend on what they are saying now. You are opposing the center closure policy of the WRA, because the WRA announced its decision to close the centers. Let us assume that the WRA announced that you can't go out of the centers at all. You will complain and complain in that case. You will say that you want to leave the centers, but you are being detained unlawfully. That's exactly the way you will behave."

"What the hell are you guys doing in a dump like this," Okamoto continued with increased vigor and zest. The audience was completely taken by a surprise; they did not expect such a speech from Okamoto. "You shouldn't stay here. You should get the hell out of here. The sooner you get out, the better it is for you. The center will become a very unpleasant place; it will become unbearable for you. In this place only old people will be left behind; people who are seventy years old and eighty years old. Even if the WRA tells you to remain here, you will not want to stay. You will try to get out as soon as possible. Such a day is coming. You might as well awaken to the reality. And you should plan to relocate immediately. This is the best time to relocate. The WRA is mobilizing every facility to help us. There are plenty of jobs. If we want to work on the outside, we can choose any kind of job we want. The economic condition of the country is most favorable to relocation of our people. If we wait until the end of the war, it will be too late. There will be many unemployed people—think of so many million soldiers coming back from the war; they will be looking for jobs, too. As I see it, depression is sure to come after the war. And this depression will be much worse than the last one. At that time, you will not know what to do, even if you wanted to earn your living."

"This center is no place to raise our children." Okamoto's shrieky voice was ringing in the room filled with the deadly silent audience. "They should go to schools on the outside. We hear so much about the kids getting bad. They will become worse if they stay here."

"Many people tell me that they want to return to Japan and want to wait until the end of the war in the center. I don't know how many of them really believe in that. I believe they are small in number. Most of them are just saying it, because they want to stay here and live easily without doing anything. You are opposing relocation. The trouble with you is that you don't have money; you are poor. At least, fifty percent of you are without adequate fund and don't know what to do. You were barely getting by before the war started. If you don't have money, you should go out of the center and should earn money. This is the best chance. If you don't now, you will be out of money always."

"They tell me that racial discrimination is severe on the outside." Okamoto seemed to be enchanted with his own speech. "The war is going on now. And what can you expect? A certain amount of discrimination should be expected. But during my trip this time I found that things aren't so bad. As a whole, my trip was pleasant, although I had two unpleasant experiences. Both at Ogden: when I was waiting for the bus to Idaho."

The City Manager then narrated the two incidents. He wanted, he stated, to drink beer and went in a place, where he was told to get out as he informed the bartender that he was Japanese. He tried another place about one block away. Here again he was asked what nationality he was. As he replied that he was Japanese, the boy shook his head signifying that he could not serve him. "I started to argue with this boy. I told him that it was all the same, because I was paying him money. I questioned him whether my money was any different from others' money. Then a big husky guy came out of the back room and told me to get hell out of the place. He looked like the boss of the place; he was tough and used cuss words. But the rest of the trip was nice. I had a good time in Las Vegas. I got to be friendly with many Caucasians and gambled with the machines with them. On the bus trip back, I made quite many friends with Caucasians. You people talk about race discrimination, but we had that before the war, too. I worked for a wholesale produce house in Los Angeles, and I had to travel extensively up and down California. Many times I was refused of hotel accommodations. I went in restaurants, and I was told that they would not serve me. There was a time when I sat in a restaurant in one of the towns in California for more than ten minutes, but no one paid any attention to me and I had to get out. That was before the war. And we expected those things then. I can't see why we can [can't?] take it now. They won't kill you."

As Okamoto paused for a moment, Katow began to speak as if he did not want the City Manager to continue with his speech. (Katow told Nishimoto afterwards that he was afraid Okamoto's opinion might be regarded as that of the Poston delegates. He did not want to give his personal point of view, but he was compelled to do so in order to clarify that Okamoto was speaking for himself and not for the others.) "Mr. Okamoto sounds like a WRA official. I doubt very much if it is wise for the Issei to relocate now. I met many Issei during this trip and during the last trip to Chicago. And I found out that they were not happy on the outside. When I went to Chicago on a Co-op's business, I stopped at Boulder on my way back (i.e., the Navy language school at the University of Colorado, where many Japanese are hired as language instructors). Many Issei, whom I knew well before evacuation, are teaching there. As soon as they saw me, they said, 'We are no worse than the Japanese in the relocation centers.' They said that before I had a chance to say anything. I surmised that they were very much on the defensive. It showed that their conscience was bothering them. They didn't have to defend what they were doing like that. (In the past, many Japanese accused these Issei instructors of betraying Japan. It has been contended that teaching the naval officers who would use the benefits of the instruction for destruction of Japan is not a proper act for any Issei who is loyal to Japan. Some of the extremists have argued that their act is that of traitors. Katow was pointing out the fact that the Issei instructors were aware of the criticism.)

The argument advanced by the Issei, whom Katow met during his trip, was obviously that the evacuees now remaining in the relocation centers were loyal to the United States, and as a corollary disloyal to Japan, by virtue of answering the loyalty questions in the affirmative. It has often been stated by such people that if the Japanese were as loyal to Japan as they would like to claim, they would have gone to Tule Lake.

Katow went on to say that the Issei whom he met on the outside were bothered with the same dilemma. "They seemed to be worried about the fact that they were working on the outside. Many of them regarded it as helping the war efforts of the United States, and wondered if that was a right thing for them to do while they remained as Japanese nationals. Some of them were worried what would happen to them after the war when they return to Japan. They were thinking whether they would not be punished in Japan for what they were doing during the war.

"These people are working hard. They are getting by as far as earning their livelihood is concerned. But I don't believe that they are satisfied with what they are doing. They are always conscious of themselves; the realization that they are Japanese is constantly on their minds. They are afraid to talk about the war. Life for them is not free like we are here. It is not a natural life; they can't say what they think. They are bothered with oppressed feeling."

"But the WRA will push its program to close the centers," Katow spoke with more strength in his voice. "We must decide now what we want to do in the future. We must decide whether or not we want to work for America. Once that is decided people can go out of the center if they are given more money. The whole thing is the matter for each individual to decide. I don't encourage relocation, because it is not pleasant on the outside. I will not say that everybody should leave the center. That is not right to say that." (Katow clarified the last statements afterwards when Nishimoto asked him what he meant. He tried to convey to the audience with these intentionally ambiguous statements that time would come for the Japanese people to decide between the two courses open to them; viz., all out affiliation with the United States or irrevocable tie with Japan. He meant to say that the people could no longer "sit on the fence". He believed that those who had forsaken the United States should not leave the center. Okamoto made a mistake in telling that every one should relocate for his own good, he thought. In his opinion, no one should persuade the people to relocate; the decision should be made by the people themselves. They should judge for themselves based on "facts" that should be presented by leaders.)

Nobuo Matsubara had been sitting in his chair uncomfortably. When Katow reached the last word, he began to speak impassionedly, as if he could not wait any longer in silence. "All these things can be decided by the conviction of each individual. It is up to what the individual believes in. Everyone should know to which country he is loyal. That's fundamental. If he is a man enough, he should know that."

Matsubara became more excited and his voice became louder. "Mr. Okamoto is wrong in advising everyone to relocate. Those who believe themselves loyal to Japan ought not to relocate. They should remain in the center. What does it matter if the WRA closes the center? There is the center at Santa Fe. There is Crystal City. It's entirely up to you. If you are really determined to return to Japan there should not be any worry. There are places to go to for those people. The whole trouble began when we answered 'yes-yes' to the questions 27 and 28. The mistakes have been made by ourselves. Not the WRA. Because we have declared ourselves loyal to the United States by answering those questions in the affirmative, the WRA has classified us as those not desiring to return to Japan. That's natural. Nothing wrong with the WRA. How can we say now that we don't want to leave the center, because we don't wish to remain in the United States after the war? Why haven't we declared so when we have been called on to decide? The persons who wish to declare themselves loyal to Japan can make such declaration; it is not too late."

"On the other hand, those people who have decided to remain in the United States ought to relocate. If they are loyal to the United States, they ought to go out and contribute to the war efforts. It's up to each individual. No one ought to push anyone out of the center. I can't understand Mr. Okamoto's point of view that we should not remain in the center. Let us decide that, instead."

Matsubara, too, urged each resident to make his own choice, avoiding adroitly, however, to reveal for which side he stood. Nishimoto became aware that arguments would ensue endlessly; he noticed that the people in the audience were tense. He could not fail to observe that they resented Okamoto's remarks—Okamoto had made tactical errors of speaking out that everyone should "get the hell" out of the center, that the center life was unwholesome, that they were poor and did not know what to do, inferring that they lacked ability and fortitude, and that so called loyal-to-Japan people were not really so. The Supervisor immediately took the situation in hand; he proposed a resolution appreciating and thanking the efforts of these delegates at the conference in behalf of the Poston residents. Without a second to the motion, he asked for passage of the resolution with clappings of hands. On the request of the Supervisor, the Block Managers obediently passed the resolution with a thunderous ovation. The meeting was adjourned immediately afterwards.

The reaction of the Managers on the meeting was surprisingly uniform—their expressions were focused on Okamoto's speech and invariably negative. One of the Managers approached the Supervisor and stated, "Good thing that you have stopped the discussion. We would have told a few things to Okamoto if we had a chance."

"What happened to that guy?" another Manager commented. "He has swallowed Dillon Myer [whole]."

"Okamoto is cocky," another Manager was visibly angry. "Look at his attitude. Who the hell does he think we are anyway?"

"How much is Okamoto getting from the WRA?" was a sarcastic remark from still another Manager.

"He is supposed to be the City Manager—a leader of the residents. How can that guy tell us to relocate with a straight face? He should quit the job."

Unit Administrator Sumida, who attended the meeting, was more to the point. "Okamoto has been talking against relocation. He has told people not to be fooled by what the WRA was saying. That was because he was a repatriate and was on the Army stop list. Now that he has been cleared by the Army, he is telling that everyone ought to leave the center. If you look back [at] his past record, you will notice that his activities here, which are supposedly for the good of the people, have been centered around his self. He is the kind of fellow who wants to drag others along if he must go to hell. He is very selfish."

Delegate Katow commented on Okamoto's speech thus: "I was surprised when Okamoto started to say those things. I don't know what to do with him. I don't know what he actually believes. He says one thing one time, and another thing at another time. I wonder whether he had any conviction of his own. He repeated what Myer had told us at the conference.

"We, the delegates, had been elected by the people to fight the policy of center closure. There is no question that we had been instructed by the people on that platform. Now we have come back, and Okamoto starts telling the people to get out of the center. To me, it doesn't make sense. If that's what he believes, he should not have gone to the conference as a delegate of the people. It is same as fooling our own people."

Matsubara was still angry long afterwards. He stated in a derisive tone, "Fool! (*Baka yaro*!) There is no medicine to cure a fool."

The resentful reaction against Okamoto could not remain within the limited circle of the Block Managers. It became known later that Okamoto's first committal in public favoring relocation permeated into the community, as the Managers reported to the residents on the conference. According to the instruction, the Managers tacked the mimeographed copies of the Salt Lake resolution on the walls of Mess Halls and on the block bulletin boards. In addition, many of them gave brief summaries of what they had heard from the delegates during the meeting to their block residents at meal times. These verbal reports varied greatly with the respective Managers, but they emphasized that an answer to the resolution had not been received from Director Myer. Some of them stressed the point that a permanent organization for the Japanese was born from this conference. As a whole, the Managers focused their emphasis on the positive efforts of the conference so that criticisms against the delegates might be diverted. However, while chatting with residents informally, many Managers, it became evident later, mentioned the fact that Okamoto had made an unexpected speech, using discourteous words, in favor of relocation. These Managers did not forget to add their own comments on the speech, unfavorable to Okamoto—similar to those that were heard after the meeting.

As a consequence of these unfavorable reactions, several attempts, albeit unofficial, were made by some of the leaders to warn Okamoto. As for an example, Manager Matsutani of Block 30, where the City Manager resided, came to the Executive Board in the morning of March 3, the next day after the Block Managers' meeting, appealing to its Chairman, Y. Katow, to warn Okamoto that he should not talk of the Japanese defeat this year and should not propagandize relocation. The Manager reported that a near fist fight almost climaxed a little discussion the night before when Okamoto discussed the war and relocation with an influential resident of the block. In the opinion of the Manager, Okamoto was unduly irritating residents who were already worried about the turn of the war and the prospect of the center closing. He believed that no leader should disturb his followers when it could be avoided. Katow, however, refused to accede to the Manager's request contending that he could not interfere with Okamoto for expressing his personal opinions.

Supervisor Nishimoto, too, received a request of the sort from another Manager, who stated that his block residents wished "someone do something about it." The Supervisor, like Katow, refused to interfere with the City Manager. Nevertheless, the dissatisfaction over Okamoto's beliefs remained unabated; with some it was of a greater importance than the outcome of the conference, and they continued to talk of the City Manager contemptuously.

As Okamoto was asked by Supervisor Nishimoto in the morning of March 2 to give his report to the Managers, he realized the necessity of calling a special meeting of the Unit I Local Council, of which he was the Chairman. He had had no intention of assembling the Council men for the purpose of hearing the delegates report on the conference. However, on the face of the new development where the Supervisor called the special meeting, he could not remain idle. Notices were immediately dispatched to the members of the Council requesting them to assemble on the next day, March 3 (Saturday).

The special meeting of the Council was called from 10 o'clock in the conference room. In addition to Y. Katow and N. Matsubara, there were about thirty Councilmen present. First, Chairman Okamoto distributed mimeographed copies of the resolution, and asked them to read them. After several minutes, the Chairman commenced to give his verbal report on the meeting with Dillon Myer, much in the same manner as he had reported to the Block Managers. He mentioned Myer's five reasons for closing the centers, then the speech made by Judge Wolfe. He explained the reason behind the belated presentation of the resolution and the circumstance why an answer had not been received. He concluded his report with an announcement of the schedule during Myer's stay at Poston. "Mr. Myer will give eloquent answers to all the points in the document. He will be very convincing."

Then Katow followed with his report. Again he covered the same grounds which had been explained to the Managers the day previously. First, he related in detail the difficulty of deciding which of the two proposals was more important—the requests of those who could not leave the centers or the various demands of those who wanted to relocate. He pointed out the sharp split on the issue among the delegates. Then Katow explained the organization established as a result of this conference and the aims which it was intending to accomplish, mentioning particularly its significance in connection with the "peace conference". The exposition on the necessity and the importance of conducting a survey initiated by evacuees in order to determine the real problems for relocation followed. The delegate concluded with the account that the various studies of other centers had revealed that the evacuee population can be divided into three groups, naming and describing in detail these three groups.

There was a relaxed lull a little while. Some of the Councilmen commented that too much could not be expected in Myer's answer to the resolution. Some others expressed that a conference of this sort could not be expected to produce any better result. Their reaction should be described as an expected realization of unsatisfactory outcome and a complete resignation to the inevitable result. This atmosphere could best be explained by the statement of a Councilman as he whispered it to another sitting next to him. "We knew from the beginning that the WRA won't budge. It couldn't be otherwise. I think they have done the best they could under the trying conditions. It's from now that will decide the issue. If we don't leave the center, the WRA can't close the center. The whole thing depends on what we will do from now on."

Suddenly, Nagano of Block 18 (a parolee) stood up and addressed the delegates, "You have spoken of three groups. Tell us now which group each one of you delegates belongs?" (Many Councilmen believed that Nagano wanted to force Okamoto to reiterate his stand in favor of relocation. His intimate friend verified this belief afterwards that it was exactly the scheme he had intended. Nagano had heard from the Manager of his block that Okamoto made the "nasty" speech before the Managers, and became incensed.) It seemed that Okamoto believed the question was directly aimed at him for an unfriendly purpose. At any rate, the Chairman began to speak in an angry tone, visibly irritated. "There are people who are saying that they will stick it out here. Those guys are saying that they will not budge even if they were plied with crowbars. You can't depend on what they say. You know that damn well, don't you? I don't have to tell you that there are a bunch of guys who say that they will not budge today, and tomorrow they will relocate as if they forgot what they have said. That's the way these people are. We fight the policy of closing of the center and spend our efforts to keep this place open. But while we are fighting, many people are leaving in droves. It's silly. As I have told the Managers, you should relocate. This place will become so unbearable and unpleasant that you won't want to stay." He repeated the speech which he had made to the Managers—this time, however, with more vigor.

Again, as the day before, Matsubara impatiently contradicted Okamoto's contention. "It is for each individual to decide—whether to relocate or whether to remain in the center. It is and must be decided depending on the true conviction of the individual. It is the question of with which of the two countries his conviction lies. What is it to some of these people if a worse depression visits America? The education of our children is a minor matter once we have decided to remain here for the duration. Suppose they can't go to school? So what?" Matsubara continued with his familiar speech with much force in an excited tone. He was shouting at the top of his voice, which rang throughout the crowded little room.

After Matsubara, Katow followed in a calmer, sarcastic tone. First, he crooked his head towards Okamoto, pointing his thumb, "Mr. Okamoto is very much for relocation . . . "

He went ahead to give the same speech that he had given to the Managers. When each of the three evacuees present at the conference had had his say, Okamoto declared that no good could be gained by arguing on the relocation issue, and began to discuss other matters on the agenda, particularly the matter of Myer's visit. While Matsubara and Katow spoke in opposition, the Chairman sat uneasily and his mannerism was haughty. The expressions on his face indicated that he was sneering at his colleagues. The Councilmen in the audience, too, were uncomfortable; they were aware of the tension as the result of revelation of the schism and the old feud between Okamoto on the one hand and Katow and Matsubara on the other hand. They seemed somewhat embarrassed of the situation, and relieved when a further development of unpleasantness was avoided by the Chairman's move to go on with the other business.

Thus, Minoru Okamoto "insulted" the Poston residents generally, and committed himself fully in accord with the new WRA post-exclusion program. Speaking in favor of relocation, however, he threw polite manner and tactful words to the wind; no one could not doubt that he held evacuees at Poston in contempt. His complete face-about in public caused a mild consternation among the evacuee leaders, and gave a tool to his enemies, which were legion, to discredit him. Indeed, many people were justifiably disgusted with Okamoto, for he had been sent to the conference as a trusted representative of the Poston residents, who desired to have the center maintained in the *status quo.* Okamoto, on the other hand, continued with similar talks; he told his point of view on the war and on the relocation program willingly and unsolicitedly to other groups of evacuees, now that he had committed once for all in public. The resultant irritation on the part of listeners was not slight, and had repercussions for a long time afterwards (see, *infra,* p. xxx).

Outside of the Councilmen and the Block Managers, who had heard the reports directly from the delegates, or other evacuees in key positions, who had a good knowledge as to what had happened at the conference, the Poston residents failed to express their reactions or their opinions on the outcome of the All Center Conference or on the accomplishments of the delegates as freely or articulately as one would expect. Comparatively few expressions were heard; many of the usually vocal people remained silent or talked only a little. It was very difficult to analyze the public opinion resulting from the conference and the reports about it; it might be described either as apathy or as complete satisfaction with inevitable unfavorable outcome. Perhaps, both the descriptions were correct; with some elements apathy prevailed, while others were satisfied with the expected incomplete outcome. In order to explain this unusual ("unusual" because a great amount of enthusiasm was evident for formulating the "demands" and for the general election) condition, the following five reasons might be advanced as the major factors.

First, the slow progress of relocation since the announcement of closing the centers (*infra,* pp. xxx). The residents had expected that many people would leave the center in droves, and the center would become noticeably thinly populated. This had been their secret fear in spite of their articulate opinions that people could not leave and would not leave the center. The Administration, too, avoided active campaigning for the post-exclusion program in the early months for fear that it would create obstructive movements and obstinate resistance to relocation among the evacuees. Because of the combination of these developments, the residents had once again been becoming complacent in the belief that it was well nigh impossible to close the center within this year, or for that matter quite a long time thereafter. This belief had been increasing, and the increase was especially noticeable during the latter part of February. It is understandable that they had supported the conference from their own accord or in response to the propaganda, for its purpose was agreeable with what they wished.

Second, through the *Poston Chronicle* and from other sources, the residents became aware of the fact that Director Dillon Myer would be at Poston on March 6 and 7, which was less than one week away. They have a great respect and admiration for Myer—some of them regard him as "the savior of the Japanese Americans". Myer's visit and his appearance before a general public, the first time in the Poston history, diverted their attention from the return of the delegates. Some of them wishfully thought that something favorable to them might be announced by Myer (*infra*, p. xxx).

Third, in advance of the conference, they had been told the difficulty of attaining the goal requested by them. They had been warned not to expect a favorable outcome. Many of them knew and realized the difficulty without being told.

Fourth, the evacuee leaders and others in the key positions realized that the results of the conference were difficult to present to the people and were not concrete and simple as one might wish. They were, therefore, sympathetic to the returning delegates, and most of them actively interpreted the results favorably in their limited spheres.

Fifth, as amply described previously, much of the potential dissatisfaction, although in restricted circles, was diverted into attacks on and criticisms against Minoru Okamoto for his new stand, which an evacuee characterized as "selling his friends down the river treacherously."

For these and other reasons, the articulate expressions were scant in number. Nonetheless, there were enough variations—varying from expressions of the pessimistic future to those signifying their sense of satisfaction with the accomplishments. Only, the usual vocal, irrational expressions and belligerent opinions were lacking. Had one wished to express a violent resentment to the delegation as a unit, he did so in whisper calmly or in a modulated, well mannered tone.

As to the lack of expressions reflected on the conference, it was not difficult to expect that the Nisei were found in the extreme position. Very few opinions were heard from them, and the Nisei in general were indifferent to the progress or the outcome of the conference. Many of them were understandably ignorant of the developments, for after all the information and the reports were dispensed being aimed particularly to the Issei. However, some interesting remarks were heard from the Nisei, generally antagonists of the Issei. For instance, a Nisei girl of about twenty years of age, the secretary in one of the administrative offices, stated: "I thought this [conference] was for all of us. I don't know what happened. They don't tell us about it. Yes, they report in Japanese, but that's no good for us, because they use difficult Japanese words."

A Nisei boy of eighteen from a rural area in Central California said: "A Caucasian asked me about the conference, but I couldn't tell him what happened. What did they do anyway?"

Another Nisei young man, probably twenty-five years of age, expressed thus: "This is the same old Issei politics. They are cooking up things among themselves, and the rest of us don't know what it's all about."

A Hawaii born Nisei in his early thirties was resentful of the fact that the matter of the All Center Conference was largely confined among the Issei and a small number of the Kibei. This Nisei had "leased" extensively for Japanese tenants in Orange County before Pearl Harbor, and was now holding a key position in the Relocation Division. He wrote in his letter to a friend of his in another center that the conference was a matter which interested only the Issei and some Kibei. Others were not all interested in the conference, which, in his opinion, could not be any more significant than idle talks, argued only among the "big shots". He could not see that the conference would accomplish any tangible purpose. (This Nisei had been regarded as *inu* in the early days here, and had been discredited. This statement is an exaggeration of the actual situation. However, it reflects well the attitude of some of the Nisei, whose ambition to be one of the leaders had been frustrated.)

Somewhat more objective than the Hawaii-born Nisei, a young evacuee from Los Angeles said: "I believe they are asking too many things. Some of their requests are reasonable, but others are entirely out of line. I think they can't get them." This Nisei obviously had read the Salt Lake resolution.

A Nisei girl of about twenty years old, formerly of Orange County, had probably heard about the requests made by the delegates at Salt Lake City: "I know something about what they asked. Do you think we will get them?"

Among the Kibei, a dichotomy existed—apathy on the one hand and antipathy on the other hand. The younger groups of the Kibei were generally indifferent or ignorant, while the older groups varied in their antipathetic attitudes from skepticism to an accusation of corruption. Few favorable expressions were heard among the Kibei.

A Kibei truck driver, probably eighteen years old, remarked: "That's an Issei politic. I don't pay attention."

Another Kibei of about twenty, working in the garage, said: "Hell. I'm ticketed to jail. (He is one of the draft evaders, and expected to be tried soon.) I don't give a damn."

A Kibei, formerly of Los Angeles, about thirty years of age, said: "I don't think anything will come out of this conference. It will end just as a lot of talks. It's hard to believe that the WRA will concede those requests."

A Kibei evacuee from Orange County, about thirty-three years old, who had at one time served as a member of the Local Council, remarked: "It's the same pattern every time with these Issei. Something happen, and they oppose. They hold a conference, and pass a resolution opposing everything. After a while, they will forget what they have said. I will bet this will be the end to the opposition to the closing of the center. The Issei don't have the spirit to go on with it to the end."

Another Kibei of about the same age commented: "What did they do? Practically nothing. Yes, they passed the resolution. But what is it? It is the same thing as the Poston resolution. And Myer will say to these demands 'no', and the whole thing will be over. It is a foolish thing."

A Kibei, who had the charge of a number of the warehouses, expressed his disgust: "They spent our money and got nothing out of it. Maybe they drank whiskey with it."

Several Kibei expressed their opinions on the results of the conference, which was similar to the prevalent attitude among the Issei. In substance they said that it was agreeable with them that such a conference had been held to discuss the common problems of the evacuees in the various centers, but the closing of the centers was an impossible venture, which the WRA would realize sooner or later. Some of them argued it on the shortage of housing on the outside, while some others pointed out the numerous incidents of violence in California.

The attitudes and opinions among the Issei on the outcome of the All Center Conference varied more widely than among the Kibei. On the pessimistic side, an Issei, an urban evacuee of about fifty years of age, commented: "It was known from the beginning that there was no point to holding this kind of conference. It was clear that nothing could be gained from it. When the Government says that it is going to do this or that, it will go ahead with it whether we like it nor not. We should better avoid a useless, foolish thing like that."

Another Issei, also from Los Angeles, remarked quietly, shaking his head, said in undertone: "After all, it wasn't any good. They wasted our money."

A young Issei, a former business man in Little Tokyo in Los Angeles, stated placidly:

> In the end, the center won't be such a pleasant place to stay. People will start leaving the center in droves this summer in spite of what they may be saying

> now. Although the conference asked the WRA to keep the center open, such a stand won't be practical. I am not interested in this sort of protest movement, although I do believe that there are many people who cannot leave the center. There are ways to take care of those people. I am leaving the center about this May. I have to look about for myself and my family before I worry about others.

In this statement, the young Issei business man expressed an important attitude, which had noticeably been increasing in the recent weeks, i.e., ". . . I am leaving the center. . . . I have to look out for myself and my family before I worry about others." Others had been heard saying the same sort of opinion—an indication of the trend moving from the communal responsibility to individualistic thinking and behaviors.

There was another Issei, a rural evacuee of about fifty-five years of age, was also pessimistic about the prospect of the WRA yielding to the requests of the conference, although he was submissively resigned to such a fate: "I think the WRA won't give in. They will just go ahead to close the center. We can't help it. It's no fault of the delegates. I guess I better be thinking about what I should do."

The majority of the Issei (and many Kibei, too, as described above) were hopeful of the future; they believed that the WRA would modify its policy of center closure before the deadline. There were many Issei who were certain of their belief that the center could not be closed; while many other Issei expressed the same attitude, although they might not be quite certain. This attitude influenced their expressions on the results of the conference; some of the representative expressions, which were legion, are recorded below:

"If we stay here and refuse to leave, the WRA cannot do anything about this closing business. Up to now, only a small number of people have relocated, and the rate of relocation cannot increase much more. At this rate, we don't need to worry; there will be a plenty of people left behind. With so many people remaining in the center, the WRA cannot close the center. This conference served the purpose of telling the WRA that that is what is going to happen."

"You can't expect the WRA to say so easily, 'We've changed our minds [about the policy of closing].' It is difficult job for the leaders, and it will take a lot of time. But there is a plenty of chance for making the WRA to change its policy. Our fight is from now."

"This is our first step. Now that the conference has been held, the WRA understands that we can't relocate even though we want to try."

"The results of the conference are not significant. It doesn't matter so much. The real purpose is to let the WRA know what we are thinking. After all, by telling the WRA that we can't leave the center its purpose was achieved."

"We must tell the WRA step by step that we can't leave the center. They can't close it anyway, but we must tell them in advance."

There were other Issei who commented on several other phases of the conference. For example, an Issei from Imperial Valley had this to say:

"If we can send our delegate to the peace conference, it will be very good."

Another Issei was appreciative of what the conference had accomplished: "It was a very good thing that the delegates from all the centers had gotten together and exchanged information. It is always important for all of us to get together and do everything together. We should depend on these delegates."

As usual, there were several Issei who spoke of the delegates contemptuously, although neither violently nor pugnaciously. "Those guys must have had a good time outside." "They must have had good things to eat."

Somewhat more cynical than the average Issei, an elderly man commented: "I bet they will leave Poston quicker than others. That's the reason that they have asked for more money and so on. They want more money to leave. As far as we are concerned, we want the center be kept open, as we said from the beginning."

However, as the news of Director Myer's coming became known to the community, the residents awaited his arrival anxiously. Their interested anticipation diverted much of their attention from the delegates and their reports. "I hear Myer is coming," was heard all over in the camp during the first week in March. With some of the more simpler people, their anticipation for Myer's visit appeared very much like hero worship. They said, in substance, "I hear he is going to speak to us," as though that was a great honor to them. It was, indeed, a sharp contrast with the cynicism of the evacuee leaders, who said, "There isn't any use listening to Myer, for we know what he will say."

An elderly Issei, probably a small scale farmer before Pearl Harbor, remarked wishfully: "Maybe Myer will tell us that we can stay here for the duration."

And he was not the only person who held such a hope.

AFTERWORD

Transition

Despite the popular sentiments and protests described in Nishimoto's All Center Conference report, as the war wound down in 1945 the Japanese Americans remaining in Poston were increasingly encouraged to leave camp. As early as 1943, select Japanese Americans who could find employment in the Midwest or the East, who made affirmative responses to key questions on the WRA's so-called loyalty questionnaire, and who agreed not to affiliate with fellow Japanese Americans had been permitted to return to the larger society. Permission gradually changed to coercion, however. After the conclusion of the war in August, the pressure increased, and finally Units II and III of Poston were officially closed on September 29, 1945, and Unit I on November 28.

Except for the lucky few who had personal property and/or businesses to return to, the period from 1943 to 1950 was largely one of slow and difficult recovery for the Japanese Americans. Often confined to blue-collar and service occupations during and immediately after the war, as well as less-than-desirable housing and neighborhood environments, Issei and Nisei families and individuals struggled to make ends meet.

During the 1950s, conditions finally began to improve for the first-generation Issei. In 1950, for example, the California Alien Land Law was finally declared unconstitutional. In 1952, provisions of the McCarran-Walter

Act gave Japanese immigrants the right to naturalization for the first time ever, thus allowing Issei access to the full rights and protections held by U.S. citizens.

For the Nisei and the Sansei, or third-generation Japanese Americans (typically born either just before the war, in camp, or afterward), the period beginning in the 1950s was one of educational achievement in terms of college and professional degrees in the midst of a postwar period of expanding economic opportunity. Further, during the 1950s and 1960s there was increasing support for civil rights and the ideal of equal opportunity for people of color in the United States. Thus the Nisei were able to make great strides in fields—such as civil service, education, and the law—that had previously been barred to their parents and themselves. In short, their reentry into the larger society provided the basis for asserting rights that had been denied them before and during the war.[1]

Nishimoto's Life from 1945 to 1956

Unlike many Japanese Americans, Nishimoto did not prosper after the war. At Poston, Nishimoto continued his regular activities until July 1945. Then, when Dillon S. Myer began to suspect that he was on the JERS staff, he had Nishimoto investigated and in mid-June ordered that he be removed from Poston. Nishimoto then joined Dorothy Thomas, the director of the Japanese American Evacuation and Resettlement Study, at the University of California at Berkeley. By the end of 1945, all the other Japanese American students and scholars with the project had either completed their work and moved on or in some cases, like Tsuchiyama's, had resigned because their views differed too greatly from Thomas's. Thus Nishimoto became increasingly important within JERS. He was the sole JERS staff person of consequence, Dorothy Thomas's only co-author of Japanese descent, and the only co-author who had also been confined in one of the camps that the JERS project personnel had studied who went on to work on and publish books with Thomas.

Beyond these basic facts, documentary evidence that would clarify Nishimoto's factual and conceptual contributions to the three JERS publications is extremely limited. Apparently, no working notes for either *The Spoilage* or *The Salvage* are extant in the libraries and archives of the two universities where they were most likely to be deposited had they been preserved: the University of California at Berkeley, where Dorothy Thomas was in residence during her

JERS directorship, and the University of Pennsylvania, where she held a position when she retired from academia. What is more, most of Nishimoto's personal papers were lost after he died. What remains is largely contained in two letters Nishimoto wrote to Dorothy Thomas in early 1952. Much of their text concerns Nishimoto's difficulty in finding a job, but they also give us the most thorough description of what Nishimoto believed his contributions had been.

Nishimoto began his reflections on *The Spoilage* by noting that the decision to make him a co-author was made by W. I. Thomas and Dorothy Thomas, not Nishimoto himself. His satisfaction in being so named did not derive from pride in the book itself but rather from his pleasure, as he said, "that my conceptualization triumphed over the others'. It concerns the trichotomy—the spoilage, the salvage, and the residue. You are the one who refined and crystallized the concepts and gave the most apt names to them. However, if you go back to the first Salt Lake City conference, you'll remember I was toying with the idea."[2]

Nishimoto observes that he proposed that the spoilage segment of the study be completed first, "because the subject matter was more definitive and easier to handle then." Reportedly, everyone on the staff except for Rose Hankey was against the idea. Nishimoto complained about "snitching and sniping," from the Japanese American staff members, who only agreed, reluctantly, when Thomas approved. "So," he wrote, "my pleasure in seeing my name on the cover of *The Spoilage* was perverted. I felt that my original concept was supported by you and that it was the best reply to the critics who said, 'What the hell does he know about Sociology? He has no training in the field.'"

A missing JERS manuscript by Nishimoto consisted of a book-length study he is supposed to have completed before he left Berkeley in 1948. Concerning this work, Nishimoto wrote to Thomas: "About 'basic economic analyses.' When I was working on the economic history, I didn't realize it was going to be an important and valuable work. My aim then was to prepare a basis for *The Salvage* for you." While admitting that this manuscript had many substantive gaps, Nishimoto also pointed out that it was one of only two works that provided a sense of the economic baseline of Japanese Americans in 1940, the other being Broom and Riemers' study *Removal and Return.*[3] The completed version of Nishimoto's manuscript appears to have been lost. Nishimoto states that "although the study was based on a 25 percent sampling, its sources are unique—the almost complete census data of a minority group." We do not know the extent to which Thomas drew upon this study, and Nishimoto himself did not comment on the topic any further in his letter of March 5, 1952, though it appears that he still had not read *The Salvage.*[4]

Regarding his work for Jacobus tenBroek, Edward Barnhart, and Floyd Matson on *Prejudice, War and the Constitution,* Nishimoto complained in correspondence that the editing process was exhausting, but he worked vigorously on the revision. He agreed completely with Thomas's desire to see them produce a book that would refute Morton Grodzins's *Americans Betrayed.* On this basis, Nishimoto worked for a number of weeks with all three authors, helping them correct and sharpen the arguments in their individually written sections of text.[5]

It is clear from this same letter, in fact, that neither Nishimoto nor Thomas spared any effort to aid tenBroek and his colleagues. At one level, support meant full access to JERS materials, including published and unpublished manuscripts. At another level, Nishimoto commented that "if the final form is satisfactory to us, they deserve any and every support you can give them. I sincerely believe they need it."[6] In fact, when the University of California Press rejected the manuscript, Dorothy Thomas wrote to the editor, advising him to consult with Nishimoto: "I should be grateful if . . . you asked Nishimoto to give you his evaluation for he is an unbiased, hard-hitting critic, whose scholarship is of the best, and who is about as 'expert' in the matters dealt with as anyone you could possibly find."[7]

Although the editor chose not to follow Thomas's advice, tenBroek wrote to Nishimoto directly, asking him to submit an independent evaluation of the work. Two days later Nishimoto sent his letter to the press, praising the manuscript and concluding that "it would be a serious loss to the world of scholarship if this book were not to be published."[8] In the end, the manuscript was accepted for publication. *Prejudice, War and the Constitution* finally came out in 1954.

In spite of these efforts, Nishimoto was unable to find any substantial employment during the 1950s. Estranged from his family for some years after the war, Nishimoto visited them in Los Angeles and reportedly had decided to rejoin his wife there. He had returned to San Francisco to pack his papers and belongings, but in late May 1956, Nishimoto died, alone, in a back room of a downtown San Franciso hotel, where he had apparently stored some of his possessions when he had worked there as a night watchman.

His death went unnoticed; no obituary appeared in newspapers such as the *San Francisco Chronicle* or the *New York Times.* The Japanese Americans who had been confined at Poston had dispersed back into the larger society and in any case were preoccupied with basic issues of survival. In short, by the time he died, Nishimoto had lost his community following from Poston, to say nothing of the support of professional academics who, during key periods when the pressure was on them to write and to publish, had depended so heavily on his insights and expertise.[9]

Nishimoto's Writings

Any evaluation of Nishimoto's contribution to the research record must first weigh his own political position as a public figure and community leader against his decision to play a simultaneous clandestine role as a fieldworker for the University of California's Japanese American Evacuation and Resettlement Study. Within this perspective and the context of the reports included in this book, it may now be noted that Nishimoto's reputation as an authority within the JERS project can be looked at from another angle: the way in which his frame of reference influenced his production and interpretation of research data. Furthermore, Nishimoto's JERS materials and interviews indicate that his biases need to be considered at three levels: personal, intellectual, and political.

To begin with a consideration of how the personal element influenced his Poston research, passages in Nishimoto's diaries reflect his thoughts on ethnicity and race relations in general, as well as the evolving nature of his own ethnic identity. Based on his reading in the sociology of race relations of his day, Nishimoto drew several explicit analogies in his journal between the situation of the Jews and the Japanese in the United States. Upon reading Louis Adamic's *From Many Lands*, for example, Nishimoto quoted extensively from the book and then made the following comment:

> Evacuation brought a drastic change in my race consciousness. . . . It was different. No longer did it feel that I am "on trial." No longer did I "look at myself in a mirror" [to see] if I have a chance among the Caucasians, nor did I care. I was resigned to the idea that I am a Japanese and am being treated as such. I began to feel that I am as good as any one of the Caucasians. . . . Should I say that with the evacuation any inward-directed race consciousness was transformed into outwardly-directed violent race consciousness?[10]

This passage indicates that Nishimoto's own sense of ethnic identity went though a transition in camp. His sensitivity about racial issues, remember, was partly a result of his own career experiences. Removal and incarceration simply reinforced Nishimoto's sense that racial discrimination was a central aspect of the Japanese American experience in the United States.

It is also clear that this understanding had an impact on Nishimoto's interpretation of events in the camps and proved to be a relative strength. For example, at one point in a JERS staff meeting he argued against James Sakoda's "labor conflict" explanation of camp rebellions. Nishimoto hypothesized that the general pattern involving protest and strikes was not simply a matter of labor or class conflict but rather defiance "against [a] caste system."[11]

JERS staff meetings—held in Chicago in 1943 and in Salt Lake City in 1944—reveal additional aspects of the intellectual bases of Nishimoto's research orientation. Nishimoto took what might be called an institutional approach to his research. At one point during the 1944 staff conference he stressed that case studies were of importance to him only insofar as they might reveal something about the whole of Poston. He seemed to be chiding other researchers for recording events simply because they had happened or for the sake of recording them. W. I. Thomas, who was present at this staff meeting, picked up on this and pointed out that Nishimoto emphasized policy at Poston and the "evolution of policy."[12]

Another bias is both intellectual and political in nature. After the war, Nishimoto claimed in his résumé that his degree specialty within engineering had been factory management. Although this was not strictly true, Nishimoto may have been exposed to this perspective while in camp through anthropologists Edward Spicer and Alexander Leighton, both of whom had a strong interest in applied anthropology. According to Spicer's later publications on applied anthropology, during the 1920s and 1930s factory management theory shifted from a focus on the "optimum physiological conditions" that would promote productivity to an emphasis on "the work groups of which individuals were a part, both in and out of the factory."[13] Specifically, productivity was considered to be a function of "[s]tatus within groups, the relative status of groups in the factory system, and morale and solidarity within the groups. . . . [W]ays of changing these elements of the industrial plants became the object of planning for attainment of goals by management and workers."[14]

Interestingly enough, the new perspective, which would be influential in such fields as industrial psychology and business administration, was partially a product of research in the nascent field of applied anthropology. A number of graduate students, including Conrad Arensberg and Solon Kimball, were involved in research in the area of factory management because it tied into their interest in how anthropology could be harnessed to practical ends. Later some of these same men and their colleagues would help the WRA plan and administer the camps. Kimball actually designed the original administrative organization of Poston.[15]

In short, factory management theory was based on the view that the social sciences were scientific enough to engage in human engineering. This orientation fit directly into Nishimoto's conception of how "human resources" should be managed at Poston, and it can be seen in his writing as early as his 1942 study of the firebreak gang. Once this context is understood, then, it is possible to see how it allowed Nishimoto to act in ways that now seem manipulative at best and Machiavellian at worst.

As far as political biases are concerned, the evidence at hand strongly supports the interpretation that Nishimoto was a political moderate at Poston. He was not a partisan of either the Japanese American Citizens League or the ostensibly pro-Japanese Issei, Kibei, or Nisei in camp, nor did he support the Nisei and Kibei draft resisters at Poston. His political orientation, however, was not simple and deserves additional explication.

While Nishimoto may sometimes have acted in a Machiavellian fashion, he carried out his actions for a larger purpose: to make life bearable for the majority of the inhabitants of Poston, who were simply trying to survive. This helps to explain his determination to eliminate the power base of his Issei and Kibei rivals during 1943 and his comments two years later concerning the Issei leader Minoru Okamoto, as documented in the All Center Conference report. Nishimoto thought that overt militancy and unrealistic demands would only cause frustration and difficulties about matters that were not resolvable. In this fashion, Nishimoto, as an activist and a moderate, believed that resistance interfered with the basic task of survival in camp.

In 1944, when a JERS staff member asked directly about Nishimoto's and his allies' stance vis-à-vis the Unit I residents of Poston, another staff member jumped into the conversation to comment: "They're people who could get things done for people." According to the conference transcripts, Nishimoto immediately agreed, saying, "That's the way they're regarded."[16] Nishimoto summed up by stating: "Last June I said that unless the community is integrated you can't get anything done at all. They can't integrate at either end of the scale. . . . [I]t has to be somewhere near the middle. [With] segregation and relocation it's become easier to organize in the middle. A good example is that it is difficult to move flakes of snow in any one direction. After making it into a ball, it's easy to move."[17]

Nishimoto's attitude toward the extremists at Poston may have influenced his interpretation of "dissidents," "resisters," and "renunciants" in *The Spoilage*. This is partly revealed in his comments regarding the subjects of the latter study:

> I realized that bitterness, frustration and anger were the major factors for the spoilage segment of Registration and Segregation. But actually bitterness, etc. were waning, and expressions reflecting such feelings were verbalized rationalization . . . their own interests being the center of the vortex of thinking. I noticed that anxiety for the future and the means to resolve this anxiety were of prime concern in evacuees' minds. And their actions and decisions as to their future seemed to be culturally determined; polarized either to their future in America or to that in Japan. For example, repatriation and expatriation moves were clear cut decisions polarized to Japan.[18]

By contrast, in a subsequent letter Nishimoto speaks very favorably about those Nisei who joined the armed forces.

> What then was the polarity of the Salvage? At one polar extreme, we had those who volunteered for the service during Registration. Registration, indeed, was the first evidence of sharp cut differentiation leading to the trichotomy [the salvage, the spoilage, and the residue]. Subsequently, many of these volunteers were taken into the army directly from the camps. . . . Many of them were very articulate; they said that their own status in America (many of them went further to say "the status of the Japanese in America") could be improved only by their serving in actual combat. They were right as later events proved. We cannot overemphasize the beneficial effect produced directly by the Nisei soldiers and their exploits. Their achievements gave the WRA and other pro-Japanese protagonists the most effective weapon with which to fight for the minority.[19]

Similarly, it is interesting to speculate whether Thomas's and Nishimoto's inclination to view politics at Tule Lake in terms of a small number of leaders (often portrayed as devious characters out to manipulate and control "the masses") represents a projection of Nishimoto's own political world view. Apart from this, Nishimoto's status as a clandestine researcher does not appear to have limited or biased his Poston data. A related question is whether Nishimoto appeared to feel any conflict or guilt over his role as a clandestine researcher. If he did, the JERS materials offer no evidence of it.

One of Nishimoto's research associates in Poston commented that a skeptic might argue that Nishimoto was "greedy for the extra money" or anxious for the "chance to remain in touch with West Coast intellectual life." While this associate was willing to allow the latter point, he also said: "I do not remember his discussing the ethics of his own activities, and I think this was significant. Perhaps he occasionally had private doubts. . . . I think he was fundamentally at peace with his research role and *did not feel that it needed discussion* [emphasis in original]."[20]

As for his own self-perceptions in this regard, in March 1952 in a long letter to Dorothy Thomas, Nishimoto reflected on his motives for conducting social research with the JERS project. Since this is the only reflection that I have been able to find, it is worth quoting at length:

> Remember those days in 1942? Many scientists were groping around in the dark. I thought I could help them to their advantage. I knew that I was one of the few experts in the field of resident Japanese problems, as good as any of the recognized authors of the secondary sources then existing. (Hell with "modesty".) I thought I could straighten out a lot of misconceptions about the Japanese, and the Nisei "scientists," too, were not getting anywhere. . . . I never expected that I would be working for you after that period, nor did I anticipate that I would later be coming to Berkeley and would participate in the publication of our findings. You never told me, and I never asked you, how long I would be working at Berkeley. I just kept on with the idea that I would be helping as long as I was needed and my assistance was of any value. . . . My purpose was therefore very altruistic. I knew I was good at the things we were doing, and was fully aware that we were producing something extremely valuable for the science. This "honorable" trait in me was also responsible for my unselfish and tireless work I did recently for Chick's [Jacobus tenBroek's] group. Yes, it is true that those two factors you mentioned, viz., (1) a "moral" obligation, and (2) a "socialized" desire, were the primary ones that motivated me to help them. But more than these, I saw an unpolished gem in their work. . . . I sensed their valuable possibility—therefore potentially a great contribution to the science—to straighten out the secondary sources and to come to a new and more valid conclusion. . . . Seeing that Chick and others were botching up this wonderful chance, I just couldn't sit still.[21]

Although this reminiscence seems idealized and must be seen in the context of Nishimoto's hope that he might find a job in the academic setting he so greatly revered, it corresponds with other evidence regarding his ability to compartmentalize his various Poston activities conceptually so that his role as a researcher had its own rationale and justification apart from his activities as head of the block managers and a community activist.

In conclusion, although Nishimoto may have been Machiavellian at times, he was never a spy in the sense of someone who was paid to pass along information to Poston's administrative staff, the War Relocation Authority, or the federal intelligence agencies, such as the FBI. In fact, as noted above, when WRA head Dillon Myer learned that Nishimoto might in fact be serving on the JERS staff, he had Nishimoto investigated and subsequently, in 1945, ordered

This group portrait of the women of Block 45 shows Yae Nishimoto, fifth from the left in the second row. Unfortunately, little information is available on how the camp experience affected Japanese American women during and after the war. (Courtesy of Roberta Shiroma)

him to be removed from Poston. Clearly, if Nishimoto was nothing more than a spy for the federal government, his residence in Poston would not have constituted a problem for the authorities.

Finally, in light of contemporary concerns about feminism and the realization that gender influences research foci and outcomes in the social sciences, I want to address the fact that Nishimoto's formal reports virtually ignore the presence, activities, and contributions of Japanese American women at Poston. To some extent this might be written off as an orientation common enough among first-generation Issei males, whose patriarchal sensibilities were framed in predominantly rural settings during the Meiji and Taisho eras. At the same time, however, it is notable that the same lack of treatment of women in Poston characterizes the journal entries and formal reports of Nishimoto's one-time friend and colleague, Tamie Tsuchiyama.

What bears remembering here is that, from the early stages of its development, the Bureau of Sociological Research had planned to study the Japanese American family in Poston, and indeed the results of such a study were published in the *Annals of the American Academy of Political and Social Science* toward the end of 1943.[22] It is thus possible that both Tsuchiyama and Nishimoto concluded that data collection and analysis pertaining to Poston's men, women, and families were already "staked out" by Nishimoto and Tsuchiyama's BSR colleagues. In any case, as previously noted, both Tsuchiyama and Nishimoto collected more-specialized data focusing on politics in Poston, although the scope of both of their journals indicates that, in a typically anthropological fashion, their vision of what constituted politics was framed within a comprehensive, holistic understanding of Poston from an institutional perspective.

Conclusion

As we have seen, Richard Nishimoto's life and work during the period he worked for the Japanese American Evacuation and Resettlement Study were rich, complex, and amazingly productive. In the end, however, the assessment of Richard Nishimoto as a research assistant to Dorothy Thomas and other JERS authors must be an ironic one. Nishimoto was, in fact, a prime mover in Poston. He was directly involved as a community leader in much of what went on there, especially between 1943 and 1945. Nishimoto's sociological journals can thus be thought of as embodying a unique combination of ethnography and auto-ethnography; that is, a good deal of his research is informed by his own plans and activities as an active participant in the affairs of Poston's Unit I.[23] Much more than a participant-observer in any ordinary social scientific meaning of the term, Nishimoto conducted research at the same time that he was acting as a power broker and community leader.[24]

In the final analysis, Nishimoto's participation in the JERS project may best be seen as his way of employing intellectual abilities and ambitions that had been completely, and unfairly, suppressed before the war. In this sense, his JERS status gave him the chance to study his environment while at the same time recording and analyzing the efficacy of his attempts to try to engineer events within it.

Notes

1. For an in-depth study of this period of transition, set within the larger context of both Japanese American and U.S. history, see Jerrold Haruo Takahashi, "Changing Responses to Racial Subordination: An Exploratory Study of Japanese American Political Styles" (Ph.D. diss., University of California, Berkeley, 1980), 221–42.

2. This and the following two quotations come from a letter Nishimoto wrote to Thomas on March 5, 1952; "Unpublished manuscripts," Dorothy S. Thomas, Papers regarding Japanese Relocation, 78/53c, Bancroft Library (hereafter cited as the Thomas Papers).

3. Nishimoto to Thomas, February 27, 1952, Thomas Papers.

4. Ibid. Two chapters from Nishimoto's lost manuscript—chapter 5, "Japanese in Domestic Service," and chapter 6, "Japanese in Personal Service and Domestic Trade"—are in the Edward N. Barnhart Papers, Japanese American Research Project Collection, University Library, University of California, Los Angeles.

5. Nishimoto to Thomas, February 27, 1952, Thomas Papers.

6. Ibid., 3.

7. Thomas to Fruge, March 27, 1952, courtesy of Roberta Shiroma.

8 Nishimoto to Fruge, May 11, 1953, courtesy of Roberta Shiroma.

9. Nishimoto's age and his status as a Japanese national may have had a bearing on why he was not encouraged to pursue graduate studies. Nevertheless, Roger Sanjek's essay "Anthropology's Hidden Colonialism: Assistants and Their Ethnographers," *Anthropology Today* 9 (1993): 13–18, which raises questions in regard to the exploitation of "native informants," is germane to Nishimoto's case.

10. Nishimoto, Journal, September 17, 1942, Japanese American Evacuation and Resettlement Study Collection, Bancroft Library, University of California, Berkeley (hereafter JERS), J 6.13A, 1–2.

11. This comment appears in the transcriptions of discussions at the JERS staff meeting in Salt Lake City in June 1944; JERS W 1.15, 83.

12. Transcript of a discussion cited in "Richard Nishimoto on the Political Organization of Poston," December 4, 1944, JERS W 1.15, 19.

13. See Edward Spicer, "Early Applications of Anthropology in North America," in *Perspectives on Anthropology*, ed. Anthony F. C. Wallace et al. (Washington, D.C.: American Anthropological Association, 1976), 116–41; quoted text is from p. 123.

14. Ibid., 123.

15. Regarding Kimball's contributions to self-government, see "Richard Nishimoto on the Political Organization of Poston," December 4, 1944, JERS W 1.15, 2–5. For another point of view on anthropologists' contributions, see Conrad M. Arensberg, "Report on a Developing Community: Poston, Arizona," *Applied Anthropology* 2 (1942): 1–21. For a critical evaluation, see Peter T. Suzuki, "Anthropologists in the Wartime

Camps for Japanese Americans: A Documentary Study," *Dialectical Anthropology* 6 (1981): 23–60.

16. Transcript of a discussion cited in "Richard Nishimoto on the Political Organization of Poston," December 4, 1944, JERS W 1.15, 19.

17. Ibid., 20.

18. Nishimoto to Thomas, February 27, 1952, Thomas Papers.

19. Nishimoto to Thomas, March 5, 1952, Thomas Papers.

20. Letter about Nishimoto by a former WRA staff member, who requested confidentiality, July 10, 1986.

21. Nishimoto to Thomas, March 5, 1952, Thomas Papers.

22. Bureau of Sociological Research, "The Japanese Family in America," *Annals of the American Academy of Political and Social Science* 229 (1943): 150–56.

23. Dorothy Thomas clearly knew about Nishimoto's activism and power; see Thomas to Nishimoto, June 30, 1944, JERS W 1.25.

24. For a thoughtful overview of this topic in sociocultural anthropology, see David M. Hayano, "Auto-Ethnography: Paradigms, Problems, and Prospects," *Human Organization* 38 (1979): 99–104.

INDEX

ABOUT THE AUTHOR

Lane Ryo Hirabayashi received his Ph.D. in anthropology from the University of California at Berkeley in 1981 and is currently an associate professor of anthropology at the University of Colorado at Boulder. His primary activities revolve around his position as a member of the core faculty at the Center for Studies of Ethnicity and Race in America (CSERA), where he teaches Asian American and ethnic studies. Hirabayashi has published articles on the Japanese American experience in anthologies, including *Views from Within: The Japanese American Evacuation and Resettlement Study* and *Through Innocent Eyes: Writings and Art from the Japanese American Internment by Poston I School Children,* and in journals such as *California History* and the *Southern California Quarterly.* He is the lead editor of the 1994 conference anthology of the Association for Asian American Studies. Also active in Latin American studies, Hirabayashi is the author of *Cultural Capital: Mountain Zapotec Migrant Associations in Mexico City* (University of Arizona Press, 1993) and is a co-editor of the anthology *Migrants, Regional Identities and Latin American Cities* (forthcoming).